Bilingualism: Beyond Basic Principles

MULTILINGUAL MATTERS SERIES
Series Editor: Professor John Edwards, *St. Francis Xavier University, Antigonish, Nova Scotia, Canada*

Other Books in the Series
Beyond Bilingualism: Multilingualism and Multilingual Education
Jasone Cenoz and Fred Genesee (eds)
Beyond Boundaries: Language and Identity in Contemporary Europe
Paul Gubbins and Mike Holt (eds)
Can Threatened Languages be Saved?
Joshua Fishman (ed.)
Community and Communication
Sue Wright
A Dynamic Model of Multilingualism
Philip Herdina and Ulrike Jessner
Identity, Insecurity and Image: France and Language
Dennis Ager
Language and Society in a Changing Italy
Arturo Tosi
Language Attitudes in Sub-Saharan Africa
Efurosibina Adegbija
Language, Ethnicity and Education
Peter Broeder and Guus Extra
Language Planning in Malawi, Mozambique and the Philippines
Robert B. Kaplan and Richard B. Baldauf, Jr (eds)
Language Planning in Nepal, Taiwan and Sweden
Richard B. Baldauf, Jr and Robert B. Kaplan (eds)
Language Planning: From Practice to Theory
Robert B. Kaplan and Richard B. Baldauf, Jr (eds)
Language Reclamation
Hubisi Nwenmely
Linguistic Minorities in Central and Eastern Europe
Christina Bratt Paulston and Donald Peckham (eds)
Motivation in Language Planning and Language Policy
Dennis Ager
Multilingualism in Spain
M. Teresa Turell (ed.)
Quebec's Aboriginal Languages
Jacques Maurais (ed.)
The Other Languages of Europe
Guus Extra and Durk Gorter (eds)
The Step-Tongue: Children's English in Singapore
Anthea Fraser Gupta
Three Generations – Two Languages – One Family
Li Wei

Other Books of Interest
Understanding Deaf Culture: In Search of Deafhood
Paddy Ladd

Please contact us for the latest book information:
Multilingual Matters, Frankfurt Lodge, Clevedon Hall,
Victoria Road, Clevedon, BS21 7HH, England
http://www.multilingual-matters.com

MULTILINGUAL MATTERS 123
Series Editor: John Edwards

Bilingualism: Beyond Basic Principles
Festschrift in honour of Hugo Baetens Beardsmore

Edited by
Jean-Marc Dewaele, Alex Housen
and Li Wei

MULTILINGUAL MATTERS LTD
Clevedon • Buffalo • Toronto • Sydney

Library of Congress Cataloging in Publication Data
Bilingualism: Beyond Basic Principles/Edited by Jean-Marc Dewaele, Alex Housen, and Li Wei.
1. Bilingualism. I. Dewaele, Jean-Marc. II. Housen, Alex. III. Wei, Li.
P115 .B5474 2003
404'.2–dc21   2002014634

British Library Cataloguing in Publication Data
A catalogue entry for this book is available from the British Library.

ISBN 1-85359-626-4 (hbk)
ISBN 1-85359-625-6 (pbk)

Multilingual Matters Ltd
UK: Frankfurt Lodge, Clevedon Hall, Victoria Road, Clevedon BS21 7HH.
USA: UTP, 2250 Military Road, Tonawanda, NY 14150, USA.
Canada: UTP, 5201 Dufferin Street, North York, Ontario M3H 5T8, Canada.
Australia: Footprint Books, PO Box 418, Church Point, NSW 2103, Australia.

Typeset by Archetype-IT Ltd (http://www.archetype-it.com).
Printed and bound in Great Britain by the Cromwell Press Ltd.

Contents

Preface. vii
Contributors ix

Introduction and Overview
Jean-Marc Dewaele, Alex Housen and Li Wei 1

1 **Who is Afraid of Bilingualism?**
   Hugo Baetens Beardsmore 10
2 **The Importance of Being Bilingual**
   John Edwards. 28
3 **Towards a More Language-centred Approach to
   Plurilingualism**
   Michael Clyne 43
4 **Bilingual Education: Basic Principles**
   Jim Cummins. 56
5 **Bilingual Encounters in the Classroom**
   Peter Martin 67
6 **Language Planning: A Grounded Approach**
   Colin Baker. 88
7 **Accepting Bilingualism as a Language Policy: An Unfolding
   Southeast Asian Story**
   Gary M. Jones. 112
8 **Markets, Hierarchies and Networks in Language
   Maintenance and Language Shift**
   Li Wei and Lesley Milroy. 128
9 **The Imagined Learner of Malay**
   Anthea Fraser Gupta 141
10 **Code-switching and Unbalanced Bilingualism**
   Georges Lüdi 174
11 **Code-switching: Evidence of Both Flexibility and Rigidity in
   Language**
   Carol Myers-Scotton 189

12 Rethinking Bilingual Acquisition
   Fred Genesee 204

Laudatio: Hugo Baetens Beardsmore – No Hyphen Please!
Eric Lee 229

Index 233

Bilingualism: The Customers' Point of View

A quarter of a century ago, when our first child was expected, Marjukka and I knew instinctively that it was important for him to be bilingual. Our problem was that, for the lay parent, if anything at all was written about bilingualism, it was about its problems. Marjukka's parents, living in Finland (then as now an officially bilingual country!), were forever reading about the problems of 'semilingualism' amongst the children of Finnish factory workers in Sweden. They were full of prophecies of doom if we followed that route.

Stubborn, as always, we decided to use our publishing connections to see if there was any, more positive, material being published. There was, but to say it was widely scattered would be a masterly understatement. To illustrate that point you only have to look in the bibliography of the first edition of *Bilingualism: Basic Principles* to find that, if you leave aside Hugo's own work, you are well into the fourth page before a single source of publication is repeated. As we pursued our investigations, it was clear that all roads were leading to two people, Derrick Sharp and of course Hugo Baetens Beardsmore. These became two of the cornerstones on which the current activities of Multilingual Matters (originally Tieto Ltd) were founded.

In the ensuing years this house has published many of Hugo's works. Each new manuscript or returned set of proofs was heralded, as the envelope was opened, by the aroma of the author's favourite cigarettes. Over these last 25 years attitudes in most countries have changed, thanks in no small way to the works of contributors to this volume and the many other researchers and teachers inspired by the example of Hugo Baetens Beardsmore.

For us, however, the biggest test of all was to watch our two sons, as fully fledged bilinguals, take a close interest and full part in recent family ceremonies, the fears of their grandparents having long since vanished.

Whether they know it or not, around the world there are millions of people who need to say 'Thank you, Hugo, for helping us to live in naturally bilingual circumstances'.

Mike Grover, Multilingual Matters

Contributors

Colin Baker, *University of Wales, Bangor*

Hugo Baetens Beardsmore, *Vrije Universiteit Brussel*

Michael Clyne, *University of Melbourne*

Jim Cummins, *OISE, University of Toronto*

Jean-Marc Dewaele, *Birkbeck College, University of London*

John Edwards, *St Francis Xavier University*

Fred Genesee, *McGill University*

Anthea Fraser Gupta, *University of Leeds*

Alex Housen, *Vrije Universiteit Brussel*

Gary M. Jones, *University Brunei Darussalam*

Eric Lee, *Institut Supérieur de Traduction et d'Interprétariat, Brussels*

Li Wei, *University of Newcastle upon Tyne*

Georges Lüdi, *University of Basle*

Peter Martin, *University of Leicester*

Lesley Milroy, *University of Michigan*

Carol Myers-Scotton, *University of South Carolina*

Introduction and Overview

JEAN-MARC DEWAELE, ALEX HOUSEN and LI WEI

The past 20 years have seen an unprecedented upsurge of research on bilingualism. A major reason for this is no doubt the acknowledgement by a growing number of researchers that bilingualism – the presence of two or more languages – is far more common than was previously thought, and perhaps even the norm. The claim that bilinguals, rather than monolinguals, prevail is particularly compelling if one allows for a broad definition of bilingualism that includes not only the 'perfect' bilingual (who probably does not exist) or the 'balanced' ambilingual (who is probably rare) but also various 'imperfect' and 'unstable' forms of bilingualism, in which one language takes over from the other(s) on at least some occasions and for some instances of language use. Also at the societal level, bilingualism prevails. With an estimated 6000 languages currently being spoken in the world (Grimes, 1992), and with only some 200 countries, simple mathematics tells us that many countries must, in one way or another, be bi- or multilingual.

Individual and societal bilingualism are neither recent nor temporary phenomena. Bilingualism has always been with us. Still, the number of bilinguals at the turn of the third millennium is probably greater than ever before and will continue to grow as a result of the combined forces of globalisation, automatisation, increased mobility and migration and, in some parts of the world at least, the blurring of political borders. Also the current advance of bilingual education movements and foreign language teaching, formerly accessible to the élite only, contributes to the spread of bilingualism.

Acknowledging the prevalence of bilingualism has brought about a growing realisation that bilingualism in itself is innocuous. For a long time, the opposite view of bilingualism as a harmful psychological and social phenomenon was held. But there is now increasing evidence that, *given the right conditions*, bilingualism can confer distinct benefits like intellectual, psychological, social, cultural and economic improvement on the individual. And countries such as Luxembourg, Norway, Switzerland, Belgium,

Canada and Singapore stand as compelling reminders that bilingual societies need not be more unstable or disadvantaged than unilingual ones. On the contrary, the number of bi- and multilingual speakers a country produces may be seen as an indicator of its educational standards, economic competitiveness and cultural vibrancy. Clearly, bilingualism may be a condition to be aspired to and cherished, rather than one to be prevented or remedied.

Current research on bilingualism is motivated by various concerns. First, the prevalence of bilingualism as an individual and societal state, and the advantages it is thought to bestow, need further documenting, as do reactions to it from all quarters. For although the two insights mentioned above may be truisms to researchers, they are not so to the wider community and therefore they still need to be defended with empirically founded arguments. In this respect, it is important for researchers in bilingualism to take an objective stance and not to turn a blind eye to the potentially detrimental correlates of bilingualism. For, surely, there are cases where the presence of two or more languages has led to unhappy consequences for the individual or for the larger community, just as there are many others causing no such negative consequences or that have led to great satisfaction and enrichment. Of course, the same is true for circumstances in which only one language is involved. The important thing is to understand what is involved in being bilingual, so that when problems arise they can be seen in proper perspective.

Public awareness-raising is a long-term process. It takes time before research findings from the social sciences trickle down to the different social layers of a society. In this sense, bilingualism researchers must play an active sociopolitical role and provide the much needed rational arguments to overcome prejudice and fear. Entrenched negative attitudes towards bilingualism are not the preserve of any particular social class, or community. Although all governments officially encourage their citizens to learn foreign languages through formal instruction, those who put policies into practice might not share exactly the same view. The following anecdote illustrates the gap between the official discourse welcoming bilingualism and the political reality on the ground. Although the setting is Belgium, it could have been any one of many other countries where tensions exist between linguistics communities.

Pauline is a talented 8-year-old Dutch-French bilingual girl who lives in Brussels. She is fond of drawing, and her parents decide to send her to a small local French-speaking arts academy in Brussels. She loves it until, suddenly, after five months, a formal notification is sent to her parents expelling Pauline from the academy. The school authorities have noticed on the admission form that the father refused to sign a declaration stating that

Pauline's mother tongue or most used language is French. The parents are told that since that omission constitutes a violation of the Belgian linguistic legislation of 1963, their daughter will no longer be allowed to attend the school or any other French-speaking school within the Brussels region. The parents are shocked and lodge an appeal before the 'Jury of Language Issues', an administrative court. The parents have to attend a hearing at which they are asked questions such as 'What language do you speak at home?', 'In what language did Pauline utter her first words?', 'Where do you intend to send your daughter for her further education?'. The parents find themselves in a situation that reminds them of the Inquisition. Their appeal is eventually rejected. The parents therefore decide to institute legal proceedings against the Belgian State. At the moment of writing the case is still pending before a Brussels court. The fact that this incredible imbroglio happened in Brussels, the officially bilingual capital of a trilingual country and administrative heart of the officially multilingual European Union, is ironical to say the least.

There are other reasons for investigating bilingualism, too. Its study has practical applicability (e.g. for speech pathology, education, communication technology) as well as general theoretical utility. Research on bilingualism contributes to theorising in other disciplines (e.g. linguistics, sociology, psychology, neurology, pedagogy) and related fields (e.g. language acquisition, speech processing). General theories of the human mind, language and behaviour must ultimately incorporate the basic facts of bilingualism if they are to be comprehensive and viable.

While bilingualism may be a very ancient phenomenon, its study is still relatively young. Looking back over the brief history of bilingualism research reveals the early 1980s as a critical juncture. It is only since that time, after an intensive but mainly descriptive initial phase, that bilingualism research has actually started to systematically process its findings theoretically. One particularly important milestone was the publication, in 1982, of Hugo Baetens Beardsmore's book *Bilingualism: Basic Principles*. This publication was a timely one, as revealed by the book's opening lines: 'As with so many introductory works the present book grew out of a pressing need. Although there is a plethora of titles in the field of bilingualism [. . .] there is no single introductory work to the study of bilingualism that is readily accessible or easily digestible [. . .].'

Bilingualism: Basic Principles has been one of the most influential books on bilingualism and is internationally recognised as a classic. The book helped to define a still nascent discipline by bringing together, for the first time, a disparate body of knowledge and research into a comprehensive introductory text that incorporates the linguistic, sociolinguistic, sociopsychological, psycholinguistic, and educational manifestations of bilingualism. *Bilingualism: Basic Principles* deserves its status as a classic not merely because of its timely publication. Like its author's other writings, it combines the qualities of enlightenment without condescension, comprehensiveness without tedium, engagement without oversimplification.

As such, *Bilingualism: Basic Principles*, and its second revised 1986 edition, has not only provided several generations of students, practitioners, policy makers and families with a first broad, balanced introduction to bilingualism but also outlined a future research agenda, giving clear directions for moving beyond the basic principles of bilingualism. In doing so, it helped to set the stage for the explosion of research and theorising that the field has witnessed since the 1980s and to which Hugo Baetens Beardsmore himself has contributed in such full measure (e.g. Baetens Beardsmore, 1983, 1985, 1987, 1988, 1991, 1992, 1993, 1995).

Scholars and teachers are just as much a product of their background and experience as the subjects they study and profess. Hugo Baetens Beardsmore, the honorand of this volume, is no exception. Born in Flanders, raised in England, educated in Wales, currently living and working in Brussels (as well as many other places), and fluent in English, French and Dutch (as well as being functionally proficient in several more languages), Hugo Baetens Beardsmore has been a staunch yet pragmatic advocate of linguistic and cultural pluralism and its study throughout his long and active academic career. Much of his work in the 1970s and early 1980s was based on the experience and insights gathered from his research on the bilingual and triglossic situation in Brussels. His later work drew heavily on his insights in bilingual acquisition, second language acquisition and, particularly, bilingual education. Many of these insights were gained from his research on bilingual education models such as those implemented in the European Schools, the Grand Duchy of Luxembourg, the Basque Country, Brunei, Singapore, California and elsewhere. In relating these insights to those from other models of bilingual education, notably Canadian-style immersion, he was able to identify general principles underlying bilingual and second-language education. At the same time, in the wake of European integration, he became interested in language planning and the maintenance of linguistic diversity, both in the individual and at the larger, community level. With a prolific output of over 150 publications in four languages, Hugo Baetens Beardsmore has made substantive contributions in domains as wide-ranging as sociolinguistics, contact linguistics, language planning, language maintenance and shift, language and identity, language and the media, language testing, language teaching, second language acquisition, and, of course, bilingualism and bilingual education.

The eleven original papers in this volume have been written by leading scholars in the field of bilingualism, honouring Hugo Baetens Beardsmore's scholarship on the occasion of the 20th anniversary of his *Bilingualism: Basic Principles* and his own 60th birthday. Reflecting his own wide-ranging contributions to the field, the papers in this volume deal with individual bilingualism, societal and educational phenomena, addressing issues such as bilingual usage, acquisition, teaching, and language planning and policy. The volume's major asset lies in its diversity, not only in depth of investigation and in topical variety but also in the range of languages and geographical regions covered, reflecting the honorand's interests, experience and influence. Another important feature of the volume is its multidisciplinary perspective. Among the contributors are linguists, sociologists, psychologists, and sociolinguists.

The volume starts with a reprint of one of Hugo Baetens Beardsmore's lesser known publications. Originally published in 1988, 'Who's Afraid of Bilingualism?' grew out of a series of lectures that Hugo Baetens Beardsmore gave in the mid-1980s. It provides a compelling account of the most popular fears and misconceptions about bilingualism, which have not changed significantly since the paper was published. Hugo Baetens Beardsmore formulates it as follows: 'Given that something which is necessary and normal for many people is considered problematic and abnormal by many others requires us to examine what fears are expressed in order to dispel antagonisms.' The paper addresses consecutively parental fears ('What have I done to my child?'), cultural fears ('Does bilingualism entail acculturation?'), educational fears ('Does bilingualism affect academic progress?'), and politico-ideological fears ('Is bilingualism a threat to the nation state?'). Referring to earlier work by several contributors to the present volume, Hugo Baetens Beardsmore points out that while some apprehensions about bilingualism may reflect legitimate concerns, they are often linked to questions of a different nature. Fears about bilingualism are also often simply fears of the unknown. Hugo Baetens Beardsmore further points out that those who express fears about bilingual education are generally not directly involved.

The papers that follow cover issues of language policy, bilingual education, code-switching and language acquisition, all of which have been dealt with by Hugo Baetens Beardsmore himself in his various publications, and geographical areas, from Southeast Asia to North America and Europe, reflecting Hugo Baetens Beardsmore's special interests.

Chapter 2, by John Edwards, 'The Importance of Being Bilingual', is a critical analysis of what it means to be bilingual. He notes that the idea that bilingualism means loss has long since been discarded by researchers. Children learning multiple languages in a natural or instructed setting do so effortlessly. Bilingualism is more than the instrumental advantage of being able to communicate in several languages; its main importance is social and psychological. Indeed, Edwards puts it succinctly: 'the psychological heart of bilingualism is identity'.

A similar argument is developed in Chapter 3, 'Towards a more Language-centred Approach to Plurilingualism', in which Michael Clyne argues that more prominence should be given to language itself in analyses of multilingualism. While acknowledging the importance of instrumental and integrative motivation, he draws attention to the importance of intrinsic motivation and metalinguistic awareness in the maintenance, acquisition and development of a language.

Chapter 4, by Jim Cummins, 'Bilingual Education: Basic Principles', formulates a number of general principles in the research and theory on bilingual education. He argues that bilingualism should not be perceived as a problem but rather as an opportunity to develop the resources of a country more fully by implementing bilingual and trilingual programmes for minority language children. Absurd claims concerning bilingualism need to be countered in order to overcome the sociopolitical obstacles.

In Chapter 5, Peter Martin investigates bilingual Malay-English classroom discourse in the primary school classroom in Brunei. He argues that switching between languages is a perfectly acceptable form of communication. While pleading for a coherent framework for an appropriate bilingual methodology, he also observes that decisions about which languages are most appropriate for different events in the classroom are ultimately in the hands of classroom participants, i.e. teachers and learners.

Colin Baker, in Chapter 6, looks at the issue of language planning and the need to maintain the diversity of language and cultures in the world before focusing on the case of the Welsh language. He outlines the successful interactive and holistic approach to language planning implemented in Wales, which he sees as the foundation of language revival. He pleads for grounded action in language planning to save the minority languages of the world.

In Chapter 7, 'Accepting Bilingualism as a Language Policy: An Unfolding Southeast Asian Story', Gary Jones focuses on the bilingual education system in Brunei. Initial difficulties were gradually overcome when findings from bilingualism research were fed into language planning and education policy. He draws parallels with other Southeast Asian countries where the situation is roughly similar, namely in the development of forms of bilingualism that include both English and the national languages.

Li Wei and Lesley Milroy in Chapter 8, 'Markets, Hierarchies and Networks in Language Maintenance and Language Shift', consider societal multilingualism in Singapore, where four languages coexist: English, Mandarin-Chinese, Malay and Tamil. The authors analyse the process of language maintenance and language shift in relation to the concomitant processes of sociocultural changes. Rather than focusing on the experiences of minority groups, the authors consider ongoing variations and change in the patterns of language use of the majority.

The next, Chapter 9, 'The Imagined Learner of Malay', by Anthea Fraser Gupta, remains within the Southeast Asian context, but travels back four centuries. Seven books designed to enable English speakers to study Malay without a teacher are analysed. She shows how the dialogues in these textbooks create an imaginary learner whose social context reflects the history and conceptualisation of the Malay region, i.e. the cosmopolitan world of work with little attention to life among Malays. Colonial-style dialogues place the imaginary learner in a superior role.

The last three chapters focus on linguistic and psycholinguistic issues of bilingual language use and acquisition. Chapter 10, by Georges Lüdi, 'Code-switching and Unbalanced Bilingualism', focuses on 'translinguistic markers' in the speech of both proficient bilinguals and foreign language learners. Although formally similar, these markers have different functions which will determine their status as code-switching or translinguistic wording respectively. Their status will also depend on the definition of the setting as endolingual/exolingual and monolingual/bilingual. He concludes that bilinguality is linked to socially constructed norms of behaviours. This means that translinguistic markers may be perceived as violations of prescriptive linguistic norms in monolingual communities, and yet be perfectly acceptable in bilingual communities.

Carol Myers-Scotton, in Chapter 11, 'Code-switching: Evidence of Both Flexibility and Rigidity in Language', discusses examples from both classic code-switching and composite code-switching that provide evidence of areas of inflexibility and flexibility in the structure of language. She develops the idea of a composite Matrix Language that structures code-switching utterances. This happens when features of abstract grammatical structure from the former Embedded Language combine with features from the original source language.

Chapter 12, 'Rethinking Bilingual Acquisition', by Fred Genesee, dispels any remaining fears about the possible detrimental effects of bilingual first-language acquisition. He shows that developing infants possess the perceptual and memory capacities necessary to acquire two languages simultaneously. Infants exposed to two languages simultaneously form differentiated linguistic systems very early, that is at the babbling stage or even prenatally. Code-mixing should not be seen as a problem but rather as the reflection of additional processing capacities. In this he clearly concurs with views expressed earlier by Lüdi and Myers-Scotton.

The book closes with a personal account of Hugo Baetens Beardsmore's life and career by Eric Lee, the honorand's first doctoral student.

If we compare current research on bilingualism as exemplified in this volume with its founding days in the 1960s, we are struck by the liveliness of questioning that characterises this field as never before. Writings deriving from recent sociolinguistic and linguistic oriented points of view have made steady and cumulative progress. And thanks to the advances in methodology, innovative work currently being done in psycholinguistics and neurocognition augurs well for the future. In more piecemeal fashion, educators and policy makers are finally offering their own type of sophistication. The current range of models, views and approaches in bilingualism research is almost staggering in its inclusiveness, a medley of all conceivable traditions in contemporary science, to the extent that no single book – the present one included – can purport to provide a comprehensive, balanced overview. In a sense, such diversity is healthy. Bilingualism, both at the individual and societal level, is a phenomenon of such complexity that the wider the lens through which it is viewed, the more complete the resultant picture will be. By the same token, however, there is a risk that the proliferation of approaches and models will obscure the path leading to a comprehensive, integrated theory. Hugo Baetens Beardsmore's life of pioneering work in linguistic and cultural pluralism should continue to serve as an inspiration for those who must now second him in this most challenging of fields.

In editing this volume, we have received contributions, encouragement and support from friends and colleagues across the world. John Edwards, the series editor, offered valuable advice. Mike and Marjukka Grover and all their staff at Multilingual Matters are exceptionally understanding and patient with our delays, inconsistencies and incompetency. Due to the time constraint, many of Hugo Baetens Beardsmore's friends and colleagues who wished to contribute articles to the present volume were unable to do so. They nevertheless made valuable contributions in terms of advice and moral support. We are especially grateful to Hugo Baetens Beardsmore himself for allowing us to reprint one of his articles in the present volume.

References

Baetens Beardsmore, H. (1982) *Bilingualism: Basic Principles*. Clevedon: Multilingual Matters.

Baetens Beardsmore, H. (1983) Substratum, adstratum and residual bilingualism in Brussels. *Journal of Multilingual and Multicultural Development* 4 (1), 1–14.

Baetens Beardsmore, H. (1992) Bilingual education. In J. Lynch, C. Modgil and S. Modgil (eds) *Cultural Diversity and the Schools: Volume One, Education for Cultural Diversity: Convergence and Divergence* (pp. 273–283.). London: Falmer Press.

Baetens Beardsmore, H. (1993) European models of bilingual education: Practice, theory and development. *Journal of Multilingual and Multicultural Development* 14 (1 & 2), 103–20.

Baetens Beardsmore, H. (1995) The European School experience in multilingual education. In T. Skutnabb-Kangas (ed.) *Multilingualism for All* (pp. 21–68). Lisse: Swets & Zeitlinger.

Baetens Beardsmore, H. and Kohls, J. (1988) Immediate pertinence in the acquisition of multilingual proficiency: The European Schools. *The Canadian Modern Language Review* 44 (4), 680–701.

Baetens Beardsmore, H. and Lebrun, N. (1991) Trilingual education in the Grand Duchy of Luxembourg. In O. Garcîa (ed.) *Bilingual Education: Focusschrift in Honour of Joshua Fishman* (pp. 107–20). Vol. I, Amsterdam/Philadelphia: Benjamins.

Baetens Beardsmore, H. and Swain, M. (1985) Designing bilingual education: aspects of immersion and 'European School Models'. *Journal of Multilingual and Multicultural Development* 6 (1), 1–15.

Baetens Beardsmore, H. and Witte, E. (eds) (1987) *The Interdisciplinary Study of Urban Bilingualism in Brussels*. Clevedon/Philadelphia: Multilingual Matters.

Grimes, B. (ed.) (2000) *Ethnologue: Volume 1, Languages of the World, 14th Edition*. Dallas: SIL International.

Chapter 1

Who's Afraid of Bilingualism?

H. BAETENS BEARDSMORE

Introduction

My reading of the literature on bilingualism and visits to different countries to lecture both formally and informally on the topic have led me to conclude that there is a deep-seated and widespread fear of bilingualism. Moreover, there is an all-pervading tendency to couple the notion of 'problems' to that of bilingualism, a connotation that never comes to mind in discussions on unilingualism. Even those positively inclined towards the phenomenon fall into this defensive position and sub-consciously attribute it with a status that at best requires cautious nurturing and at worst remedial intervention. Such connotations arise from the assumption that unilingualism is the norm and that bilingualism represents some sort of deviation. Yet as Haugen (1972: 309) has stated, 'necessity is the mother of bilingualism'; the majority of people who manipulate two languages do so because to them it is a natural corollary to functioning efficiently as a human being, be it because of residence patterns, family circumstances, employment opportunities or intellectual needs. To the average bilingual his linguistic status is the norm, though he may well be made to feel that this is not so.

Given that something which is necessary and normal for many people is considered problematic and abnormal by many others requires us to examine what fears are expressed in order to dispel antagonisms. Although much research undertaken in the second half of this century has been positive both in approach and outcome yet it has failed to affect general opinions on bilingualism. Two reasons may explain this situation. First, the message from research is not getting across, partly because many of us implicitly accept the problematic connotation. Secondly, we are not sufficiently aware of the nature and extent of the fears evoked by bilingualism so that we do not know how to direct the research findings to the right adversaries. Hence we need to investigate the multiple levels of connotation so as to confront fears squarely, distinguish the rational from the unfounded, review the types of fears expressed and examine the evidence that surrounds them.

Two broad kinds of fears come to the fore, those that reflect societal preoccupations and those centring on the individual, though they are often intertwined. What is striking, however, is how few bilinguals share such fears, when compared with unilinguals. Grosjean (1982: 268) surveyed bilingual and trilingual individuals about the inconvenience of having more than one language and found that 52% of the bilinguals and 67% of the trilinguals simply replied 'no inconvenience' while not a single subject felt that there were no advantages. Further, many bilinguals feel that the apparent difference between them and unilinguals is a figment of the latters' imagination (Grosjean, 1982: 273).

Four groups of fears will be discussed here as representative of the most prevalent types encountered. Others may well come to mind but appear as less widespread or are less significant to the general debate. Two will be considered as individual in nature, namely parental and cultural fears, the two others as more societal, namely educational and politico-ideological fears, though the division is somewhat arbitrary. The discussion will focus on an analysis of the literature since the results of an enquiry designed to tap the prevalence of fears are not available at the time of going to print, though they will be presented orally as an annex to this paper.

Parental Fears

Here one must deal with a variety of apprehensions which may arise in parents who either (1) come from unilingual backgrounds and when confronted by bilingualism tend to transfer the difficulties of their own adult experience to what they suspect affects their children, or (2) although bilinguals themselves are isolated in a generally unilingually environment which pressurises them into worrying about bilingualism in their children. The very existence of the *Bilingual Family Newsletter* testifies to the presence of parental fears, with its regular series of readers' questions requiring advice and reassurance. De Jong's (1986) investigation into parents affected by bilingualism in their children revealed how friends, neighbours and teachers who know nothing about the subject instill worry in parents through bad advice. The folklore influence of non-specialist opinion was often decisive among parents who chose against bringing up their children bilingually when they were in a position to do so; such parents related horror stories of bilingual children who were disturbed, had problems with stuttering or were behind at school.

> However, in my search for material I did not go by hearsay information
> and I myself have not come across any children with serious problems
> resulting from their bilingual home environment. (de Jong, 1986: 33)

Harding and Riley's (1986) report of 16 case studies came to the same
conclusion, even in complex circumstances. Their comments on a French/
Austrian couple who had lived in Brazil and France and brought up their
children in Portugese, German and French, are revealing – 'the problems
seem to be the parents' not the children's' (Harding & Riley, 1986: 33). I
myself have never come across a child whose problems can unequivocally
be attributed to bilingualism, though there are cases where bilingualism
has compounded other difficulties, for example divorce by parents of
mixed language backgrounds followed by remarriage with a partner using
a new language leading to the introduction of a new lingua franca for
family interactions.

Parents sometimes transfer their own difficulties in coping with a new
language environment to their children, as illustrated by an English couple
who withdrew their children from a French language school in Belgium
when they appeared to make little progress in French after a few months.
The parents, educators themselves, worried about their girls' withdrawal
and silence in school which they attributed to lack of French; the parents
themselves however, were critical of the new school's teaching practices,
disciplinary codes and socialisation patterns. The parents' difficulties in
adapting to their children's new educational system were interpreted in
terms of language problems where these were probably only one of several
causes of silence and withdrawal. The girls were removed to an English
language school and never learnt French after several years in the French
environment. This fact, however, was not seen as a problem.

Some parents harbour guilt feelings if their careers make them move to a
new linguistic environment and ask themselves 'What have I done to my
child?' The assumption is that coping with one language is simpler than
living with two, that they have taken an unknown risk and put an extra
burden on the child (de Jong, 1986: 33). Yet Saunders (1982) and Fantini
(1985) have clearly shown how their own children had no more difficulties
with two languages than with one, echoed by Cummins' (1984: 285) review
of a large body of evidence. Nowhere in the specialist literature are any
grounds for fears on this count to be found as long as the family background is stable, relaxed and positive towards the languages involved.

Some parents fear that bilingualism stunts the linguistic development of
young children in particular. This fear fails to appreciate the developmental stages in dual language acquisition, particularly the significance of
input factors. A child who receives input divided across two languages,

often in unequal proportions, should not be compared with a child who receives input in one language, as is often the case, or we could be expecting the bilingual to live twice. Swain (1981) has shown that it may take a little longer for the bilingual child to acquire the equivalent competence of monolingual peers, depending on the amount of input and the particular circumstances of the bilingual experience. With time bilingual children catch up and sometimes surpass their unilingual peers in competence in one of their languages. To this end, ' . . . the specific language of communication is much less significant than the quality and quantity of communication' (Cummins, 1984: 271).

Some parents fear that a child who does not have a single language fails to forge firm emotional ties with a given linguistic-cultural community. Lambert and Aellen (1972) compared middle-class children of mixed ethnic parentage with those from homogeneous backgrounds, noting that the former had developed a dual allegiance to the two language groups in their lives and manifested healthy personality and social characteristics. Enquiries among multilingual adolescents in the European School system (Housen & Baetens Beardsmore, 1987) revealed that the majority of subjects had no polarised stances towards the language groups they were involved with, lacked stereotyped attitudes towards members of other groups, and maintained dual or multiple language loyalty patterns.

Certain parents experience feelings of regret that their bilingual children's linguistic and cultural allegiance is not as strong as their own, particularly if the older child preferentially opts for a language group other than that of the parents. This is sometimes the case with immigrant parents whose children slip away from the values the immigrant brought with him in favour of those of the mainstream society. Tensions may arise if parents attempt to resist this tendency which may be no more than an assertion of individuality and independence expressing itself in terms of language and culture.

However widespread parental fears about bilingualism may be, the literature shows that most of them are unfounded. Such fears are never mentioned in accounts of multilingual societies where bilingualism is the norm.

Cultural Fears

These represent an area difficult to circumscribe because of the lack of consensus on what the attributes of culture are, how these are absorbed, transmitted and measured. The difficulty of distinguishing between language and culture has been shown by Miller (1983) who describes how her

enquiry into the role of language in the lives of her bilingual subjects was
constantly deflected onto other issues:

> . . . my somewhat dogged insistence that my interlocutors keep to the
> subject of language was defeated time and time again. Only later did I
> realise that these speakers' evading of my questions about language in
> order to talk about immigration, culture, family conflict, social and po-
> litical dilemmas, constituted, in fact, and significantly, answers to my
> questions. (Miller, 1983: 17)

Fitouri (1983: 214–15) attempted to differentiate between language and
culture among Arabic–French bilinguals in Tunisia by discussing four
types of individual: (1) monocultural monolinguals, (2) monocultural
bilinguals, (3) bicultural monolinguals, and (4) bicultural bilinguals. The
first type is irrelevant to the present discussion. The second type is typical
of the adult learner of a foreign language in his home country, for example
the university graduate who develops dual language abilities while retaining monocultural values and attitudes. The third category of bicultural
monolinguals refers to the children of immigrants who do not use the parents' original language but who have maintained the customs, beliefs and
value systems of their parents, transmitted within the home through the
medium of the language of the outside community. The fourth category of
bicultural bilinguals reflects the speakers who have acquired an additive
form of bilingualism, who can function in either language community with
ease, can appreciate the diversified cultural facets of both groups and does
not engender or perceive any frictions in interacting with speakers of either
language

There is a further category which does not fit into the above breakdown,
though Fitouri's book devotes considerable attention to the type in question. This involves bilinguals who undergo a form of disorientation or
acculturation brought about by cultures in conflict. In Tunisia, where
Arabic and French are used in education, it appears that people from upper
social groups have no problems with the bicultural values implicit in Tunisia's Arabic–French education system, whereas those from lower social
strata have difficulties in reconciling the two cultures embodied in the different languages:

> . . . tant qu'on ne vise que le sommet de la pyramide sociale, le
> bilinguisme et le biculturalisme ne peuvent être perçus que comme un
> bien. Ils deviennent le mal personifié dès qu'on regarde la base de cette
> pyramide. (Fitouri, 1983: 282)

This 'evil personified' is explained by the fact that whereas upper level
groups are orientated towards cosmopolitan values which makes bilin-

gualism stimulating and enriching lower level groups in Tunisia are more orientated towards traditional, indigenous cultural values which makes them perceive bilingualism as a profound cultural aggression (Fitouri, 1983: 49–50). Garmadi (1972: 319) uses equally strong terms to describe cultural destabilisation brought about by bilingualism in developing nations, where he talks of linguistic and cultural mutilation. Such statements reveal that cultural fears cannot be dismissed lightly.

To avoid problems of acculturation, or as T'Sou (1985) strikingly puts it in his discussion of Anglo-Chinese bilinguals in Hong Kong, the cultural eunuch syndrome, before the second culture gets imposed: 'il faut, au préalable, être bien enraciné dans la sienne propre' (Fitouri, 1983: 285).

This conclusion coincides with that expressed with reference to lower level immigrant populations in Europe who undergo subtractive bilingualism through inadequate educational provision. Skutnabb-Kangas (1984) argues that without maintenance of the mother tongue and culture there is a risk of conflicts of identity, rootlessness, marginality and alienation. Miller's (1983) investigation of immigrant teenagers in Britain brought out similar cultural problems:

> There is the presence of contradiction, duality, ambivalency, which characterises the girls' experiences and attitudes and their accounts of them. Language meant for them the things they used it for, so that relationships, cultural differences, their efforts to bridge gaps between their own age group and their families, the past, the present and the future, were easier to talk about than language in isolation. (Miller, 1983: 45)

The parallelisms between lower level groups in developing nations and similar immigrant groups in industrialised nations is striking, as is the fact that cultural questions are discussed in terms of conflicts between traditionalism and modernism, and in the last example in generation gap difficulties. It seems that the class factor plays a primary role which determines to some extent whether bilingualism is additive or substractive and which affects biculturalism. With elite bilingualism conflicting cultural pressures seem to be absent.

Paulston (1982) warns about bicultural expectations among immigrants in her example of Turkish girls from traditional villages who later grew up in Sweden:

> It is difficult to see how these girls can internalize both their fathers' value system of women and that of Swedish society. In fact, they can't, and that situation casts many serious doubts on the many glib statements of biculturalism as one objective of bilingual education. (Paulston, 1982: 43)

If the bilingual's two cultures are mutually exclusive it is impossible to harmonise them, though McLaughlin (1985: 39) feels that this does not necessarily mean that immigrant children are more emotionally disturbed or have higher rates of psychopathology than do comparable groups. As Ekstrand (1981) points out, when socio-economic class variables are controlled immigrant children differ little in social and emotional adjustment from comparable indigenous children. Moreover, it is often difficult to separate the stresses caused by biculturalism from those due to urbanisation, whether in the developing world or industrial nations.

McLaughlin believes that the solution for immigrant children is to opt for one culture or the other. This assumes there is a choice, which may be the case if bilingual education is fully developed but not in the majority of circumstances where few schools provide dual language provision for immigrants that goes beyond surface features. Moreover, where bilingual education is fully developed there appear to be few problems of biculturalism, at least in industrialised nations. Bentahila (1983) examined cultural fears among Arabic–French balanced bilinguals of middle-class origins between the ages of 15 and 45 in Morocco. Results were mitigated. To the statement, 'The Moroccan bilingual is divided between two cultures (Arabic and French), and he does not seem to fully belong to either', a small majority of respondents agreed, as did a similar slight majority with the statement, 'Arabic–French bilingualism produces in Moroccans a cultural crisis and lack of identity'. On the other hand, a slight majority of respondents disagreed with the stronger statement that, 'Arabic–French bilingualism produces in Moroccans a lack of culture and originality'. In spite of the above responses there was still an overwhelming majority in favour of bilingualism, as can be seen from responses to the following two questions:

> 'Do you regret being bilingual?'
> Yes 8.25% No 87.15% Blank 4.58% No. of respondents 109
> 'Are you for bilingualism or Arabization?'
> For bil. 62.5% For Arab. 32.5% Blank 5% No. of respondents 120.
>
> (Bentahila, 1983: 146–7)

For these middle-class Moroccans then, the utilitarian value of bilingualism seems to outweigh the cultural fears or the totality of responses would have been more consistent. Bentahila (1983: 152) explains his findings in terms of a conflict between ideology and practicality, between Arabisation for idealistic and patriotic reasons and bilingualism for practical reasons.

An examination of the literature reveals that there may well be some ground for cultural fears in certain circumstances. With middle-class populations in both developing and industrialised nations such grounds seem slight. With lower level groups in both types of society the grounds seem more justified. Remedies for alleviating such fears are not self-evident, given the incompatibilities of the cultures in conflict. The least traumatic solution seems to be the provision of fully developed bilingual education in both developing and industrialised nations so as to provide the recipients with at best bicultural potential and at worst an option. Whether the option the individual takes is not that of the mainstream society may well lead to further difficulties but at the least it avoids the imposition of linguistic imperialism so that the problem ensuing will be less of an individual than a societal one.

Educational Fears

In this section one needs to examine both the populations that express fears and the types of fears expressed, since the two do not appear to coincide. On the one hand there are those who have undergone bilingual education or who experience it indirectly as parents, on the other there are those who have little experience of the phenomenon but are often most vocal in expressing negative opinions as to its effects. There is almost no mention in the literature of fears about bilingual education by those who are directly involved. Many research workers express dissatisfaction about inadequate bilingual education provision, though they never suggest its radical replacement by unilingual education. This is because where children are involved in bilingual upbringing it is either by choice or necessity; those involved by choice are lucky recipients of what Fishman (1976: 28–9) has called enrichment programmes. Those involved by necessity are usually immigrant populations or ethnic minorities (except in developing nations) where the bilingual provision is frequently temporary, often inadequate and usually stigmatised as marginal.

Elite bilingualism is that which has been entered upon as a conscious option by parents from stable, middle-class backgrounds who are in a position to support the educative process with back-up involvement. With these populations there is no conflict between the values of the home and the wider environment. Global outlines of bilingual provision for these populations can be found in Mackey (1972), Fishman (1976), Swain & Lapkin (1982), Baetens Beardsmore and Swain (1985). Few fears are recorded among the populations referred to in the above publications.

With ethnic and immigrant minorities bilingual education is usually remedial or transitional, i.e. where the ultimate goal is to move the recipients into unilingual education, unlike in enrichment programmes. The recipients are usually grateful for the bilingual provision, even though it may not have been entered upon voluntarily and they do not come from middle-class backgrounds. Often the parents are not in a position to provide the back-up involvement in the educative process from which the schools benefit and there may be cultural conflict between the values of the home and those of the school or between those of the home and the wider environment. It is with reference to these populations that most fears have been expressed about bilingual education, though not by the recipients themselves.

Cummins (1984: 101ff.) provides an overview of the types of fears expressed, together with commentary. They can be summarised into the following: bilingualism will handicap a child's speech development, intellectual progress, educational chances, emotional stability; may cause character difficulties so that children become aggressive and anti-social; bring about schizophrenia; make children ambivalent; cause cultural disorientation or opposing pulls of loyalty; make children morally untrustworthy and engender linguistic sloppiness. If these dangers have any basis in reality one wonders how there can be any children present in the enrichment bilingual programmes referred to earlier, amazed that the voluntary Canadian immersion programmes involve more than 100,000 children or that parents are clamouring for access to the restricted entry, multilingual European Schools (Baetens Beardsmore & Kohls, 1988). Obviously the fears expressed cannot refer to these programmes, even though individual parents may well have some misgivings. Where misgivings have arisen, however, they are usually dispelled by the reassurance that the schools in question know their business and that the outcome is positive both for the individual and society.

Since minority populations have no choice about their bilingual status it is futile to allow fears about bilingualism to impede its proper development. The bilingual status must be taken as given and fears eliminated by ensuring adequate educational provision; the enrichment programmes clearly indicate that this is feasible. This does not imply that identical solutions are applicable to majority and minority populations engaged in bilingual education, as has been amply demonstrated by Cummins (1984) and Skutnabb-Kangas (1984), to which we refer for detailed discussion of differentiated circumstances. Our concern being more with fears than with models we must turn to an examination of evidence to dispel anxieties.

Cummins (1984: 44) points out that there is no evidence that bilingualism, in the form of a home–school language switch, exerts any negative effects on children's academic development, in spite of the misguided assumptions of many school personnel. He illustrates the mistaken advice schools give to parents, such as abandoning the home language or providing extra tuition in the language of the wider environment. The real educational problem lies with biases in test measurements, bias in cultural indices of learning styles, an inadequate appreciation of the amount of time required to achieve academic and conceptual skills in a second language, and the erroneous assumption that eliminating the first language as quickly as possible will help promote the learning of the second language when in fact the opposite may be true. Note than none of these factors intervene in enrichment bilingual programmes for the elite.

Bruck (1984) also shows how a home–school language switch, here in the case of immersion programmes, need have no negative effects on academic progress. She points out that in Canada between 10% and 20% of the school population have learning difficulties which cannot be attributed to socio-economic status and that between 7% and 10% of the total school population exhibit some specific type of learning problem. Hence one can expect similar proportions among any population in bilingual education and that such proportions cannot be directly attributable to bilingualism. Bruck also notes that minority children are often classified as handicapped when their primary difficulty lies in an inadequate knowledge of the school language. Hence, no distinction is made between those who have general learning problems and those with specific difficulties due to language. Bruck examined cases where language disabled children were placed in immersion education and compared them with similar children in unilingual education or with those who had been transferred from immersion to unilingual schools. Results showed that the children who were transferred continued to have the same problems as when they were in immersion. Changing the language of instruction did not alleviate the problem. Children who made the most successful adjustment in the unilingual stream were those who received the most intensive and individualised remedial help. Children with problems who remained in bilingual education and who received remedial assistance in the second language, French, fared particularly well.

Genesee (1976) came to similar conclusions with children of below average IQ ratings in French immersion programmes, showing that the bilingual nature of their education has no negative effects if one compared with low IQ unilingually educated children. On the contrary, the children in immersion had the edge on their unilingual counterparts in that they also learnt French.

What the above studies show is that bilingual education need neither cause nor compound educational problems but that tailor-made solutions are required to overcome the learning difficulties of specific children, not the elimination of bilingualism.

If we turn to who expresses fears about bilingual education it is noteworthy that the vast majority represent people who are not directly involved. Hakuta (1986: 224) notes the virulence of its detractors in the United States, observing that the fears expressed have less to do with education than with perceptions concerning national unity. In other words, bilingual educational provision is seen by some as a threat to the status of the majority language. These fears will be dealt with in the next section (Politico-ideological fears). Of interest here is the poll Hakuta conducted to discover whether public opinion as reflected in newspaper accounts of a four-to-one bias against bilingual education was a mirror of general feeling. Of 179 respondents contacted only 18% felt that bilingual education provision should be decreased while 50% felt it should be increased, 58% believed it should be developed into an enrichment programme and 70% were in favour as a means of helping minority immigrants. Negative feelings were expressed with greater virulence than positive opinions and interestingly negative opinions were often expressed by immigrants who were themselves bilingual but who had not benefited from bilingual educational provision.

All the findings in the literature show that we need a precise picture of the types of fears expressed and of those who express them. They also show that the majority of fears are unfounded if one is dealing with truly bilingual education, properly developed and long-term in nature. Investigations show that fears about inadequately developed bilingual provision are warranted and these are shared by committed specialists but that in no case are the worries about bilingualism itself. The picture is not quite so clear-cut with reference to developing nations using a dual language education system, as can be seen from the research conducted by Bentahila (1983) in Morocco, or by Fitouri (1983) and Riguet (1984) in Tunisia where a social cleavage seems to determine the outcome of nationally imposed bilingual education.

Politico-ideological Fears

In this area it is important to bear in mind the symbolic significance of language which tends to mask issues that may be expressed through language but which are not necessarily directly related: 'Unease about language is almost always symptomatic of a larger unease' (McArthur, 1986: 87).

Many fears expressed about the negative aspects of bilingualism tend to be overtly directed towards questions of culture, aesthetics, education, which hide the covert preoccupations of those involved: 'The issues in question, I would suggest, are much more likely to be such things as dominance, elitism, ethnicity, economic control, social status and group security' (McArthur, 1986: 88).

Great care must be taken in the interpretation of fears of a politico-ideological nature surrounding bilingualism, for even when the facts warrant apprehensions one must be cautious not to extend arguments relevant for one context in applying them to another. In cases where the co-existence of different linguistic communities has led to tensions it is important to analyse the background context. Nelde (1987) believes that language contact means language conflict and that language conflict arises from the confrontation of differing standards, values and attitude structures which strongly influence identity image, education and group consciousness Nelde does not make it clear, however, whether by language contact he is referring to bilingualism on the group level or to contiguous unilingual elements. For often the very tensions arise because of a *lack* of bilingualism among segments of mixed heritage communities, or else because of attempts to eradicate bilingualism attendant on the co-existence of different linguistic communities within one political entity. Again this raises the question as to whether fears are really about bilingualism or whether they should be about unilingualism. Where tensions have arisen in mixed language political entities they have often done so because of inadequate language management at the macro-sociological level. It should also not be forgotten that certain mixed language political entities have successfully avoided tensions, though these tend to be ignored in the analysis of bilingual problems.

Let us assume for the moment that unilingualism is desirable for the cohesion of a given nation-state. History has shown that wherever this goal has been promoted by political intervention in the form of encouraging language shift to a dominant language, this has rarely succeeded. Welsh has not been eradicated from the United Kingdom in spite of the Act of 1535 forbidding its use in official life, Breton has not disappeared from France in spite of its elimination from education and the public sphere since the French Revolution, Catalan and Basque did not die out in Spain under the Franco regime in spite of severe repression. Official attempts to destroy a language have often merely promoted tension without achieving language shift.

Calvet's (1987) *La guerre des langues* with its portentous imagery of language war, analyses language conflict and linguistic imperialism in theoretical terms and concludes:

> . . . derrière cette guerre des langues, se profile une lutte pour le pouvoir; c'est la langue de la capitale, ou celle de l'ethnie dominante, qui tente de s'implanter comme langue unique, exclusive des autres, ce sont ses locuteurs qui tentent d'imposer leur culture aux autres. (Calvet, 1987: 181)

Marshall's (1986) analysis of attitudes towards bilingualism within the United States clearly brings out the political and ideological fears that underlie hostility. Lord and T'Sou's (1985) *The Language Bomb* uses explosive imagery to analyse language contact in Hong Kong, though rather than portending doom and gloom it represents a plea for properly managed promotion of bilingualism. Whether they be advocates or opponents of bilingualism all those who discuss problems treat questions of socio-economic status, of power, of education and ideology expressed in terms of language. These factors are clearly brought to the fore when one examines political entities where language tensions exist.

Belgium is a trilingual nation notorious for its linguistic tensions. These have occurred because of an imbalance in prestige and public recognition between the language of the statistical majority, Dutch, and that of the statistical minority, French. (It is noteworthy that there are few problems with the tiny German minority, which tends to be bilingual anyway.) For years economic and political power, together with intellectual prestige, coincided with the functions of the French language, thereby imposing bilingualism on those Dutch speakers who aspired to upward social mobility. This one-way pattern of bilingualism led to language loss, most significantly in the Belgian capital where there was massive language shift from Dutch to French predominance (Witte & Baetens-Beardsmore, 1987). This shift had been promoted by means of widespread bilingualism among Dutch speakers and its absence among French speakers. Increasing political awareness of the relationship between language and socio-economic status led to the gradual redress of the imbalance between Belgium's two major communities whereby today upward social mobility is no longer coupled with language shift from Dutch to French. The creation of structural equality between the two major communities by political means has brought a halt to language shift via the intermediary of one-way bilingualism. Hence, present-day fears about bilingualism within the Dutch community are justified by historical precedent since past experience has shown that bilingualism leads to language loss in the community that uses a socially, economically and politically stigmatised language (Willemyns, 1984: 250). On the other hand, since the root causes of the stigma have now been eliminated there should no longer be any fear of the consequences of bilingualism on the Dutch language community, though there are at present few signs of a more confident attitude.

It has already been seen (cf. Cultural Fears, above) that in certain developing nations where bilingualism pertains in the form of an ex-colonial language co-existing with indigenous languages certain fears of acculturation have been expressed. Both Fitouri (1983) and Riguet (1984) discuss the ideological debate around the role of bilingualism in education in Tunisia and reveal how the superimposition of French on Arabic alienates the middle-class elite from the rest of the population, drives a wedge between social groups and engenders language determined class tensions. Whether similar circumstances give rise to analogous fears in other developing nations is not clear from the literature. Calvet (1987) surveys such multi-ethnic nations as Burkina Faso, the Central African Republic, Guinea, Chad and Zaire which distinguish between an official language, French, the language of state functions, national languages of varied status with regional and symbolic functions, and a variety of vernaculars. In such multi-ethnic states there seems no option but for bi- and multi-lingualism and linguistic diversity has long been a fact of life. The widespread bilingualism which of necessity prevails in such countries does not at present appear to warrant fears, or if so they do not come to the forefront of preoccupations.

The attitudes towards bilingualism in the United States, as documented by Marshall (1986), illustrate a perceived threat to national identity under the influx of massive immigration from mainly Spanish-speaking countries. The Californian senator Hayakawa maintains that: 'A common language can unify, separate languages can fracture and fragment a society' (quoted in Marshall, 1986: 23).

This standpoint is debatable since Northern Ireland has a common language but is divided on religious ideology, whereas Luxembourg, Switzerland, Finland and Singapore all use several languages without social fragmentation. But assuming Hayakawa were correct then it is precisely by promoting bilingualism among the immigrant population that linguistic unity with the English-speaking majority can be attained, not the opposite. It is not bilingualism which should be feared, but the absence of bilingualism in the immigrant population. Hostility towards bilingualism in the United States is based on assimilationist arguments of the type recorded in Marshall (1986: 25): 'Linguistic minority groups . . . must learn English if they are to become fully integrated into American society', which may be perfectly true but need not imply that bilingualism should be feared since there is no reason why the acquisition of English should lead to the disuse of another language. Those hostile to bilingualism fear that in tolerating the use of other languages immigrants are not motivated to learn English. This argument puts the cart before the horse since it implies that language is the key to integration when in fact it is integration that is the key to language acquisition according to Schumann's (1986) acculturation model. It is impossible to learn a language without using it, impossible to use it without interaction, impossible to interact without social integration. Hence if integration between immigrants and the host population is achieved this enhances language acquisition among immigrants which allows bilingualism to develop, thereby avoiding the fragmentation alluded to earlier. Moreover, since the immigrant requires time to acquire the new language if not already known prior to resettlement it is absurd to fear his bilingualism by envisaging the immediate disappearance of his first language, as expressed in an outrageous statement quoted from a San Francisco newspaper in Marshall (1968: 61):

> The new immigrants seem less willing to give up their native tongue. They gave up their homeland, why do they resist giving up their language? A little intolerance is good for the soul. If you go around tolerating everything all the time, you get walked all over. I personally enjoy being intolerant once in a while. I'm intolerant of people who come here to live and don't want to learn to speak English.

The idea that the immigrant should discard his original language on entry to a new country implies he must become a mute until such time as he can operate in the new language! But even after acquiring the new language he is not likely to forget the one he has carried in his head for years before so he is still likely to remain bilingual. Calvet (1987: 76) notes that: '. . . l'homme accepte mal la différence', and shows advocates of unilingualism as representing an ideology of superiority which uses the weapon of deprecation against bilingualism.

Although one cannot ignore the fears expressed about bilingualism with reference to immigration in countries like the United States it is felt they are exaggerated and largely unwarranted. In no way do the political and social circumstances resemble those found in countries like Belgium (or Canada, or India for that matter, where tensions have prevailed) because of the presence of contiguous unilingual populations. Nor are they in any respect similar to those of developing nations like Tunisia where a second ex-colonial language imposed on the total population drives a socio-economic wedge between different social groups. The situation is more akin to that which prevailed in Brussels in which socio-economic and prestige factors have led to massive language shift from a minority to a majority language, where majority is to be understood in terms of politico-ideological factors. This shift has occurred over time by the very means of bilingualism and has also been arrested in recent decades by the non-encouragement of bilingualism. Hence instead of discouraging bilingualism as implicit in American hostility to the phenomenon it appears that by encouraging it amongst the immigrant population one is more likely to achieve the desired goal of integration. There are no simplistic arguments which oppose the advantages of unilingualism over bilingualism in any given political entity. Unilingualism cannot be achieved by decree, as has been seen in Catalonia and the Basque country. Bilingualism may or may not provoke tensions, depending on socio-economic, political and ideological circumstances. Linguistic courtesy, on the other hand, can do much to dispel the fears surrounding bilingualism.

Conclusion

The above examination has not gone into all the fears expressed about bilingualism. We have ignored purist fears concerning the effects of bilingual usage on language norms (Milan, 1982), moral fears concerning a supposed relativisation of moral standards due to a weakening of certitude brought about by the comparability inherent to bilingualism. One fear not examined is that concerning the cost of bilingualism. But if we can accept that 'necessity is the mother of bilingualism' then there is very little choice and it is not clear anyway that provision for bilingualism need cost any more than unilingualism. Moreover, in the ever-shrinking world of the global village there is no way of escape from the increasing prevalence of bilingualism so that whatever fears get expressed must be faced squarely and adjudged in terms of the inevitable changes in society to which we must all adapt.

Acknowledgement

This chapter is based on a paper presented at the 2nd World Basque Congress, San Sebastian, Spain, 31 September to 4 October 1987.

References

Baetens Beardsmore, H. and Kohls, J. (1988) Immediate pertinence in the acquisition of multilingual proficiency. The European Schools. *The Canadian Modern Language Review* 44 (2), 680–701.

Baetens Beardsmore, H. and Swain, M. (1985) Designing bilingual education: Aspects of immersion and 'European School' models. *Journal of Multilingual and Multicultural Development* 6 (1), 1–15.

Bentahila, A. (1983) *Language Attitudes among Arabic-French Bilinguals in Morocco.* Clevedon: Multilingual Matters.

Bruck, M. (1984) *The Suitability of Immersion Education for Children with Special Needs.* In C. Rivera (ed.) *Communicative Competence Approaches to Language Proficiency Assessment: Research and Application* (pp. 123–31). Clevedon: Multilingual Matters.

Calvet, J.-L. (1987) *La guerre des langues et les politiques linguistiques.* Paris: Payot.

Cummins, J. (1984) *Bilingualism and Special Education: Issues in Assessment and Pedagogy.* Clevedon: Multilingual Matters.

De Jong, E. (1986) *The Bilingual Experience: A Book for Parents.* Cambridge: Cambridge University Press.

Ekstrand, L. (1981) Unpopular views on popular beliefs about immigrant children. Contemporary practices and problems in Sweden. In J. Bhatnagar (ed.) *Educating Immigrants* (pp. 184–213). London: Croom Helm.

Fantini, A. (1985) *Language Acquisition of a Bilingual Child: A Sociolinguistic Perspective.* Clevedon: Multilingual Matters.

Fishman, J. (1976) *Bilingual Education: An International Sociological Perspective.* Rowley: Newbury House.

Fitouri, C. (1983) *Biculturalisme, bilinguisme et education.* Paris: Delachaux and Niestlé.

Garmadi, S. (1972) *Les problèmes du bilinguisme en Tunisie.* In A. Abdel-Malek (ed.) *Renaissance du Monde Arabe: Colloque inter-arabe de Louvain* (pp. 309–22). Gembloux: Duculot.

Genesee, F. (1976) The suitability of immersion programmes for all children. *Canadian Modern Language Review* 26, 267–80.

Grosjean, F. (1982) *Life With Two Languages: An Introduction to Bilingualism.* Cambridge, MA: Harvard University Press.

Hakuta, K. (1986) *Mirror of Language: The Debate on Bilingualism.* New York: Basic Books.

Harding, E. and Riley, P. (1986) *The Bilingual Family. A Handbook for Parents.* Cambridge: Cambridge University Press.

Haugen, E. (1972) The stigmata of bilingualism. In E. Haugen and A.S. Dill (eds) *The Ecology of Language* (pp. 307–44). Stanford: Stanford University Press.

Housen, A. and Baetens Beardsmore, H. (1987) Curricular and extra-curricular factors in multilingual education. *Studies in Second Language Acquisition* 9 (1), 83–102.

Lambert, W. and Aellen, C. (1972) Ethnic identification and personality adjustment of Canadian adolescents of mixed English-French parentage. In W. Lambert (ed.) *Language, Psychology and Culture* (pp. 266–89). Stanford: Stanford University Press.

Lord, R. and T'Sou, B. (1985) *The Language Bomb.* Hong Kong: Longman.

Mackey, W. (1972) *Bilingual Education in a Binational School.* Rowley: Newbury House.

Marshall, D. (1986) The question of an official language: Language rights and the English Language Amendment. *International Journal of the Sociology of Language* 60, 7–75.

McArthur, T. (1986) Comment: Worried about something else. *International Journal of the Sociology of Language* 60, 87–91.

McLaughlin, B. (1985) *Second Language Acquisition in Childhood: Volume 2, School-Age Children.* Second edition, Hillsdale: Lawrence Erlbaum.

Milan, W. (1982) Spanish in the inner city: Puerto Rican speech in New York. In J. Fishman and G. Keller (eds) *Bilingual Education for Hispanic Students in the United States* (pp. 191–206). New York: Teachers College, Columbia University.

Miller, J. (1983) *Many Voices: Bilingualism, Culture and Education.* London: Routledge and Kegan Paul.

Nelde, P. (1987) Language contact means language conflict. *Journal of Multilingual and Multicultural Development* 8, 1–2, 33–42.

Paulston, C. (1982) *Swedish Research and Debate About Bilingualism Skoloverstyrselen.* National Swedish Board of Education.

Riguet, M. (1984) *Attitudes et représentations liées à l'emploi du bilinguisme. analyse du cas tunisien.* Paris: Publications de la Sorbonne.

Saunders, G. (1982) *Bilingual Children: Guidance for the Family.* Clevedon: Multilingual Matters.

Schumann, J. (1986) Research on the acculturation model for second language acquisition. *Journal of Multilingual and Multicultural Development* 7 (5), 379–92.

Skutnabb-Kangas, T. (1984) *Bilingualism or Not: The Education of Minorities.* Clevedon: Multilingual Matters.

Swain, M. (1981) Time and timing in bilingual education. *Language Learning* 31, 1–16.

Swain, M. and Lapkin, S. (1982) *Evaluating Bilingual Education: A Canadian Case Study.* Clevedon: Multilingual Matters.

T'Sou, B. (1985) Chinese and the cultural eunuch syndrome. In R. Lord and B. T'Sou (eds) *The Language Bomb* (pp. 15–19). Hong Kong: Longman.

Willemyns, R. (1984) Bilingualism, diglossia and language planning. Three major topics of sociolinguistic concern in Belgium. *Handelingen der Koninklijke Zuidnederlandse Maatschappij voor Taal- en Letterkunde en Geschiedenis* XXXVIII, 253–72.

Witte, E. and Baetens Beardsmore, H. (1987) (eds) *The Interdisciplinary Study of Urban Bilingualism in Brussels.* Clevedon: Multilingual Matters.

Chapter 2

The Importance of Being Bilingual

JOHN EDWARDS

Why should bilingualism (or multilingualism) be particularly important? After all, most people in the world have some sort of facility in more than one language and, as we are regularly informed nowadays, it is mono-lingualism that is an aberration, an affliction of the powerful, a disease to be cured. Older ideas that bilingualism meant a splitting of finite cognitive po-tential or, worse, a diminution of intellectual capacities, have long since been retired by research, to be replaced by the view that bilingualism does not mean loss; indeed, some have argued that increases in linguistic reper-toire correlate with heightened sensitivity, enhanced cultural awareness, perhaps even greater cognitive flexibility and all-round *nous*. Studies in language acquisition, particularly those focusing upon very young chil-dren, demonstrate the ease with which varieties can be added, or learned simultaneously with others. Academic and popular treatments devoted to the production and maintenance of bilingual children abound – and, again, there is little suggestion of any cognitive price to be paid for this in normal circumstances. The very idea of separate languages is clearly a construction unfamiliar to the four-year-old who simply makes different selections, from a larger pool, according to the presence of either English-speaking mother or German-speaking father. And if this little family leaves Berlin, or Birmingham, and goes to live in Paris, then the pool deepens a bit and, indeed, the child may (initially, at least) be the bridge into *francophonie*. A ??? demonstration of such linguistic elasticity is found in immer-??? an ability possessed by the majority of human ??? atively uneducated, many of them illiterate – and ??? rtlessly acquired by the youngest of them seems to ??? in its share of academic attention. I don't mean to ??? that language *per se* is a completely open book to us, ??? facility – which sets us apart, in tremendous degree ??? , from even those clever apes and dolphins – is trans-??? lopment or use. But it might seem as if, within the broader study of language, what happens once could easily be seen as, *mutatis mutandis*, happening again: why should a second or subsequent language warrant more than an extending footnote to the broader linguistic enquiry? Why should bilingualism occupy its own niche in the larger enterprise?

Second-language acquisition cannot, in principle, be a precise replica of mother-tongue learning, for the simple reason of being second. Heraclitus told us, a very long time ago, that you can't step into the same river twice. So those 'necessary changes' mentioned above become of some interest. For instance, knowing one variety may make it easier to learn subsequent ones (particularly if they are closely related, but theoretically even if they aren't). Linguistic interference and the presence of *faux amis* may complicate the process (again, particularly among near relations). Code-switching and borrowing of various sorts are predictable. Complete 'balance' among varieties is rare, perhaps non-existent. In some circumstances, bilingualism may lead to outright language replacement. And so on.

These, and many other issues, can account for a great deal of what we may call the technical literature on bilingualism, a literature largely concerned with the variations among linguistic gears and axles occasioned by bilingual competence (see Edwards, 1995). The point I wish to make here, however, is that the technicalities of this broad enterprise – vital and interesting as they are – cannot, themselves, fully explain its depth and its appeal. To understand these, we have to move beyond language itself, beyond developmental psycholinguistics, beyond experimental studies and educational programmes that illuminate and facilitate repertoire expansion. We have to go beyond instrumental matters altogether, and consider issues of psychology and sociology, of symbol and subjectivity. In a word, we must think about the relationship between language and identity, and how this relationship may alter when more than one variety is involved.

Identity is, itself, a many-faceted phenomenon. Broadly speaking, we could isolate two obvious levels here: *personal* and *social*. Personal identity – or personality – is essentially the summary statement of all our individual traits, characteristics and dispositions; it defines the uniqueness of each human being. But it is important to realise that our individuality does not arise through the possession of psychological components not to be found in anyone else. On the contrary, it is logical to assume that all personalities are assembled from the same pool of human possibilities. Logical, and also widely accepted as a philosophical and psychological principle: *homo sum,* wrote Terence, *humani nihil a me alienum puto.* This is one of the classical lines Montaigne had carved into the ceiling beams of his study, a statement of human solidarity among a collection emphasising human limitations and frailties (see Frame, 1965). The sentiment underpins all intellectual, literary and clinical enquiries into human behaviour.

The uniqueness of the individual surely comes about through the particular combination or weighting of building blocks from that common pool. To accept this is to accept that no rigid distinction can be made between personality and social identity and, again, this is a view of very long standing: no man is an island. Social scientists put it rather differently, of course, but the essence is the same. Our personal characteristics derive from our *socialisation* within the group (or groups) to which we belong; the social context defines that part of the larger human pool of potential from which personal identity can be constructed. Thus, for example, individual identities will be both components and reflections of particular social (or cultural) ones – and the latter will always be, to some extent at least, stereotypic in nature because of their necessary generality *across* the individual components.

Language can certainly be considered as a marker at the individual level. The detail and nuance of psycholinguistic acquisition patterns, for instance, lead to the formation of the *idiolect*. But, while this microscopic approach has undoubted validity – notably in clinical or forensic investigations – it is generally only of anecdotal interest or concern. The comic element is often central here: think, for example, of the odd lexicon and pronunciation of Sara Gamp, in *Martin Chuzzlewit*, with her 'when I'm so dispoged . . .' or 'the torters of the Imposition'. Indeed, one could argue that even idiolectal usage is a social, or group phenomenon – on the simple grounds that all language implies someone to talk to, a communicative intent, a linking of the individual to others. Apart from this sort of argument, it is common to consider the linguistic associations with identity as group matters: the jargon of the club, the class or regional dialect, the language of the wider community. There are, however, one or two points to be made at the more or less personal level – and we can approach them most easily by returning to our bilingual theme.

Speaking a particular language means belonging to a particular speech community and, as suggested above, this implies that part of the *social* context in which one's *individual* personality is embedded, the context which supplies the raw materials for that personality, will be linguistic. Disentangling the linguistic features from all others is not, of course, an easy task and so it has always been difficult to make a compelling case that membership in a given speech community has – in theoretical isolation, as it were, from other socialising threads – concretely specifiable consequences for personality. Whorfianism, at least in its 'weaker' forms, is of course relevant here, but its implications are of more direct interest at the level of the group – the broadly stereotypic linguistic patterning of the thoughts, attitudes and habits of the collectivity, of what Cattell (1948,

1964) referred to as the *syntality*. Indeed, a Whorfian perspective has been extended to cover paralinguistic features, too. Any cultural package which connects language and thought must also involve all sorts of accompanying communicative gestures (see Birdwhistell, 1970) and, by extension, virtually all aspects of the personal repertoire In general, an influence of language upon personality may be assumed, if not easily demonstrated, but it will tend to link personalities and operate upon their socially overlapping spheres, rather than distinguishing between them or producing idiosyncratic dispositions.

We might reasonably argue, however, that membership in more than one speech community could produce more immediately observable results at the individual level: if two or more languages are exercising some influence, then an individual could conceivably display an interesting pattern woven from several linguistic threads, a pattern which might look quite distinctive against a more unidimensional one. Arguably, any distinctiveness here would be most apparent in social settings where bilingual individuals are relatively rare, or where – if more numerous – they are at least similar amongst themselves (in terms, say, of degree or type of bilingual capacity). The fact that neither of these conditions occurs particularly frequently is a complication. And there is another important factor here, too. A line of argument which is at least implicit in the relevant literature suggests that the joint influence of more than one language upon individual psychologies is best understood as a sort of *tension* – i.e. that the individual effects will reflect one language working against the other, as it were. In any event, it is clear that this sort of tension would, indeed, produce the most observable results; after all, if the joint linguistic influences were to seamlessly merge, to pull in harness, then the results might logically be thought to be, at best, a heightening or a strengthening of influences traceable to each speech community singly. This is one way, indeed, of thinking about that alleged consequence of bilingualism to which I have already alluded: increased cognitive capabilities and intellectual sensitivities.

Much of interest rests upon the degree to which bilinguals possess either two (theoretically) separately identifiable systems of language – from each of which they can draw, as circumstances warrant – or some more intertwined linguistic and, perhaps, cognitive duality. As Hamers and Blanc (2000) point out, we are far from having compelling empirical data here. There is a difficult circularity at work, one that confounds all scientific attempts to link the observable to the intangible: the ambiguous or unclear results of the relatively few studies of the non-verbal repertoires (for example) of bilinguals do not provide clear indications of likely underlying mechanisms; on the other hand, plausible variations in rational accounts of these mechanisms make the interpretation of subtle behavioural differences hard to assess. Whether we are interested in verbal communication, its paralinguistic accompaniments or the broader reaches of personality traits generally, we find very little experimental evidence. It is interesting that, in their massive study of bilingualism, Baker and Jones (1998) give only six pages (out of more than 750) to a section on personality.

Consider, for instance, the 'popular' (and, sometimes, academic) view that bilinguals must have some sort of split mentality – two individuals in one, as it were. Grosjean (1982) and others have reported that bilinguals sometimes feel, themselves, that language choice draws out, and draws upon, different personalities. But, as Baker and Jones (1998) and Hamers and Blanc (2000) note, the evidence here is anecdotal at best. Indeed, we could go a bit further, and point to the large logical and rational difficulties which some two-in-one arrangement would create. There is certainly, however, evidence that language choice may implicate different *aspects* of the personality: bilinguals responding to interviews and questionnaires are liable to give slightly different pictures of themselves, depending upon the language used. They may make different responses to objective or projective probes, responses may be more emotional through one variety (typically, but not inevitably, their maternal language), they may more strongly affirm their sense of ethnic identity in one language than in another, and so on (see, for example, studies by Ervin, Guttfreund, Bond and others, usefully summarised in Hamers and Blanc, 2000). The fact that different social settings and variations in language-affect linkages lead to different patterns of self-presentation clearly does not imply separate personalities, although it does suggest an enhanced repertoire of possibility.

Language 'tensions' at the individual level have been seen to contribute to emotional strains – *anomie* and lowered self-esteem, for example. These are often most pronounced in immigrant or minority-group situations, a fact which suggests very strongly that the stresses are essentially not linguistic in origin but, rather, result from broader pressures associated with cultures in contact, with cross-group antagonism and prejudice, with poverty and disadvantage. It is not so very long ago that an American study concluded that 'the use of a foreign language in the home is one of the chief factors in producing mental retardation' (Goodenough, 1926: 393), and Weinreich, in his classic *Languages in Contact* (1953), produced a long list of disorders allegedly suffered by bilinguals: moral depravity, stuttering, left-handedness, idleness, excessive materialism – to name but a few of the more bizarre examples. Some of these are simply stupid, of course, and reflect anti-'foreign' prejudices of the wildest nature. Where emotional problems *are* linked with bilingualism, we have a classic instance of the fallacy that correlation implies causation; as noted above, the more likely explanation is that social and sociological pressures lead to psychological manifestations. Among immigrant and minority populations, as Diebold (1968) pointed out, bilingualism is often, itself, a response to the social contact which also produces psychological stresses and strains. (It is worth noting that the beneficiary of this *festschrift* has, as part of a lengthy devotion to language study, provided guidelines for minimising conflict and alienation; see, e.g. Baetens Beardsmore, 1982.)

We have once again, then, linked the individual to the group, and have seen how the psychological intertwines with the sociological. When Baker and Jones, Grosjean, Hamers and Blanc, and other able commentators suggest that those problems which seem particularly characteristic of bilinguals are social in nature, and not linguistic *per se*, they are reminding us of a broader set of relationships which embed the individual in his or her society. So it is apposite at this point to move more directly to that wider realm, and to consider the social implications of bilingualism itself. In so doing, we complete another loop of the circle: the bilingualism which results from particular settings, which reflects cultural contact, is at the same time a contributor to one or more 'mainstreams' – which are, themselves, neither watertight nor static.

People belong to many groups, and all groups – all, at least, that have boundaries possessing some degree of permanence – have characteristics which mark their identity. This marking is, of course, more or less visible at the level of the individual member. The implication is that each of us may carry the tribal markings of many groups, that our 'group identity' is itself a mosaic rather than a monolith. Still, it is clear that, where language issues are central, the pivotal group is the ethnocultural community: overlaps of importance may occur because of simultaneous membership in gender, socioeconomic, educational, occupational and many other categories, but the base here is an ethnic one.

The point at issue, then, is the significance of a bilingualism which links an individual to more than one ethnocultural community. How does it feel, we might ask, to have a foot in more than one camp? Is it this that could lead to that psychological splitting which we have rejected on more purely cognitive grounds? Or is such duality the origin of the expanded acuity and awareness that some have claimed for bilinguals? The short answers to these sorts of questions are all positive, or potentially positive, in a world where complicated patterns of social relations are made more intricate still by a very wide – theoretically infinite, in fact – range of linguistic capabilities. Of course, a great deal of bilingualism has very little emotional significance: the purely instrumental fluencies needed to conduct simple business transactions do not, after all, represent much of an excursion from one's ethnic base camp. This is probably a rather larger category than is often thought. For example, breadth of multiple fluencies does not, *per se*, imply emotional or psychological depth – it may, more simply, reflect the exigencies of a complicated public life. On the other hand, it is certainly possible to hold dual (or multiple) allegiances, involving different-language groups, in the absence of personal bilingualism. The attachment felt by the English-speaking Irish or Welsh to a culture and an ancestry whose language they no longer possess is a psychologically real one, and demonstrates the continuing power of what is intangible and symbolic. Indeed, there often exists a continuing attachment to the 'lost' language itself, seen as perhaps the most important specific aspect of that more general ancestry, and as the point of entry into cultural tradition. The fact that such attachments rarely lead to actual linguistic revival is regrettable in the eyes of those who feel that language is *the* pillar of culture, but this is not the place to explore the reasons why passive sympathies do not become active ones: the point is, again, that these attachments – however attenuated or residual – have a meaning, and represent a sort of symbolic bilingual connectivity.

The argument has been made elsewhere (in Edwards, 1985, for instance) that a continuing sense of ethnic-group identity need not inevitably depend upon the continuing use of the original language in ordinary, communicative dimensions – again, this a matter of considerable complexity which cannot detain us further here – but it can hardly be denied that linguistic continuity is a powerful cultural support. It is not the only pillar, but it is obviously an important one. There are many bilinguals whose competence is more deep-seated and whose abilities go beyond commercial instrumentality. These are the more 'typical' individuals one usually has in mind when considering the relationship between bilingualism and identity. And, if we are to think about this socio-psychological relationship, it may be useful to consider the manner in which bilingualism arises. Yet again we are confronted with a topic whose complexity can only be acknowledged in passing. Still, there are two broad divisions of relevance: the first comprises those bilinguals who have a kinship attachment to each group (detouring once more around a large and often vexed literature, we can accept either real or perceived attachments for our present purposes); the second is made up of people who have, in a more formal way, acquired another linguistic citizenship, as it were (there is a redolence, here, of the *integrative* motivation once much discussed in the literature).

The latter division involves what has been referred to as *élite* bilingualism, a variety best exemplified by members of the educated classes whose formal instruction would, historically, have been seen as incomplete without the acquisition of another language or two. Typically, then, élite bilingualism involves prestigious languages – although the term could reasonably be extended to cover the competence of those whose maternal variety is of lesser-used status, as well as of those lucky, or intelligent, or industrious enough to have achieved upward mobility through education. Élite bilingualism is usually discussed in comparison with *folk* bilingualism – where the latter signifies that necessity-induced repertoire expansion already touched upon – and, indeed, the distinction seems apt, particularly when one considers that, historically, the élite variety often had as much to do with social-status marking as it did with a thirst for knowledge and cultural boundary crossing. In earlier times, not to have known Latin or Greek or French in addition to one's vernacular would have been unthinkable for educated people – but often unthinkable, perhaps, in the same way that it would have been unthinkable not to have had servants. Among those fortunate élite bilinguals, of course, there were – and are – many driven by purer scholastic motives. But acknowledging this also means acknowledging that élite bilingualism need not rule out motives of necessity more usually associated with the folk variety. It is just that necessity itself becomes a little more rarefied. Your intellectual pursuits and desires may demand, for example, the acquisition of other languages and the acquaintance of other cultures.

It is not difficult to see that the life's work of a sensitive scholar could depend upon or, at least, produce – as an incidental result of more specific researches – an extended allegiance or sense of belonging. Indeed, this scenario also theoretically applies to those whose excursions across boundaries are motivated by nothing more than interest. After all, given a threshold of intelligence and sensitivity, the difference between the scholar and the amateur lies in formality of focus. The general point here is that we can ally ourselves, by more or less conscious effort, with another group – and that a formally cultivated bilingualism can act as the bridge here. And it is important, I think, to acknowledge the depth that can be attained by such effort. Boundaries are really crossed, cultural and linguistic sensitivities are really enlarged, and allegiances are both refined and broadened. Sometimes, indeed, the scholar shows astonishing capacities in these connections:

> I possess a general acquaintance with the languages and literature of the Aryan and Syro-Arabic classes . . . with several [languages] I have a more intimate acquaintance . . . Italian, French, Catalan, Spanish, Latin and in a less degree Portuguese, Vaudois, Provençal . . . I am tolerably familiar with Dutch . . . Flemish, German, Danish. In Anglo-Saxon and Moeso-Gothic my studies have been much closer . . . I know a little of the Celtic . . . with the Sclavonic [sic] . . . of Russian . . . of

> Hebrew and Syriac . . . to a less degree I know Aramaic Arabic, Coptic
> and Phenician [*sic*]. (Murray, 1977: 70)

Can anyone doubt that James Murray – who, after describing his linguistic abilities and interests in an unsuccessful letter of application for a job in
the British Museum, went on to become the editor of the *Oxford English Dictionary* – through this remarkable broadening of his capabilities, must
necessarily have achieved a heightened cultural awareness, an exploded
sense of 'groupness'? It seems unlikely. But, if one reads the biography
written by Murray's granddaughter – or, indeed, if one merely looks at the
pictures of this quintessential Victorian scholar – one also realises that
Murray always retained an unshakeable sense of his original Scottishness,
which became allied to a wider British sense of identity. (This was not at all
unusual at the time, and in the circumstances of an educated and ambitious
life.)

In fact, the picture is a little more interesting still. I thought of Murray
here, not only because of his linguistic breadth – and the motivations
behind it, and the sensitivities it nourished – but also because he felt himself
the possessor of a special sort of identity. Scholars have recently turned
their attention to 'border identities' – see, for example the work of Thomas
Wilson and Hastings Donnan (1998, 1999) – and Murray would have endorsed this. His granddaughter tells us that he never felt really English –
but his Scottishness was also qualified. He was a Borderer, born and raised
in Teviotdale:

> within three hours walk of English ground . . . very near to that nonde-
> script tract which in older times was known as the Debateable [*sic*]
> Ground – because it was claimed by both England and Scotland and
> whose inhabitants were neither English nor Scotch [*sic*] but simply Bor-
> derers. (Murray, 1977: 3)

All who grow up as 'borderers' have an awareness of others and a pro-
pensity for heightened cultural sensitivity that may be denied to their
counterparts in the heartland. This applies even where – as in Murray's
case – the border is not a linguistic one (prescinding here, of course, from
matters of dialect and accent variation). It is likely to be particularly striking in settings where borders mark status differentials and is, relatedly,
more noticeable among those borderers who are on the 'weaker' side of the
divide; this 'weakness', however, is often a complicated element, and may
be a subtle one. Given this qualification, Murray's Scottish–English frontier
is a case in point, but there are many others: the Canadian–American
boundary, for example. Where the border *does* have language significance
the effects are of course amplified.

   The broader point about borders is that, for those whose bilingualism is of the more 'formal' variety, they are more often intellectual than geographical – but the effects may be just as consequential as those associated with commerce and customs-posts. Murray's case is interesting because it reflects both physical boundaries and scholarly ones. It is an intriguing idea – one worth some pursuit, perhaps – that those nurtured along the former might be more disposed, as adults, to wish to cross the latter.

   But we must pass now to a brief consideration of the other broad category, those bilinguals who have some real or understood blood attachment to more than one language community. There is a large literature on varieties of bilingualism, which concerns itself with onset and timing, and with the consequences for fluency to which technicalities of acquisition lead. In terms of identity, it is surely the case that the deeper the linguistic and cultural burrowing into another community, the greater the impact upon identity. This in turn suggests that those whose bilingual competence is nurtured early will, other things being equal, have a firmer foot in the two (or more) camps. It will usually be the case, of course, that one camp will have psychological and emotional primacy. If we return for a moment to Murray, as an example, we can see that his Victorian solidity, expressed – whether as Scottish, British or Borderer – in English, always remained of pivotal centrality. This is not to belittle in the slightest those cross-group sensitivities that were so marked in his case, but it does remind us that – however many camps we may visit with ease and comfort – the fires typically burn brightest at home.

   But there are some cases where home itself is difficult to establish, at least in any simple unidimensional sense. There are some cases, that is, where bilingual or multilingual capacities, linked to their several cultural bases, develop so early and so deeply that a primary allegiance is hard to discover. There are generally two ways to consider the situations of those whose bilingualism begins at the parental knees. The first is simply that two or more base camps are home simultaneously; the second is that one primary home indeed exists, but it is constructed – in a manner unique to the individual – from materials taken from the several sources. The writer and critic George Steiner (1992) claims early and continuing competence in German, French and English. He also notes that careful self-examination – of which variety emerges spontaneously at times of emergency or emotion, of which language is dreamt in, of which is associated with earliest memories – shows that no one of the three seems dominant. He is by his own account maternally and perfectly trilingual. And Steiner has suggested that such 'primary' multilingualism is, as I have implied above, an integral state of affairs in itself. There has been virtually no research on the consequences for identity of multilingual tapestries so closely woven, but one imagines that there are subtleties here that go far beyond simple additive relation-ships. It is of course difficult to define and assess perfectly and fully balanced bilingualism, and it may be that even polyglots like Steiner would fall short under the most rigorous examination; nonetheless, more atten-tion to deep-seated multiple fluencies is indicated.

As we move towards the bilingualism of more ordinary individuals, we move more obviously towards the idea of a unitary identity – woven from several strands, to be sure, but inevitably influenced by one language and culture more than by others. But, if we move from the Steiners (and Conrads, Nabokovs, Kunderas, Stoppards and all the rest) – whose literary power, and the ability to reflect in meaningful ways upon its multifaceted origin, are simply unavailable to most people – we must not imagine that we have moved away from enlarged identities *per se*. It is both the obliga-tion and the fulfilment of intellectual life, after all, to express what less articulate souls may somehow feel or possess. When we consider that the language competences of most bilinguals are shallower than those of the Steiners of the world – broader, sometimes, but rarely as deep – and that neither the capacity nor the inclination to think much about identity is a widely distributed quantity, we realise again what important questions remain to be asked, what research – more psychological than linguistic – still needs to be undertaken. The intellectuals can look after themselves here: Steiner (1975) has written famously about the 'extraterritoriality' of multilingual writers; Ilan Stavans argues that monolingualism is a form of oppression (see Kellman, 2000); others, from Goethe to Eliot, have argued over the ability – particularly the poet's ability – to be fully expressive beyond the *muttersprache*. We need reports from more mundane quarters, too.

As it is, we rely largely upon inference to support the contention that it is the identity components, the symbols of the tribe, that energise languages beyond their instrumental existences. One large and obvious example here is the powerful association between language and nationalism. Since the latter is, among other things, a pronounced and often mobilising sense of groupness, it follows that any language component will be carefully delin-eated. And so, historically, it is. The language in which you do your shopping, and which – if you thought much about it – is also the variety in which your group's tradition is inscribed, can become a symbol of your op-pressed state, a rallying-point, a banner under which to assemble the troops. Would people be so ready to sacrifice for something that was of purely mundane importance? We might regret that circumstances encour-age us to put aside a familiar tool, and learn to use another – but we go to war over histories, not hammers.

The important associations of a particular language with a particular base camp are made clearer – and here we move from languages in general to languages in tandem – when we think about translation. This is an exercise driven by obvious necessity and, if language were not invested with emotion and association, its operation would be unremarkable. While employing them, we might applaud those whose expertise allows them the access denied the rest of us, but we would rarely be suspicious. And yet the old proverb says *traduttori, traditori*. We would hardly equate translation with treason unless we feared that (as Steiner has put it) 'hoarded dreams, patents of life are being taken across the frontier' (1992: 244). And what are 'patents of life', if not the psychological collections of past and present that are unique – or are felt to be unique, at any rate – to ourselves? An informal Whorfianism tells us that every language interprets and presents the world in a somewhat different way, that the unique wellsprings of group consciousness, traditions, beliefs and values are intimately entwined with a given variety. So, translation may mean the revealing of deep matters to others, and cannot be taken lightly. The translator, the one whose multilingual facility permits the straddling of boundaries, is a necessary quisling. But necessity is not invariably associated with comfort, and not even their employers care very much for traitors.

The tenor here is one of psychological privacy and coherence, one which – while not necessarily secretive – nonetheless wraps its hoarded dreams in a particular linguistic package. Many have gone further, arguing that concealment is more central to language than is communication. Talleyrand said that '*la parole a été donnée à l'homme pour déguiser sa pensée*' and he should have known. (*Larousse* used to describe him as '*plein d'esprit et de ressource, mais sans valeur morale*'.) But Popper also noted that 'what is most characteristic of the human language is the possibility of story telling'. Steiner, with his usual felicity, speaks of the 'enclosure and willed opaqueness' of language (1992: 300: Talleyrand and Popper cited on pp. 235 and 236). *Und so weiter*. Privacy, the construction of myths, legends and stories, and outright dissimulation are at once central to a group's self-identity and threatened by translation. A modern theme is 'voice appropriation' – the telling of native stories by outsiders. In many societies, particularly those having rich and powerful oral traditions, stories *belong* to the group or, indeed, to some designated story-teller.

Stories are what constitute our identity. Some are sacred and, indeed, the power of words themselves has often attained mythic or religious significance: 'in the beginning was the Word, and the Word was with God, and the Word was God.' In Christian tradition, the scriptures are divinely incarnate in Christ – as the *logos* – but many religions view tampering with the Word as sinful. The stain which mortal utterance of the *arcana verba* would represent, and the three days of darkness caused by the translation of

Jewish law into Greek – these are examples of the potency here. The stories are sacred but so too is the language which clothes them. The perspective here is not only biblical: Irish, for example, has been described in contemporary times as 'the casket which encloses the highest and purest religion' and as the 'instrument and expression of a purely Catholic culture' (Fullerton, 1916: 6; O'Donoghue, 1947: 24). Similar equations can be readily found elsewhere.

Not all chapters in our stories are sacred, of course; legends and literatures are in the province of the profane. Still, it is often the case that the central and the most enduring narratives achieve a sort of sacred status: what was lying outside the *fanum* has now been given an inside niche, and canonical literatures can be as important as religious canons themselves. The point of general interest here is that group identity is based on both stories *and* the language in which they are told. Small wonder, then, that translation can be blasphemous, and that multiple linguistic capabilities may be suspect. Such potentials need not worry bilinguals themselves, of course, but they clearly reinforce – from a negative perspective, in this case – the central theme: the psychological heart of bilingualism is identity.

So, both contemporary observation and the historical record suggest that language and identity can be powerfully intertwined. The particular importance of this, for bilingualism, arises from the division within the former. And this, in turn, leads to a final inferential context of special relevance. For monolingual majority-group speakers in their own 'mainstream' settings, the instrumentality and the symbolism of language are not split and, for most such individuals, the language-identity linkage is not problematic – indeed, it is seldom considered. Minority-group speakers, however, rarely have this luxury; for them, matters of language and culture are often more immediate. Now, while it is true that no simple equation exists between bilingualism and minority-group membership, it is also true that many bilinguals are found in the ranks of 'smaller' or threatened societies. The implication is that a link will often exist between bilingualism and a heightened awareness of, and concern for, identity. Specific linguistic manifestations include attempts at language maintenance or revival, the use of language in ethnic or nationalist struggles, the efforts to sustain at least some domains in the face of external influence, and so on. A more general consequence is that the position and the responses of minority groups focus attention on the possibility – and, in many instances, the inevitability – of a split between the communicative and the symbolic functions of language: you may have to live and work in a new language, a medium that is not the carrier of your culture or the vehicle of your literature. In these sorts of settings we see, in fact, an extended value to the study of bilingualism and identity. First, the attitudes and actions of bilinguals in situations of risk and transition have a special poignancy and visibility – identities, like everything else, are thrown into sharper relief when threats are perceived. Second, these same attitudes and actions can galvanise others, and can remind a larger and often unreflective society that matters of language and identity are not relevant for 'ethnics' and 'minorities' alone.

The importance of bilingualism is, then, of both intrinsic and generalisable value. We need to know more about it because it is an issue in its own right – with all the ramifications and technicalities to which I have only alluded here – and, as well, because it may illuminate wider patches of ground. More specifically, I have tried to argue here that the importance of being bilingual is, above all, social and psychological rather than linguistic. Beyond types, categories, methods and processes is the essential animating tension of identity. Beyond utilitarian and unemotional instrumentality, the heart of bilingualism is belonging.

References

Baetens Beardsmore, H. (1982) *Bilingualism: Basic Principles*. Clevedon: Multilingual Matters.

Baker, C. and Jones, S.P. (1998) *Encyclopedia of Bilingualism and Bilingual Education*. Clevedon: Multilingual Matters.

Birdwhistell, R. (1970) *Kinesics and Context*. Philadelphia: University of Pennsylvania Press.

Cattell, R. (1948) Concepts and methods in the measurement of group syntality. *Psychological Review* 55, 48–63.

Cattell, R. (1964) *Personality and Social Psychology*. San Diego: Knapp.

Diebold, A. (1968) The consequences of early bilingualism in cognitive and personality information. In E. Norbeck, D. Price-Williams and W. McCord (eds) *The Study of Personality: An Interdisciplinary Appraisal* (pp. 164–89). New York: Holt, Rinehart & Winston.

Donnan, H. and Wilson, T. (1999) *Borders: Frontiers of Identity, Nation and State*. Oxford: Berg.

Edwards, J. (1985) *Language, Society and Identity*. Oxford: Blackwell.

Edwards, J. (1995) *Multilingualism*. London: Penguin.

Frame, D. (1965) *Montaigne*. New York: Harcourt, Brace & World.

Fullerton, R. (1916) *The Prudence of St Patrick's Irish Policy*. Dublin: O'Brien & Ards.

Goodenough, F. (1926) Racial differences in the intelligence of school children. *Journal of Experimental Psychology* 9, 388–97.

Grosjean, F. (1982) *Life With Two Languages*. Cambridge, MA: Harvard University Press.

Hamers, J. and Blanc, M. (2000) *Bilinguality and Bilingualism* (2nd edition). Cambridge: Cambridge University Press.

Kellman, S. (2000) *The Translingual Imagination*. Lincoln: University of Nebraska Press.

Murray, K. (1977) *Caught in the Web of Words: James Murray and the Oxford English Dictionary*. New Haven: Yale.

O'Donoghue, D. (1947) Nationality and language. In Columban League (ed.) *Irish Man – Irish Nation* (pp. 20–8). Cork: Mercier.

Steiner, G. (1975) *Extraterritorial: Papers on Literature and the Language Revolution.* Harmondsworth, Middlesex: Penguin.

Steiner, G. (1992) *After Babel: Aspects of Language and Translation* (2nd edition). Oxford: Oxford University Press.

Weinreich, U. (1953) *Languages in Contact.* The Hague: Mouton.

Wilson, T. and Donnan, H. (eds) (1998) *Border Identities: Nation and State at International Frontiers.* Cambridge: Cambridge University Press.

Chapter 3

Towards a More Language-centred Approach to Plurilingualism

MICHAEL CLYNE

Introduction

When my daughter was aged seven, one of her friends, knowing that my daughter and I communicated in German, asked her if she was German. 'Oh no,' replied Joanna, quite offended, 'I'm bilingual'. There was no doubt that she saw her bilingualism as providing the basis for her identity and not the other way around. This motivated her early interest in languages and other cultures, something that later receded under the pressure of other interests or perhaps due to relatively little stimulation of this by her schooling. Similar interest in languages and cultures motivated by bilingual language acquisition is reported by Saunders (1988: 221–5). Bilingual children are often totally convinced of the importance of knowing several languages and the superiority of bilinguals (Clyne, 1997: 241–3). Is there still an environment in which such young people can thrive or is our attitude towards language becoming too pragmatic?

We 'contact linguists' have, for some time, been successful in demonstrating the centrality of language to social life and human development in plurilinguals. But we still project language as being determined by identity, attitudes and motivation, and social needs. What role does language itself play in shaping these, apart from the well-known aspect of regarding language as a surrogate for ethnicity?

In the following remarks I will begin by discussing some of the ways in which language has been rightfully constructed as a tool of social needs, and then, without denying the significance of such a relation with cultu or the social functions, offering some alternative ways of viewing lang in the plurilingual in which language is an end in itself. My comme apply not only to childhood bi- and trilinguals and immigrants emerging bilinguals who have acquired second languages the home environment. Drawing on various research projects undertaken in Australia, I will contend that intrinsic motivation may be just as significant to the maintenance, acquisition and development of a language as are instrumental and integrative motivation. Some communities are built around commonality of language. Relationships develop through and with a language in the home environment. It will be argued that the interests of the structurally oriented in the era of communicative language teaching need to be addressed alongside those of the functionally oriented. The transfer of metalinguistic awareness and intrinsic motivation across languages may benefit both language maintenance and the subsequent acquisition of other languages.

Social Bias

The social significance of language in a contact situation has been argued in a number of ways:

(1) *Language choice as a reflection of societal patterning*. Fishman (1965) poses the question: 'Who speaks which language to whom and when?' as an indicator of the way a bi- or mulilingual society is structured and what the functions of the languages are within it.

(2) *Language as a medium of identification*. The very use of one language (or variety) rather than another or a mixed code fulfils an indexical function (e.g. Auer, 1998; Gumperz, 1982). That is, the choice of the language and the way in which resources from the languages are juxtaposed becomes part of the message and not just a vehicle for it.

(3) *Diglossia*. Two languages/varieties are employed in a society or community and code choice is determined by fairly rigid rules of appropriateness (e.g. Ferguson, 1959; Fishman, 1967, 1991). (It is becoming increasingly apparent that the division between H and L is (now) not as clear-cut – or restricted in the case of L – than had originally been described (see e.g. Clyne, 1995: 42–55; Gorter, 2001; Pauwels, 1986: 9–11)).

(4) *Factors in language maintenance and shift*. The literature (e.g. Clyne, 1991; Fishman, 1965, 1985, 1991, 2001; Giles *et al.*, 1977; Jaspaert & Kroon, generally shows how language maintenance and through factors outside language itself, e.g. demo- perceived or objective status of group, language ing, functions of the language in public life or edu- is seen as an indicator of ethnicity (Broeder *et al.*,

nning of language for 'nationalist' ends. Languages, like ed. The creation or development of a corpus of the language to be declared the language may be the response to a need to claim nationhood. Sometimes the corpus of a language will be replanned as a result of substantial sociopolitical change as in former Soviet bloc nations or post-Apartheid South Africa. Corpus and status planning usually go hand in hand (see e.g. Clyne, 1997).

(6) *Integrative, instrumental and intrinsic motivation in SLA.* Literature on motivation in SLA (e.g. Gardner & Lambert, 1972; Gardner & Smythe, 1975) emphasises the dichotomy, 'instrumental' and 'integrative' motivation. However, this dichotomy is an incomplete choice. In sociolinguistic studies of adult second language acquisition (e.g. Klein & Dittmar, 1979), for instance, social use of the language outside the workplace is identified as the key factor in successful SLA.

Attachment to other people's language for integrative reasons is discussed in some of Rampton's writings on crossing, featuring ethnolects as inter-group markers of youth solidarity (e.g. Rampton, 1997). However, in his innovative study of the use of German elements in the interaction of children, especially boys, in an East London school where German was taught (Rampton, 1999), ritual performance in the 'neutral' language German, which is no-one's L1, becomes an expression of solidarity. Here there is no German-speaking community into which they are integrating.

Another aspect of the emphasis on language as a means rather than an end is to be found in the assessment of the Canadian French immersion programmes. Although they were intended to lead to a higher incidence of effective bilingualism among Anglo-Canadians, the emphasis in the evaluation over the first two decades was overwhelmingly on the achievement and skills in the subject areas taught in the language (as well as English skills) and cognitive skills, to ensure that no deficit occurred (Swain & Lapkin, 1982).

Beyond Instrumental and Integrative Motivation

I would like to propose an additional dimension which gives more prominence to *language* itself. This can be argued in the following ways:

Intrinsic motivation

While intrinsic motivation (i.e. motivation to achieve in the task) does rate a mention (Ellis, 1995: 515–16), there is very little research on *languages themselves* motivating learners. A survey of Australian teachers of languages other than English (Nicholas *et al.*, 1993: 124–34) found their strongest motivational factor to be their love of languages and the desire to pass on this love to others. It is this kind of intrinsic motivation that makes people seek out speakers of the language with whom to practise it and to get to know them better, so that integrative motivation may sometimes result from intrinsic motivation. Some of the linguaphiles I have known in Australia began acquiring community languages through immigrants living in their neighbourhood or the families of school friends, some from prisoners-of-war working on their farm, many at school or university. I am acquainted with Australians from monolingual English-speaking families who 'got hooked' on Dutch, German, French, Italian or Latvian because they were languages that were used around them by postwar immigrants, and there are many who are now acquiring the languages of more recent immigrants. Having found the opportunity to acquire a second language, most of them not only achieved native-like proficiency and got to understand the intricacies of the grammar, but they also proceeded to acquire other languages as well. Some of those linguaphiles whose contact with a second language started at school would seek out a community of speakers because they wanted to use the language and not vice versa. They were high input generators (Seliger, 1977). They also often developed an emotional attachment to the language rather than to a culture or an ethnic group, becoming a kind of native speaker, due to their unusual proficiency in the language being conferred a type of 'honorary member' of the speech community (rather than the ethnic group). This is especially where the language is a less commonly used language which is considered by its speech community impenetrable by members of out-groups. Nevertheless, finding functions for the new language so that the learner who is intrinsically so strongly motivated in order to acquire it well enough to gain this 'honorary membership' may be problematic. Formal learning of a language may equip learners with an academic or other formal register or higher sociolect which impresses rather than solidarises community members.

On the other hand, the community with whom the language is used may well be one of non-native speakers, the kind of group which meets in the Alliance Française in many parts of the world. One language that lends itself especially to acquisition for its own sake is Esperanto since the language has hardly any native speakers and the language community is not limited or defined by territory. What links the community of speakers is the enthusiasm for the language. In some immigrant minority languages, it is the 'non-ethnic' speaker of the language who is more supportive of language maintenance than the 'ethnic' one (as has been discussed for Dutch in Australia in Pauwels, 1985). Saunders (1988) is a case of a linguaphile plurilingual from a monolingual background who became the father of a generation of bilinguals and an example to others like him wanting to raise bilingual children. Döpke (1992) shows that highly competent speakers of a language who acquired it as L2 can be more successful than L1 speakers in transmitting the language to their children as long as they employ appropriate communication strategies. The intrinsic motivation can thus sometimes be more important than ethnic background in the transmission of a language in the family.

In his collection *In Praise of the Beloved Language*, Fishman (1997) records what those with a strong ethnic identity consider praiseworthy about their 'mother tongue'. Some of the statements focus on proprietary rights and a duty to maintain, rather than an intrinsically linguistic attraction. But uniqueness, beauty and effectiveness are also prominent among the praise. Similarly, the sounds, the script, the shape of the letters, the sequences of graphemes, the idiomatic expressions, are all elements that can attract an attachment to a language among the intrinsically motivated.

Structural orientation

Nicholas (1985) differentiates between two orientations in language learners – functional orientation (interest mainly in getting the message across) and structural orientation (an additional layer – an interest in how the language is structured). I would suggest that we would find among the intrinsically motivated (rather than instrumentally or integratively motivated) to acquire or maintain a language those who have a structural orientation.

Some bilingual children do not obtain high grades in the minority language to which they are exposed at home but in which they also receive formal instruction. This is due largely to assessment procedures which discriminate against them (cf. Clyne *et al.*, 1997 for a discussion of such practices). But part of the reason is that they have little interest in grammatical structures or grammatical accuracy or in the separation of the languages – they can communicate with reasonable ease and that is the important thing. Other bilinguals, however, are fascinated by the structure of their two languages and they want to learn more about it. Their interest leads on to the acquisition of more languages or to the study of linguistics. One question to consider is whether today, with an emphasis on communicative methods and syllabuses at primary and junior secondary schools, welcome as it is to promote second language acquisition, there may be little opportunity to develop the linguistic interests and talents of structurally oriented learners.

Functional specialisation and intrinsic motivation

Various writers (e.g. Grosjean, 1982; Romaine, 1995) remind us that bilinguals are not double monolinguals. They employ the resources of both their languages, so that each language has certain functions, and various combinations of the languages have particular social and communicative meaning. Similarly, trilinguals are not triple monolinguals. In a recent study of three groups of trilinguals, Dutch-German-English, Hungarian-German-English and Italian-Spanish-English (Clyne, 2000), it was found that most of them assigned specific functions to each language not only for social reasons but to give them practice, e.g. by joining clubs and choirs using the language, watching films and TV programmes, subscribing to magazines, reading books and writing letters in the language.

Metalinguistic awareness/language apprenticeship/language awareness programmes

Hawkins (1986) has developed the concept of 'language apprenticeship', which emphasises the value of acquiring one language as a basis for later acquiring further languages. Central to this is the acquisition of metalinguistic awareness. Various authors have commented on the earlier metalinguistic awareness of bilinguals than of monolinguals (e.g. Ben Zeev, 1977), their increased metacognition and metalinguistic awareness (De Avila & Duncan, 1979; Heeschen, 1989; Tunmer & Myhill, 1984), and their greater separation of form and content (Leopold, 1939–49). Cognitive advantages attributed to plurilinguals by psychologists, e.g. advantages in conceptual development (Bain, 1974; Cummins & Gulutsan, 1974; Liedke & Nelson, 1968; Peal & Lambert, 1962), higher verbal intelligence and greater psycholinguistic skills (Cummins & Gulutsan, 1974; Kittell, 1963; Lambert & Tucker, 1972; Peal & Lambert, 1962), and more divergent thinking (Balkan, 1970; Landry, 1974) are all related to metalinguistic awareness as well as to the practice of switching between languages.

On the basis of experience and observation, I would speculate that the acquisition of a third language could have a positive effect on the languages of a bilingual. It can provide both metalinguistic awareness and the kind of intrinsic motivation that encourages a young person to value better the asset that bilingualism is. What we now need is more specific findings on what it is that can be transferred to the acquisition of other languages. We also need to explore what transfer of positive attitudes towards languages in a general way occurs from a third language acquired through formal instruction to a community language, which may have an enhancing effect on language maintenance.

Language awareness programmes based on Hawkins's notion of 'language apprenticeship' have been introduced into primary and early secondary education in many countries. However, awareness programmes have often been established where there are limited resources available for actual second language teaching and new programmes have to be maximally efficient (e.g. in some German states today) or where actual language programmes are considered to be unsuccessful or too expensive (e.g. Australia in the 1980s, predating Hawkins's 1986 book). They are most effective where they offer an additional dimension alongside actual early second language acquisition. Unfortunately, sampling courses (where pupils take three months of each of three languages to decide which they wished to study the following year) and general language programmes (learning a few snippets of a large number of languages) were the reason why second language teaching was reduced to a shadow in Australia and took many years to recover. The sampling and general language courses replaced any more thorough study of a specific second language. More recently, most states of Australia have reinstated actual second language programmes in languages other than English. The best way to acquire metalinguistic awareness is through exposure to a second language (cf. Peal & Lambert (1962) for Canadian immersion programmes, Yelland, Pollard & Mercuri (1995) on the advancement of reading readiness in the L1 of young children exposed to a limited programme in a second language).

Community building function of language

The general assumption is that a language will be maintained around a group of people of common culture and ethnicity and that it will have an integrative function within the culture (cf. for instance the core culture theory of Smolicz, 1981). But there is also evidence of a group of people forming a community around a language. This applies particularly to pluricentric languages, languages with several interacting centres, each providing a national variety with at least some norms of its own with which its people identify (Clyne, 1992: 1). In third countries, such as immigration countries where different national varieties of a language meet, the language will frequently have a community building function, uniting groups from different source countries or parts of the world, religious and cultural backgrounds beyond a common ethnicity. In the immigration country, they come into contact with people whom they recognise as speaking the same language but in a different way. They feel at ease with people using the same language with whom they have some ways of communicating in common. In Australia, for instance, this has occurred among speakers of languages such as German, Spanish, Arabic, Cantonese and Mandarin. Often the groups using a common language constitute different vintages, and older established groups speaking a language help resettle newer ones. Together they set about the task of running part-time language schools for their children, propagating their language as a school subject and organising radio and television programmes in the language together. Many social welfare services run by communities are organised according to language-based groups. (Cf. Clyne, 1991: 99–100 for German; Clyne and Kipp, 1999 for Arabic, Chinese and Spanish).

Developing relationship through a language and with a language

Studies of bilingual language acquisition employing the one parent, one language approach (e.g. Döpke, 1992; Saunders, 1988, Taeschner, 1983), have demonstrated how in the very early period of a child's life, they develop a relationship with a parent through a particular language. This relationship is strong enough to form the basis of a strong command of the language and a lasting commitment to it without membership of or the support of any community – i.e. there is no need for other speakers. Often this initial relationship instils positive attitudes towards the language for its own sake (cf. Clyne, 1997). So intrinsic motivation can be achieved partly through an integrative function.

There is an increasing interest, even in predominantly monolingual countries of European background, in bringing up children bilingually, often using the one parent one language approach. It is intriguing that, in similar social situations, some children become and remain bilingual, others don't (Döpke, 1992). There are many factors involved in this, not the least being the child's willingness to be different, the attitude of the wider community, the consistency of the parents' approach. I would argue that the intrinsic significance to the child of being bilingual should be taken into account far more. This is expressed in metalinguistic comments which reveal that it is language that gives them a chip on their shoulders. Bilinguals are considered to be special people, while monolinguals are quite impoverished, such as:

> *Weisst du, Daddy, nur mich im Kindergarten kann deutsch sprechen. Andrew sollte, weil seine Mummy deutsch spricht, aber er spricht nicht deutsch.* (Bilingual child, aged 4,7) 'You know, Daddy, only me at kindergarten can speak German. Andrew should, because her mummy speaks German, but he doesn't speak German'.

> *Danusha kann besser lesen als ich, aber sie kann keine andere Sprache.* (Aged 6,11) 'Danusha can read better than me, but she doesn't know another language'.

> (To a monolingual adult telephone caller who had forgotten his L2): Don't you get bored speaking only English? You could go to another land, then you could learn a second language. If you go to Frenchland, you can learn it again, and you can write it down on a piece of paper, then you won't forget it. (Aged 4,11). (Clyne, 1997: 240–2)

The importance of catering for intrinsic motivation and students with a structural orientation in language programmes

Intrinsic motivation and metalinguistic awareness should be very significant outcomes of bilingualism, bilingual education and, in fact, of any second language programme. It can never be gauged which language or languages the individual may need or wish to acquire in the future. If a language programme leads to transferable metalinguistic skills and an interest in languages, the student can continue to learn more and more languages effectively in the future, even for instrumental reasons. In a predominantly English-speaking country such as Australia in which many languages are learnt and taught, it is not unusual for children from geographically mobile families to change schools several times and acquire a different language in each school. However, neither the students nor the teachers are trained for the transfer process necessary to make it possible for the skills acquired through an earlier language experience to benefit a subsequent one. The findings of a pilot project by Kipp (1996) suggested that children who had taken French or German at primary school performed better in Japanese in secondary school and continued longer with the language than those without a primary school second language acquisition. There is no doubt that communicative methods have achieved an improvement in communicative competence, aural-oral skills, and the students' confidence in using the target language. However, it has served functionally oriented learners far more than structurally oriented ones.

Research Areas

The above considerations entail a research agenda that, in some ways, extends beyond what is currently the focus of attention. What kind of person is likely to be a more structurally oriented learner and what kind of person tends to be a functionally oriented one? Achieving the aims of language learning needs to be underpinned by an understanding of individual students as well as processes. Here are a few examples of research issues:

(1) What is the relation between intrinsic motivation and the development of structural orientation? Are learners (adults or adolescents) with a structural orientation likely to start off with a more intrinsic motivation than those with a mainly functionally orientation? Are they likely to develop such a motivation?

(2) Can one predict an intrinsic motivation for language maintenance/bilingualism from any other information, such as biography, personality? Can it be tested?

(3) Case studies of learners carried to high levels of competence through intrinsic motivation.
(4) Exactly how does transfer of metalinguistic skills proceed from one language to another in the structurally oriented? How can this be stimulated at the individual level or through school programmes?
(5) What is it about a language that attracts linguaphiles? Is it the uniqueness of any aspect of a language? Is it sound or script or the shape of the written language? For instance, what is the role of: phonemes/phones/clusters that have no equivalent in any other language acquired; otherwise unknown graphemes (e.g. ü, é, å), intonation, an unusually complex case system, idiomatic expressions that are unknown in any other language encountered by the person? (Some of these would scare off other potential acquirers.) This calls for comparative case studies of adults and adolescents who have acquired different languages and in different ways.
(6) Does early exposure to a L2 at home, in the country, in a community situation or in kindergarten or primary school affect intrinsic motivation and structural orientation?
(7) How does a structural orientation affect results in formal language learning? Is it better protection from attrition than a more functional orientation? Does it mean that a language-object approach is more successful or useful with such learners than an immersion/content based programme? What does a teacher or a curriculum need to do to enable such learners/bilinguals to move more swiftly into the acquisition of other languages as they have a cognitive apparatus to help them along?

Implications for International Communication

There has recently been much discussion on the most efficient means of communicating across cultures and language communities internationally, especially in Europe. Among the options suggested have been *polyglot dialogue* (Posner, 1991), where everyone speaks their language and understands that of a number of other people, and *multilateral competence*, where people acquire a number of related languages (Munske, 1972; Schmid, 1994) through contrastive programmes. Both of these require an interest in and commitment to languages and language acquisition. The first capitalises on structural and/or a functional orientation, but for the second approach, a structural orientation is vital because it involves an understanding of language distance and the construction of conversion formulae for convergence and divergence. Another imperative of international communication is competence at communicating in a lingua franca, and understanding the relativism of language and how language works is a good start. Thus intrinsic motivation and a structural orientation can lead to instrumental and functional uses of languages.

Whether in the acquisition, development or maintenance of plurilingualism, it is important to consider language itself as an important factor.

Acknowledgement

I thank Sandra Kipp, Howard Nicholas, and some anonymous reviewers for helpful suggestions.

References

Auer, P. (ed.) (1998) *Code-switching in Conversations*. London: Routledge.

Bain, B.C. (1974) Bilingualism and cognition: Toward a general theory. In S. Carey (ed.) *Bilingualism, Biculturalism and Education. Proceedings from the Conference at College Universitaire Saint-Jean*. Edmonton: University of Alberta Press.

Balkan, L. (1970) *Les effets du bilinguisme français-anglais sur les aptitudes intellectuelles*. Brussels: AIMAV.

Ben Zeev, S. (1977) Mechanisms by which childhood bilingualism affects understanding of language and cognitive structures. In P. Hornby (ed.) *Bilingualism: Psychological, Social and Educational Implications* (pp. 29–56). New York: Academic Press.

Broeder, P., Extra, G., Habraken, M., van Hout, R. and Keurentjes, H. (1993) *Taalgebruik als indicator van ethniciteit*. Tilburg: Tilburg University Press.

Clyne, M. (1991) *Community Languages: The Australian Experience*. Cambridge: Cambridge University Press.

Clyne, M. (ed.) (1992) *Pluricentric Languages*. Berlin: Mouton de Gruyter.

Clyne, M. (1995) *The German Language in a Changing Europe*. Cambridge: Cambridge University Press.

Clyne, M. (1997) Retracing the first seven years of bilingual and metalinguistic development through the comments of a bilingual child. In S. Eliasson and E.H. Jahr (eds) *Language and its Ecology: Studies in Memory of Einar Haugen* (pp. 235–59). Berlin: Mouton de Gruyter.

Clyne, M. (2000) What is it that is special about trilinguals? In A. Grotans, H. Beck and A. Schwob (eds) *Consolationae philologicae* (pp. 585–96). Göttingen: Kümmerle.

Clyne, M., Fernandez, S., Chen, I. and O'Connell, S. (1997) *Ba̅ ͐und Speakers*. Canberra: Language Australia.

Clyne, M. and Kipp, S. (1999) *Pluricentric Languages in an Ir* ʼin: Mouton de Gruyter.

Cummins, J.P. and Gulutsan, M. (1974) Some effects of ʼ functioning. In S.T. Carey (ed.) *Bilingualism and Educ* ton: University of Alberta Press.

De Avila, E. and Duncan, S. (1979) Bilingualism and tʼ *tional Association for Bilingual Education* 3, 1–20.

Döpke, S. (1992) *One Parent One Language – an Intera* Benjamins.

Ellis, R. (1995) *The Study of Second Language Acquisiʼ* Press.

Ferguson, C.A. (1959) Diglossia. *Word* 15, 325–44

Liedke, Journal Munske, H.H. unter Berück Dialektologie und L

Fishman, J.A. (1965) Who speaks which language to whom and when? *Linguistique* 2, 67–88.

Fishman, J.A. (1967) Bilingualism with and without diglossia, diglossia with and without bilingualism. *Journal of Social Issues* 23, 29–38.

Fishman, J. A. (1985) *The Rise and Fall of the Ethnic Revival*. Berlin: Mouton de Gruyter.

Fishman, J.A. (1991) *Reversing Language Shift*. Clevedon: Multilingual Matters.

Fishman, J.A. (1997) *In Praise of the Beloved Language*. Berlin: Mouton de Gruyter.

Fishman, J.A. (ed.) (2001) *Can a Threatened Language Be Saved?* Clevedon: Multilingual Matters.

Gardner, R.C. and Lambert, W. (1972) *Attitudes and Motivation in Second Language Learning*. Rowley: Newbury House.

Gardner, R.C. and Smythe, P. (1975) Motivation and second language acquisition. *Modern Language Review* 31, 218–30.

Giles, H., Bourhis, R.Y. and Taylor, D.M. (eds) (1977) *Language, Ethnicity and Intergroup Relations*. London: Academic Press.

Gorter, D. (2001) A Frisian update of reversing language shift. In J.A. Fishman (ed.) *Can Threatened Languages Be Saved?* (pp. 215–33). Clevedon: Multilingual Matters.

Grosjean, F. (1982) *Life with Two Languages*. Cambridge, MA: Harvard University Press.

Gumperz, J.J. (1982) *Discourse Strategies*. Cambridge: Cambridge University Press.

Hawkins, E. 1986 *Language Awareness*. Cambridge: Cambridge University Press.

Heeschen, V. (1989) The metalinguistic vocabulary of a speech community in the highlands of Irian Jaya. In A. Sinclair, R. Jarvella and W.J.M. Levelt (eds) *The child's Concept of Language* (pp. 155–87). Berlin: Springer.

Jaspaert, K. and Kroon, S. (1991) Social determinants of language shift among Italians in the Netherlands and Flanders. *International Journal of the Sociology of Language* 90, 77–96.

Kittell, J.E. (1963) Intelligence-test performance of children from bilingual environments. *Elementary School Journal* 64, 76–83.

Kipp, S. (1996) How will learning French get me a job in Japan? *Australian Language Matters* 4, 16.

Klein, W. and Dittmar, N. (1979) *Developing Grammars*. Heidelberg: Springer.

Kloss, Heinz (1967) German American language maintenance efforts. In J.A. Fishman (ed.) *Language Loyalty in the United States* (pp. 206–52). The Hague: Mouton.

Lambert, W. and Tucker, G.R. (1972) *Bilingual Education of Children: The St. Lambert Experiment*. Rowley: Newbury House.

Landry, R.G. (1974) A comparison of second language learners and monolinguals on divergent thinking tasks at the elementary school level. *Modern Language Journal* 58, 10–15.

Leopold, W.F. (1939–49) *Speech Development of a Bilingual Child* (4 vols). Evanston, IL: Northwestern University Press.

W.W. and Nelson, L.D. (1968) Concept formation and bilingualism. *Alberta f Educational Research* 14, 225–32.

(1972) Vorschläge zu einer multilateralen kontrastiven Grammatik ichtigung differenzierter Sprachkompetenz. *Zeitschrift für nguistik* 39, 284–299.

Nicholas, H. (1985) Contextually defined queries: Evidence for variation in orientation to second language acquisition processes. Paper given at the 9th conference of the Applied Linguistic Association of Australia, Alice Springs.

Nicholas, H., Moore, H., Clyne, M. and Pauwels, A. (1993) *Languages at the Crossroads*. Canberra: Australian Government Publishing Service.

Pauwels, A. (1985) The role of mixed marriages in language shift in the Dutch communities. In M. Clyne (ed.) *Australia, Meeting place of languages* (pp. 39–55). Canberra: Pacific Linguistics.

Pauwels, A. (1986) *Immigrant Dialects and Language Maintenance in Australia*. Dordrecht, Holland: Foris Publications.

Peal, E. and Lambert, W.E. (1962) The relation of bilingualism to intelligence. *Psychological Monographs, General and Applied* 76, 1–23.

Posner, R. (1991) Der ployglotte Dialog. *Der Sprachreport* 3/91, 6–10.

Rampton, B. (1997) *Language and Ethnicity among Adolescents*. London: Longman.

Rampton, B. (1999) Deutsch in Inner London and the animation of an instructed foreign language. *Journal of Sociolinguistics* 3, 480–504.

Romaine, S. (1995) *Bilingualism* (2nd edn). Oxford: Blackwell.

Saunders, G.W. (1988) *Bilingual Children from Birth to Teens*. Clevedon: Multilingual Matters.

Schmid, S. (1994) *L'italiano degli Spagnoli*. Milan: Franco Angeli.

Seliger, H. (1977) Does practice make perfect? A study of interaction patterns and second language competence. *Language Learning* 27, 63–78.

Smolicz, J.J. (1981) Core values and cultural identity. *Ethnic and Racial Studies* 4, 75–90.

Swain, M. and Lapkin, S. (1982) *Evaluating Bilingual Education*. Rowley: Newbury House.

Taeschner, T. (1983) *The Sun is Feminine*. Berlin: Springer.

Tunmer, W.E. and Myhill, M.E. (1984) Metalinguistic awareness and bilingualism. In W.E. Tunmer, C. Pratt and M. Herriman (eds) *Metalinguitsic Awareness in Children* (pp. 169–87). Berlin: Springer.

Yelland, G.W., Pollard, J.P. and Mercuri, A. (1995) The metalinguistic benefits of limited contact with a second language. *Applied Psycholinguistics* 14, 423–44.

Chapter 4

Bilingual Education: Basic Principles

JIM CUMMINS

Introduction

In 1982, Hugo Baetens Beardsmore published the book *Bilingualism: Basic Principles*. According to the cover description, this book was designed 'to provide a clear introductory guide to the fascinating queries that arise in connection with what is involved in knowing more than one language and the effect this has on the personality'. The book more than succeeded in accomplishing this goal; in effect, it set the stage for the explosion of research on bilingualism and bilingual education that has occurred during the past 20 years and to which Hugo Baetens Beardsmore has contributed substantially (e.g. Baetens Beardsmore, 1993, 1995).

When *Bilingualism: Basic Principles* was published, few people could have anticipated the intense controversies and divisive public policy debates that the phenomena of bilingualism and bilingual education would engender over the next 20 years. At the same time as our knowledge of these phenomena has increased dramatically as a result of both basic and applied research in countries around the world, public policy in many countries has either ignored or repudiated this research and implemented policies, directed at minority language children, designed to *minimise* children's opportunities to develop bilingual and trilingual abilities. While favourable policies towards some 'lesser used languages' spoken by national linguistic minorities have been implemented in a handful of European Union countries, the languages of immigrant children have generally been targeted for extinction.

In this paper, I examine research and theory on bilingual education with the goal of establishing some 'basic principles' that hold across sociolinguistic and sociopolitical contexts. In other words, what can we say with confidence about the effects of bilingual education and the optimal conditions for its implementation? The complexity of the process of bilingual development in home and school was clearly expressed by Hugo Baetens

Beardsmore (1982) and this complexity accounts for some of the confusion and controversy in this area. He notes that a host of variables need to be taken into account in any appraisal of the effects of bilingual development:

> These include the type of linguistic knowledge the child brings to school, the relative status of the two languages involved, the socio-economic background of the parents, the nature of the bilingual programme being applied, the sequencing of instruction, the make-up of the group undergoing bilingual instruction and particularly its homogeneity, the expectancies and attitudes of the teachers, the extent of parental involvement and understanding of the bilingual process, the attitudes and motivations of the learners, the pressures of the outside environment in the development of anomie; this list is by no means exhaustive. (1982: 146)

Although partially captured by the notion of the status of the two languages involved, the experience of the past 20 years suggests that it would be important also to include as a central variable the historical and current power relations operating between majority and minority groups in the society. Power relations are not highly salient in the case of bilingual programmes for dominant or majority language groups for the simple reason that the programmes serve the interests of these groups. However, they constitute a critical variable in understanding the outcomes of various bilingual and monolingual programmes for minority language or subordinate group students. The recent history of debate on bilingual education in the United States and elsewhere illustrates how power relations are infused into the public discourse concerning this issue. These power relations, constituted discursively, obscure the fact that research in this area is extremely consistent and supports a set of theoretical principles that have emerged across a wide range of social contexts in programmes for both minority and majority language students. Excerpts from the recent discourse on this issue illustrate the point.

The Discourse on Bilingual Education

The intersection of societal power relations and bilingual education for minority students is most obviously illustrated in the United States. Proposition 227, passed in June 1998 in California by a margin of 61% to 39%, severely restricted the extent to which children's first language (L1) could be used as a medium of instruction. Teachers who continue to use children's L1 in the classroom can be held legally liable and sued. In November 2000, the citizens of Arizona followed California's lead in severely restricting bilingual education for linguistic minority children by an even greater margin.

Many teachers and parents of minority language students have resisted these coercive measures and bilingual education struggles on in both California and Arizona despite a significant decline in the number of programmes offered. Ironically, so-called 'dual language programmes' (also termed 'two-way bilingual immersion programmes'), the form of bilingual education endorsed by virtually all researchers who have carried out research on bilingual education, has expanded in California. In the year 2000, there were 119 dual language programmes in California, an increase of 11 programmes since 1999 and 24 programmes since 1998 (California Department of Education, 2000). These programmes involve both language minority students and English-dominant students in the same programme with the intent of developing fluent bilingualism and biliteracy among both groups of students. Between 50% and 90% of instruction is conducted in the minority language in the early grades. By the end of elementary school, approximately 50% of instruction is conducted in each language: 91% of these programmes operate in Spanish and English followed by Korean-English (six programmes), Cantonese-English (four programmes) and Japanese-English (one programme).

During a visit to Denmark in September 2000, I was surprised to find that a major issue of interest to the media was the supposed 'failure' of bilingual education in California and the fact that this clearly showed that mother tongue programmes for minority groups in Denmark should be halted immediately. In Greece, to take another European example, parents of bilingual children report that teachers frequently advise them to use only Greek in the home and teachers attribute any difficulties children might experience in school to their bilingualism (personal communication, parents of children attending the International School, Rhodes, May 1997–April 2001; see also, Skourtou, 1995).

Suspicion in relation to linguistic diversity also exists in contexts that pride themselves on their multiculturalism. In Ontario, Canada, for example, which proudly claims to have 'the most multicultural city in the world' within its boundaries (Toronto), it is still illegal to teach through the medium of any language other than English or French, except for short-term transitional purposes (American Sign Language (ASL) and indigenous languages are partial exceptions to this prohibition). International languages are taught with provincial funding as subjects for two-and-one-half hours per week outside of the regular five-hour school day but that's as far as linguistic imagination is permitted to roam in 'the most multicultural city in the world'. This legal prohibition on enrichment bilingual education through any language other than the two national official languages persists despite the widespread implementation and success of French–English bilingual programmes for English speakers and minority francophones respectively (see Cummins & Danesi, 1990; Swain & Lapkin, 1982). As in other contexts, bilingual programmes that serve the interests of dominant groups are not viewed as problematic whereas bilingual or mother tongue programmes designed to promote multilingualism among 'non-official' language groups are resisted strenuously.

The media have played a significant role in spreading disinformation about bilingualism and bilingual education. Reporters in both North America and Europe often seem ready to abdicate scepticism, logic, and journalistic responsibility in their zeal to 'solve the problem' of bilingualism. In March 2000, *The Economist* treated its readers to the following assessment of bilingual education in the United States:

> New York is the next target for Ron Unz, a Silicon Valley millionaire who was the guiding force behind California's Proposition 227. This measure replaced bilingual education, which around half the students with poor English were receiving, with crash courses in English. Bilingual education, originally invented as a way to steer funds to poor people in the southwest, has always produced disappointing results. It is now merely a sop to the teachers' unions. Since bilingual education was banned in California about a year ago, test scores have risen. Even more tellingly, the students who were put on the English crash course or into mainstream classes are well ahead of those still stuck in bilingual ones (which a few students have waivers to continue). (Micklethwait, 2000: 15)

Out of six sentences in this passage, five are blatantly false. Going through them in order:

- Prior to Proposition 227, only 30% of English language learners in California were in any form of bilingual programme and less than 20% were in classes taught by a credentialled bilingual teacher.
- Bilingual education was not originally 'invented' in the United States – these programmes have been operating since Greek and Roman times; furthermore, the spread of these programmes in countries around the world, including the spread of dual language programmes in the United States, is hardly consistent with the claim that they have 'always produced disappointing results' (see Baker & Jones, 1998).
- Contrary to the claim that bilingual education is a 'sop' to teachers' unions, teachers unions in California and elsewhere have tended to be very ambivalent about bilingual education for the simple reason that only a small fraction of their members are in fact bilingual teachers.
- The implication that test scores rose in California as a result of the

banning of bilingual education is without foundation. Changes in scores occurred in districts in ways that appeared to be completely unrelated to what kind of programme a district implemented (Hakuta, 1999).

- There is absolutely no data to support the claim that students put into all-English classes made better progress than those who were 'still stuck in bilingual ones' (Hakuta, 1999).

The reason for analysing these claims in some detail is to illustrate the shallowness of the typical journalistic inquiry into the issues (see also Crawford, 2000; Tse, 2001). It is sufficient to note that Micklethwait's sketch of bilingual education would receive an 'F' grade in any assessment of journalistic competence or responsibility. He has taken the views of Ron Unz, or one of his associates, and has reported them as 'fact' rather than attributing them as the particular perspective of his source (e.g. 'Ron Unz claims that bilingual education has always produced disappointing results, etc.). He has obviously not checked out any of the data that might back up his claims nor even bothered to note that there are any alternative viewpoints other than those he reports as 'fact'. Even a five-minute excursion into the Encyclopedia of Bilingualism and Bilingual Education (Baker & Jones, 1998) or into journalist James Crawford's well-known web site on Language Policy (http://ourworld.compuserve.com/homepages/jwcrawford), would have indicated to him that the vast majority of academic analysis of bilingual education is at variance with what he reports as undisputed fact.

One other example illustrates the impunity with which the evidence on bilingualism and bilingual education is distorted in the United States context. The following statements were made by Arthur Schlesinger Jr (1991) in his book The Disuniting of America:

> In recent years the combination of the ethnicity cult with a flood of immigration from Spanish-speaking countries has given bilingualism new impetus . . . Alas, bilingualism has not worked out as planned: rather the contrary. Testimony is mixed, but indications are that bilingual education retards rather than expedites the movement of Hispanic children into the English-speaking world and that it promotes segregation rather than it does integration. Bilingualism shuts doors. It nourishes self-ghettoization, and ghettoization nourishes racial antagonism . . . Using some language other than English dooms people to second-class citizenship in American society . . . Monolingual education opens doors to the larger world . . . institutionalized bilingualism remains another source of the fragmentation of America, another threat to the dream of 'one people'. (1991: 108–9)

The claims that 'bilingualism shuts doors' and 'monolingual education opens doors to the wider world', are laughable if viewed in isolation, particularly in the context of current global interdependence and the frequently expressed needs of American business for multilingual 'human resources'. Schlesinger's comments become interpretable only in the context of a societal discourse that is profoundly disquieted by the fact that the sounds of the Other have now become audible and the hues of the American social landscape have darkened noticeably.

Despite its disdain for empirical evidence, this discourse is broadcast through the media into every classroom in the nation. There is anger that schools have apparently reneged on their traditional duty to render the Other invisible and inaudible. Under the guise of equity programmes initiated in the 1960s, diversity infiltrated into the American classroom and became legitimated. In view of demographic projections that diversity will increase dramatically during the next 30 years, many Americans view it as extremely urgent to curtail the infiltration of diversity and particularly one of its most visible manifestations, bilingual education. As noted above, this opposition to bilingual education and mother tongue promotion for minority students is not by any means confined to the US context.

What does the research say about bilingualism and bilingual education? Is there any empirical support for the claims that 'bilingualism shuts doors' and bilingual education retards children's academic progress? For minority language children, continued mother tongue development during the school years is a necessary condition for the development of bilingualism and thus the questions can be rephrased in relation to what we know about mother tongue development.

What We Know About Bilingual Education and Mother Tongue Development

The research is very clear about the importance of bilingual children's mother tongue for their overall personal and educational development. More detail on the research findings summarised below can be found in Baker (2000, 2001), Cummins (2000), and Skutnabb-Kangas (2000).

Bilingualism has positive effects on children's linguisti
development. More than 150 research studies conducted
years suggest that when children continue to develop th
or more languages throughout their elementary or pri
they gain a deeper understanding of language and how
They have more practice in processing language, es;
develop literacy in both, and they are able to compa

ways in which their two languages organise reality. The research also suggests that bilingual children may also develop more flexibility in their thinking as a result of processing information through two different languages.

The level of development of children's mother tongue is a strong predictor of their second language development. Children who come to school with a solid foundation in their mother tongue develop stronger literacy abilities in the school language. When parents and other caregivers (e.g. grandparents) are able to spend time with their children and tell stories or discuss issues with them in a way that develops their mother tongue vocabulary and concepts, children come to school well prepared to learn the school language and succeed educationally. Children's knowledge and skills transfer across languages from the mother tongue they have learned in the home to the school language. From the point of view of children's development of concepts and thinking skills, the two languages are interdependent (Cummins, 2000). Transfer across languages can be two-way: when the mother tongue is promoted in school (e.g. in a bilingual education programme), the concepts, language, and literacy skills that children are learning in the majority language can transfer to the home language. In short, both languages nurture each other when the educational environment permits children access to both languages.

Mother tongue promotion in the school helps develop not only the mother tongue but also children's abilities in the majority school language. This finding is not surprising in view of the previous findings that (1) bilingualism confers linguistic advantages on children and (2) abilities in the two languages are significantly related or interdependent. Bilingual children perform better in school when the school effectively teaches the mother tongue and, where appropriate, develops literacy in that language. By contrast, when children are encouraged to reject their mother tongue and, consequently, its development stagnates, their personal and conceptual foundation for learning is undermined.

Spending instructional time through a minority language in the school does not hurt children's academic development in the majority school language. Some educators and parents are suspicious of bilingual education or mother tongue teaching programmes because they worry that these programmes take time away from the majority school language. For ample, in a bilingual programme where 50% of the time is spent teaching children's home language and 50% through the majority school surely children's learning of the majority school language must suffer? One of the most strongly established findings of educational research, conducted in many countries around the world, is that well-implemented bilingual programmes can promote literacy and subject matter knowledge in a minority language without any negative effects on children's development in the majority language. Within Europe, the Foyer programme in Belgium which develops children's speaking and literacy abilities in three languages (their mother tongue, Dutch and French) in the primary school most clearly illustrates the benefits of bilingual and trilingual education (see Byram & Leman, 1990; Leman, 1993).

The same phenomenon of positive multilingual academic outcomes is demonstrated in the experience of trilingual education in Luxembourg (Lebrun & Baetens Beardsmore, 1993) and in the European Schools model (Baetens Beardsmore, 1993).

We can understand how this happens from the research findings summarised above. When children are learning through a minority language (e.g. their home language), they are not only learning this language in a narrow sense. They are learning concepts and intellectual skills that are equally relevant to their ability to function in the majority language. Pupils who know how to tell the time in their mother tongue understand the *concept* of telling time. In order to tell time in the second language (e.g. the majority language), they do not need to re-learn the concept of telling time; they simply need to acquire new labels or 'surface structures' for an intellectual skill they have already learned. Similarly, at more advanced stages, there is transfer across languages in academic and literacy skills such as knowing how to distinguish the main idea from the supporting details of a written passage or story, identifying cause and effect, distinguishing fact from opinion, and mapping out the sequence of events in a story or historical account.

Children's mother tongues are fragile and easily lost in the early years of school. Many people marvel at how quickly bilingual children seem to 'pick up' conversational skills in the majority language in the early years at school (although it takes much longer for them to catch up to native speakers in academic language skills). However, educators are often much less aware about how quickly children can lose their ability to use their mother tongues, even in the home context. The extent and rapidity of language loss will vary according to the concentration of families from a particular linguistic group in the school and neighbourhood. Where the mother tongue is used extensively in the community outside the school, language loss among young children will be less. However, where language communities are not concentrated or 'ghettoised' in particular neighbourhoc children can lose their ability to communicate in their mother to within two to three years of starting school. They may retain receptive (understanding) skills in the language but they will use the majority language in speaking with their peers and siblings and in responding to their parents. By the time children become adolescents, the linguistic gap between parents and children has become an emotional chasm. Pupils frequently become alienated from the cultures of both home and school with predictable results.

Negotiation of identity is a crucial factor in minority children's academic success. When the message, implicit or explicit, communicated to children in the school is 'Leave your language and culture at the schoolhouse door', children also leave a central part of who they are – their identities – at the schoolhouse door. When they feel this rejection, they are much less likely to participate actively and confidently in classroom instruction. In order to promote active participation in learning, it is not enough for teachers to passively accept children's linguistic and cultural diversity in the school. Rather they should be *proactive* and take the initiative to affirm children's linguistic identity by means of activities such as having posters in the various languages of the community around the school and encouraging children to write in their mother tongues in addition to the majority school language (e.g. write and publish pupil-authored bilingual books). In general, minority language children will benefit academically when teachers create an instructional climate where the linguistic and cultural experience of the whole child is actively accepted and validated.

When educators affirm the value of minority children's culture and language in the school context, they simultaneously challenge the societal discourse that devalues children's cultural and linguistic capital. If a bilingual programme does not incorporate this challenge to societal power relations, it is unlikely to be successful in promoting strong bilingual and biliteracy development (Cummins, 1996).

Shaping a Dynamic Identity for the Future

When educators within a school develop language policies and organise their curriculum and instruction in such a way that the linguistic and cultural capital of children and communities is strongly affirmed in all the the school, then the school is rejecting the negative attitrance about diversity that exist in the wider society. In ercive relations of power, the school is holding up to bilin-positive and affirming image of who they are and who they within this society. As Hugo Baetens Beardsmore has emphasised consistently during the past 25 years, minority language children have an enormous contribution to make to their societies, and to the international global community, if only the educational system puts into practice principles that are almost universally taken for granted for majority language children:

- Children's cultural and linguistic experience in the home is the foundation of children's future learning and the educational system should build on that foundation rather than undermine it;
- All children have the right to have their talents recognised and promoted within the school.

In short, the cultural, linguistic and intellectual capital of our societies will increase dramatically when we stop seeing culturally and linguistically diverse children as 'a problem to be solved' and instead open our eyes to the linguistic, cultural, and intellectual resources they bring from their homes to schools and societies. Bilingual and multilingual education programmes are necessary to develop these resources fully. At this point, these programmes are supported by a vast amount of research and practical experience and their educational legitimacy is no longer in question among researchers and policy-makers who consult the empirical evidence. Unfortunately, however, bilingual programmes for minority language children are intertwined with debates about issues of identity, culture and racism in many societies. As a consequence, the empirical evidence regarding the potential benefits of bilingual education for both minority and majority language children and for the society as a whole typically plays a subordinate role in policy-making in comparison to ideological considerations related to managing and curtailing diversity. Thus, the future of bilingual and trilingual education depends not just on demystifying the research findings but also challenging the operation of coercive relations of power that operate to limit the educational options and opportunities afforded to many minority children. A good place to start in this regard is to highlight some of the more absurd claims that have been made to rationalise the extinction of minority languages such as Schlesinger's statements that 'bilingualism shuts doors' and 'monolingual education opens doors to the wider world' (1991: 108–9). Statements such as these cannot be accounted for by ignorance or irrationality. Rather they reveal the surface façade of a coercive power structure and highlight the fact that successful implementation of bilingual and trilingual programmes for minority language children must address sociopolitical as much as psycholinguistic issues.

References

Baetens Beardsmore, H. (1982) *Bilingualism: Basic Principles.* Clevedon: Multilingual Matters.

Baetens Beardsmore, H. (1993) The European School model. In H. Baetens Beardsmore (ed.) *European Models of Bilingual Education* (pp. 121–54). Clevedon: Multilingual Matters.

Baetens Beardsmore, H. (1995) The European School experience in multilingual education. In T. Skutnabb-Kangas (ed.) *Multilingualism for All* (pp. 21–68). Lisse: Swets & Zeitlinger.

Baker, C. (2000) *A Parents' and Teachers' Guide to Bilingualism* (2nd edn). Clevedon: Multilingual Matters.

Baker, C. (2001) *Foundations of Bilingual Education and Bilingualism* (3rd edn). Clevedon: Multilingual Matters.

Baker, C. and Jones, S. (1998) *Encyclopedia of Bilingualism and Bilingual Education.* Clevedon: Multilingual Matters.

Byram, M. and Leman, J. (1990) *Bicultural and Trilingual Education.* Clevedon: Multilingual Matters.

California Department of Education (2000) *California Two-way Bilingual Immersion Programs Directory.* Sacramento: California Department of Education.

Crawford, J. (2000) Proposition 227: A new phase of the English-only movement. In R.D. González and I. Melis (eds), *Language Ideologies: Critical Perspectives on the Official English Movement,* Vol. 1. *Education and the Social Implications of Official Language* (pp. 28–61). Urbana, IL: National Council of Teachers of English.

Cummins, J. (1996) *Negotiating Identities: Education for Empowerment in a Diverse Society.* Los Angeles: California Association for Bilingual Education.

Cummins, J. (2000) *Language, Power, and Pedagogy. Bilingual Children in the Crossfire.* Clevedon: Multilingual Matters.

Cummins, J. and Danesi, M. (1990) *Heritage Languages: The Development and Denial of Canada's Linguistic Resources.* Toronto: Our Schools Ourselves/Garamond.

Hakuta, K. (1999) SAT-9 scores and California's Proposition 227: Drawing legitimate inferences regarding its impact on performance of LEP students. *NABE News* 22 (8), 1–7.

Lebrun, N. and Baetens Beardsmore, H. (1993) Trilingual education in the Grand Duchy of Luxembourg. In H. Baetens Beardsmore (ed.) *European Models of Bilingual Education* (pp. 101–20). Clevedon: Multilingual Matters.

Leman, J. (1993) The bicultural programmes in the Dutch-Language school system in Brussels. In H. Baetens Beardsmore (ed.) *European Models of Bilingual Education* (pp. 86–100). Clevedon: Multilingual Matters.

Micklethwait, J. (2000, March 11–17) Survey: The United States. Oh, say, can you see? *The Economist* 1–8 (insert).

Schlesinger, A.J. (1991) *The Disuniting of America.* New York: W.W. Norton.

Skourtou, E. (1995) Some notes about the relationship between bilingualism and literacy concerning the teaching of Greek as a second language. *European Journal of Intercultural Studies* 6 (2), 24–30.

Skutnabb-Kangas, T. (2000) *Linguistic Genocide in Education – or Worldwide Diversity and Human Rights?* Mahwah, NJ: Lawrence Erlbaum Associates.

Swain, M. and Lapkin, S. (1982) *Evaluating Bilingual Education: A Canadian Case Study.* Clevedon: Multilingual Matters.

Tse, L. (2001) *Why Don't they Learn English? Separating fact from fallacy in the U.S. language debate.* New York: Teachers College Press.

Chapter 5

Bilingual Encounters in the Classroom

PETER MARTIN

Introduction

It is well-attested that the discourse of classrooms in many multilingual contexts includes the use of an indigenous language as well as the use of the official language(s) of the education system (for example, Adendorff (1996) in South Africa; Arthur (1996) in Botswana; Canagarajah (1995, 1999) in Sri Lanka; Gonzalez (1996, 1998) in the Philippines; and Lin (1996, 1999) in Hong Kong). It is the purpose of this chapter to highlight some of the bilingual encounters in one particular multilingual context, and to show how the participants in such classrooms make use of the resources available to them in order to accomplish lessons bilingually within a bilingual educational context. While I will mainly draw on observations from classrooms in Brunei, I will also make reference to other educational contexts where similar bilingual encounters occur.

In seeking to investigate this salient feature of classroom discourse in the primary school classroom in Brunei, the paper will give due emphasis to language policy issues in a country which purports to value two languages simultaneously. In other words, the bilingual classroom encounters discussed in this paper are seen in the light of a bilingual system of education which is 'a means of ensuring the sovereignty of the Malay language, while at the same time recognising the importance of the English language' (Government of Brunei, 1985: 2).

The bilingual system of education in Brunei has received considerable attention in the literature in the last decade or so (Baetens Beardsmore, 1993, 1996; Edwards, 1993; Jones *et al.*, 1993; Tucker, 1996). Focusing more specifically on classroom practices, certain themes have emerged. The apparent success of the development of literacy skills through projects such as the Reading and Language Acquisition (RELA) programme has led to a discussion as to whether such a programme should be introduced in the students' first language (Ng, 1996). There have also been debates on policy decisions about the language medium for different subjects at different stages of the primary school curriculum (Baetens Beardsmore, 1996; Jones, 1996). A third area of interest has been the use of the first language in disciplinary teaching and learning in classrooms where English is planned as the medium of instruction. The focus of this paper is very much on the third issue but, as noted earlier, such discussion cannot be divorced from other issues to do with literacy and biliteracy, and language policy in Brunei.

Any discussion of language use in the classroom needs to be considered in the context of the social conditions outside the classroom. As pointed out by Martin-Jones (1990: 102), it has been common to approach classrooms as if they were 'independent cultural domains', and this has resulted in the failure to take into account language behaviour outside the classroom which clearly has an important bearing on what goes on inside the classroom. The importance of the link between the schools and the society at large has not gone unrecognised. Das (1987: v), for example, in the introduction to a volume on classroom interaction in Southeast Asia, states that 'the classroom, in any society, represents a microcosm of the sociocultural patterns existing outside it'. Similar views have been expressed by Mehan (1981) and Tucker (1996), with specific reference to bilingual education situations. Fishman (1977: 32), too, argued that what he calls 'social dimensionality' should be 'recognised *within* the bilingual education classroom, rather than merely *outside* it'. The following section of this paper therefore gives some emphasis to the language environment in Brunei, including a brief review of the sociolinguistic context.

The Language Environment in Brunei

Brunei is a multilingual country with five indigenous languages. These include several varieties of Malay, and four regional, non-Malay languages (Tutong, Belait, Murut and Dusun-Bisaya). These four non-Malay languages are spoken by a decreasing number of the population (Kershaw, 1994; Martin, 1995). Provision of education through the medium of these languages, none of which has a written tradition, was never given serious consideration (Annual Report 1939: 32–33). In contemporary Brunei, they have come to be regarded as 'Malay' dialects and, as such, there has been little need to develop them. Linguistically, however, they are clearly separate from Malay.

The official language of Brunei is *Bahasa Melayu*, often referred to as 'Standard Malay', or 'Malay'. The other Malay dialects used in the country include Royal Malay, Kedayan, Kampong Ayer, Bazaar Malay and Brunei Malay. The only one which need concern us here is Brunei Malay, the variety of Malay used by the politically and numerically dominant group in the country, the Brunei Malay. A form of this variety, which I have called Colloquial Brunei Malay, has become the major code in the country, the lingua franca *par excellence* and the *de facto* national dialect, a code which functions as an important marker of rapport and solidarity in all but a few interior regions of the country (Martin, 1996a).

The relationship between Brunei Malay and *Bahasa Melayu*, the official language, has not been explored in any depth. An understanding of this relationship is critical if the goals of the bilingual system of education are to be met. In Brunei society, Colloquial Brunei Malay is not only the usual code for informal communication but it is used in a number of formal contexts, too, including the classroom. Use of *Bahasa Melayu* among Bruneians in day-to-day interaction would be very marked indeed. In the small and close-knit Brunei community, face-to-face encounters with 'strangers' are uncommon and there is little need or desire to use *Bahasa Melayu*.

Within the bilingual education system, *Bahasa Melayu* and English have clearly defined roles. It is significant, though, that neither of these two languages is the home language of all but a small number of Brunei students. A successful bilingual programme depends on the opportunity for individuals to use the languages for genuine communication (cf. Cummins, 1988: 272). Baetens Beardsmore (1993: 20–21) compares the situation in Europe with that in Brunei and points out that in Europe 'it is far easier and more natural [. . .] to use the target language as output, both because of the environment, because of attitudes, and because the school circumstances help to create many opportunities for *individual practice* and output' (original emphasis). Such opportunities for either of the target languages – English and *Bahasa Melayu* – are clearly much less available in Brunei.

One significant feature of communication patterns in Brunei is the abundance of switching between codes. Among the younger generation, switching between Malay and English is becoming increasingly common (Ozóg, 1996). As well as switching between Malay and English, there is also switching between Brunei Malay or Colloquial Brunei Malay and *Bahasa Melayu*. Use of the term 'code-switching' could be seen as problematic here and it might be argued that what actually occurs is style-shifting, or moving along a continuum from Colloquial Brunei Malay towards the standard variety. I accept this, but nevertheless argue that the two varieties have what I would call a 'social distinctiveness', which is clearly perceived by the speakers themselves. A switch to the standard variety in many situations would be extremely marked. Incorporation of Standard Malay lexis, phonologically adapted to Colloquial Brunei Malay, however, would be unmarked. Space does not allow an in-depth analysis of the dialect versur standard argument. I do, however, feel that the distinction is importan the Brunei context. The whole question of what language the young l brings to the classroom is hugely significant for the subsequent acquisition of literacy and for the bilingual education system in Brunei.

Teaching and Learning Bilingually in Classrooms

In the last two decades, code-switching in the classroom has become an important area of study (Martin-Jones, 1995). Numerous functions have been identified to account for a switch to the first language. These include translation, clarification, checking comprehension, giving directions, maintenance of discipline, aiding weak students, saving time and for solidarity purposes, in other words, acting as a 'we-code' (see, for example, Atkinson, 1987; Canagarajah, 1995; Garrett *et al.*, 1994; Guthrie, 1984: 45). Merritt *et al.* (1992: 118), in their study into the social determinants of code-switching in Kenyan primary classrooms have summarised the four major factors which account for code-switching: '(1) official school policy, (2) cognitive concerns, (3) classroom management concerns, (4) values and attitudes about the appropriate use of [the languages] in society at large'. Such taxonomic approaches to code-switching are centred around the teacher. Martin-Jones (1990) itemises work which takes into account the learners' as well as the teachers' contribution to the complex sequences of classroom discourse. Auer's (1984, 1990) neat distinction between discourse-related and participant-related code-switching is discussed by Martin-Jones (1995). The former is speaker-oriented, serving as a 'resource for accomplishing different communicative acts at specific points within interactional sequences' (Martin-Jones, 1995: 99). Making an aside, specifying a particular addressee or moving in and out of the teaching/learning frame are examples of discourse-related code-switching. Participant-related code-switching, on the other hand, is hearer-oriented and is common where speakers face communicative problems. It is particularly relevant in Brunei where many students and some teachers have a limited grasp of English.

Brunei's bilingual system, referred to as *dwibahasa*, is based on the principle of 'bilingualism through monolingualism' (Swain, 1983: 41). In this approach, English and 'Malay', ostensibly *Bahasa Melayu*, are used separately depending on the subject content. There are clear guidelines on the language of instruction for all subjects in the school curriculum at all levels of education (Government of Brunei, 1985). In the first three years of ˌ ˌˌˌ ˌ˗ˌˌˌˌˌˌˌˌˌˌˌˌtion all subjects are taught through the medium of Malay. In
ʳ of primary education, there is a transition to English-
tion for a number of subjects: geography, science, mathe-
til 1995, history.
lementation in 1985, a number of studies have looked at atti-
the bilingual system of education in Brunei. I will report

briefly on one of these studies here as it suggests a number of potential 'drawbacks' to the system, based on the views of a 'representative cross-section of Principals, Headteachers and teachers' (Ahmad, 1992: 25). Among the drawbacks are problems at the operational level, including factors such as a syllabus which is too demanding, difficulties with the language of the textbooks, a lack of a sufficient number of bilingual teachers, and the 'too abrupt' transition from Malay to English at Primary Four level (Ahmad, 1992: 27–29).

Braighlinn (1992) has pointed out what he refers to as an 'extraordinary paradox' in that 'the development of the Malay language as a medium of literary expression and analytical thought' has been thwarted by the introduction of the *dwibahasa* system. So much so that he suggests that 'the majority of non-middle class youth receive virtually no education at all, because the medium of instruction [English] cannot be understood' (Braighlinn, 1992: 21). However, as this paper will show, Braighlinn's statement is only partially true. What classroom practices actually show is a complex mesh of language selection and code-switching as teachers and students try to cope with the constraints imposed by concerns of language competency, the language policy and the values of and attitudes to the languages in the environment outside the classroom. In other words, students in these classrooms do receive some education in that they and their teachers are not constrained by the English-only policy.

Classroom observation and numerous reports and case studies indicate that 'Malay' is commonly used in the subject classroom where ostensibly English is the medium of instruction. More precisely, there are several studies by local authors which refer to the fact that a form of Brunei Malay is often used in the classroom alongside *Bahasa Melayu* and English. I have discussed these studies elsewhere (Martin, 1996b).

This paper focuses on observations from the primary classroom in the years immediately after the transition from *Bahasa Melayu* to English as the medium of instruction for subjects such as geography, science, mathematics and history (the latter up until 1995 when the medium of instruction changed to Malay). This is clearly the stage at which the greatest linguistic pressure occurs and consequently, an investigation of classroom language use at this level is deemed to be particularly useful. Observations and recordings were made in a number of primary schools, two in the region of the capital city, Bandar Seri Begawan and one in Temburong, a rural and isolated area of the country. Content lessons were observed and recorded with the permission of the Ministry of Education, the headteachers, teachers and pupils.

I make no claim that the classrooms in which the observations were made are necessarily representative of the situation in Brunei. Indeed, it is likely that classrooms in different types of schools and in different geographical areas will provide distinct models of language use. In addition, individual teachers will make use of the first language to different degrees. However, given individual differences, the fact remains that code-switching is a striking feature of the classroom, particularly the primary classroom. Based on the quantifiable data from the present study, code-switching was most common in history and then science lessons, and least common in mathematics lessons. It must be noted, though, that the two mathematics lessons which I observed and recorded were revision lessons in which, I was informed, no new information was given. If further studies of a larger sample of classrooms showed that, for example, in mathematics lessons there was little use of 'Malay', this would surely be of significance. There has been considerable discussion (for example, Baetens Beardsmore, 1993; Jones, 1996) about a possible change of language of instruction (from English to Malay) for the so-called 'cognitively difficult subjects' such as science and mathematics. The amount of dependence on the first language in such lessons might prove to be a useful guide for future language policy. I certainly feel it is worthwhile to look into the 'nature, frequency and functions' of code-switching at the different levels of the school system in Brunei (Baetens Beardsmore, 1993: 58). However, there is a danger that in trying to do so one might attempt to fit instances of code-switching into neat, pre-ordained categories, without any reference to either the participants in the interaction or the wider social and institutional order. In sum, it is clear that code-switching in the classroom needs to be considered as situated social practice rather than decontextualised practice.

Code-switching in Brunei Primary Classrooms

I do not believe it is possible, or, indeed, useful, to attempt to assign a 'cause' for every instance of code-switching that occurs in a given set of data. Although it might appear clear what the particular function of a switch is, for example, the provision of a gloss for a particular lexical item, in many cases a switch might carry a lot more meaning than a simple translation. Thus, to take one example, teachers' language behaviour in the classroom also needs to be seen in the light of their role as socialising agents (cf. Canagarajah, 1995; Merritt *et al.*, 1992). This is particularly relevant in the close-knit Brunei community. There is also the factor of linguistic insecurity: many teachers openly admit that they are aware of their own limitations in English. The lesson transcripts show that teachers do, indeed, resort to the first language when they have linguistic or conceptual problems.

The aim of the discussion below, then, is not to provide a rigid typology of the code-switching that occurs in Brunei classrooms. I will, nevertheless, highlight below some salient practices in order to give some idea of the range of uses to which 'Malay', both *Bahasa Melayu* and Colloquial Brunei Malay are put in content lessons where the medium of instruction is English. In the examples of code-switching which follow, switches into Malay are given in bold print (with translations provided in italics in pointed brackets). The type of Malay used in the extracts is identified in the discussion. Further transcription conventions are provided at the end of the paper.

The first two extracts provide examples of switching into Malay to unpack the meaning of text. In the first example, the text is history and in the second it is geography. In both extracts, the students are reading aloud from the textbook, in chorus in Extract 1, and a single student in Extract 2. In both extracts, the teacher orchestrates the reading process, and this orchestration includes negotiating the meaning of difficult words. It will be noted that, particularly in Extract 1, the words are extremely difficult. In a study referred to above, Ahmad (1992) noted the high lexical load in the textbooks. Baetens Beardsmore (1996) has also made the point that there is very often little comprehension on the part of the students. This is particularly apparent in Extract 1. The teacher provides one-word glosses for three difficult items of vocabulary: 'dependency', 'tribute' and 'embraced'. At the same time, the students are instructed to write the Malay equivalents of these words in their books.

Extract 1 (Primary 5: History)

Ss:	'In the early period of his rule, Brunei was still a dependency of'
T:	dependency .. **apa itu**? < *what's that?* >
Ss:	[No response]
T:	Write in your books .. dependency **ialah jajahan** < *is 'jajahan'* > .. 'Brunei was still under the' **jajahan** < *dependency* > of ..
Ss:	'of Majapahit. Many countries paid tribute'
T:	Now what is tribute?
Ss:	[No response]
T:	Find the word tribute .. put there **penghormatan** < *tribute* > .. OK .. Before
Ss:	'Before Sultan Muhammad Shah embraced Islam'
T:	embrace .. **apa maksud**? < *what's the meaning of it?* > embrace .. it means **memeluk agama** < *embracing religion* > Islam.

In Extract 2, the teacher has more success negotiating the meaning of the terms 'farm', 'self-employed' and 'vegetables' with the students. They are able to provide the appropriate labels, in Malay. The discourse in Extract 2 demonstrates a collaborative bilingual engagement between teacher and students. Having elicited the Malay label, the teacher orchestrates the whole class to respond in chorus. The teacher does this by using prosodic clues such as raised intonation and vowel lengthening in order to alert the students that it is their cue to come in. This is represented in Extract 2 by the symbol (^).

Extract 2 (Primary 4: Geography)

S: 'Zainal bin Ahmad'
T: 'is a farmer'
S: 'is a farmer'
T: Aah . a farmer . **di mana tempat** farmer **bakaraja**? < *where does a farmer work?* >
Ss: **kebun** < *garden/farm* >
T: **kebun** .. 'he is self-employed'
S: 'he is self-employed'
T: **apa** self-employed **ini**? < *what does* 'self-employed' *mean?* >
S: **berkerja sendiri** < *works by himself* >
T: **berkerja^** < *works^* >
Ss: farmer
T: **sendiri . bekerja^** < *himself . works^* >
Ss: **sendiri** < *by himself* >
T: Aah . **bekerja sendiri** . < *works by himself* > 'and works on his farm'
S: 'and works on his farm'
T: 'growing vegetables'
S: 'growing vegetables'
T: **apa** vegetables **ani** < *what's the meaning of* 'vegetables'? >
Ss: **sayur** < *vegetable* >
T: **sayur-sayuran . sayur^** < *vegetables . vegetable^* >
Ss: **sayuran** < *vegetables* >
T: Aah . 'he must work'

The bilingual unpacking of text which occurs in these two extracts is, I would argue, the default mode of talking around content area texts in the Brunei classroom, an issue discussed in more detail elsewhere (Martin, 1999). Studies in other contexts indicate similar bilingual annotation strategies to those shown in the extracts above. For example, Lin (1996) in the Hong Kong context, relates how Cantonese is used to annotate texts in English, and Camilleri (1996) notes the way teachers and learners in secondary schools in Malta switch between Maltese and English in interacting with English texts.

Similar bilingual encounters occur in interaction around textbook pictures. In Extract 3 below, using both English and Malay, the participants negotiate the meaning of 'grasshopper', and the teacher checks that the students understand the term 'insects'.

Extract 3 (Primary 4: Science)

T: millipede . and one more .. what's that .. **apa tu**? < *what's that?* > [pointing at the picture]
S: hopper
T: grasshopper .. **belalang bah dalam Bahasa Melayu** < *grasshopper in Malay* > OK some of these insects are .. **tau** insects < *do you know?* [insects] >
S: **tau** < *yes* >
T: **dalam Bahasa Melayunya apa**? < *what's the meaning in Malay?* >
Ss: **serangga** < *insects* >

Teachers also switch between English and Malay to reformulate or restate an idea which is first expressed in the other language. Two examples are given below. In Extract 4, the restatement is from English to Colloquial Brunei Malay. In Extract 5, English follows Malay.

Extract 4 (Primary 4: Science)

T: Now when we eat too much .. eh .. no .. when we eat these foods .. these vegetables .. OK **kalau kitani makan** < *if we eat* > vegetables ..

Extract 5 (Primary 4: Science)

T: This one .. **dengarkan lagi** < *listen again* > .. **kalau makan banyak ani .. kalau makan banyak** chicken < *if you eat too much of this, too much* chicken > chicken .. if you eat too much . **ada dengar** cholesterol? < *have you heard of* cholesterol? >

Extracts 4 and 5 exemplify switches which function to reformulate an idea previously expressed. However, many switches do actually develop the discourse, introducing new content or providing exemplification or clarification, as in the two extracts below. In Extract 6, the teacher introduces the topic 'cholesterol' in Malay, restates part of her exposition in English and then switches to a mixture of Colloquial Brunei Malay and *Bahasa Melayu* to provide some clarification.

Extract 6 (Primary 4: Science)

T: **ada pernah mendengar** cholesterol? < *have you ever heard of* cholesterol? >

Ss: **ada** < *yes* >

T: **maksudnya orang bercholesterol atu .. maksud orang atu** < *the meaning of people who have high cholesterol, those people* > .. **banyak bah cholesterolnya .. banyak lemak bah . dalam badannya bah .** [inaudible] < *they have a lot of cholesterol, a lot of fat, in their bodies* > OK **jangan makan** < *don't eat* > too much of these .. **kitani boleh . tapi jangan selalu .. baik jangan makan anu ani banyak banyak** < *we can eat a little, but not always, eat a little of this and a little of that* >

In Extract 7, the type of Malay used to develop the meaning of 'envoy' and 'diplomat' is clearly not the standard variety. One particularly notice-able feature of this extract and, indeed, Extract 6, is the use of Brunei Malay pronouns such as *kitani* and *diurang* (as opposed to *kita*, 'us'; and *mereka* 'they', 'these', the respective *Bahasa Melayu* and English equivalents).

Extract 7 (Primary 4: History)

T: How many envoy?

Ss: three

T: three . envoy **atu macam** diplomat **bah** < envoy *is like* diplomat > OK . **ia manghantar urang ani** < *he sent these men* > **ia mambawa** < *he brought* > letter and gifts .. ah .. **barang** < *things* > .. ah **mambagi barang kapada Raja Cina** < *he gave things to the King of China* > **Raja Cina macam kitani bah .. kalau kitani pergi ka rumah urang kitani selalu mambawa barang kan buah tangan** < *like us .. if we go to someone's house we always bring things or gifts* > **sama jua macam diurang ani** < *it was the same with these people* >

The choice of pronouns and other terms of address in the classroom in Brunei would make an interesting study. Observation shows that teachers use English, *Bahasa Melayu* and Brunei Malay pronouns depending on context. Teachers commonly use 'you' and the standard Malay equivalent of *kamu* to address their students. They address themselves as 'teacher' and very rarely as *cikgu* (the Malay equivalent), even when using Malay. Thus a switch to English, as in the utterance '*Apanya kata* teacher *tadi*?', 'What did I say just now?' is common. Students always use 'teacher' both as a term of address and a pronoun. Use of the Brunei Malay pronoun *kitani* (the inclu-sive form of 'we') also occurs regularly in the data, as can be seen in Extracts 6 and 7 above and Extract 8 below. It is interesting to note that the *Bahasa Melayu* equivalent, *kita* is hardly ever used. One reason could be that the pronoun *kita* functions in Colloquial Brunei Malay as the second person singular pronoun 'you'. Extract 8 below provides examples of the use of a number of Brunei Malay pronouns. In particular, there are two examples where -*nya* functions as a second person pronoun, 'you' as in *bini bininya*, 'you girls' or 'the girls among you' and *mamaknya* 'your mothers'.

Extract 8 (Primary 4: Science)

T: [Talking about green vegetables] now . they contain much fibres . **tau** fibres? < *do you know* fibres? >

S: **tau** < *yes, we know* >

T: for example . **kalau sakiranya kamu mengarat** .. < *if you're cutting* > **apa namanya ni bini bininya** < *what's the name of it you girls?* > .. **menulong mamaknya mengarat ah .. sawi .. tau sawi?** < *helping your mothers cut* **sawi** *[a green vegetable] .. do you know* **sawi**? >

Ss: **tau** < *yes, we know* >

T: now .. **bila kitani karat** . < *when we cut up* > **ada macam .. kadang kadang ..** < *it's like . when we sometimes* > **kalau kitani memakai tangan . memutong** . < *if we use our hands to cut up* > **pakai tangan memulak .. ah mengatuk** < *to use hands to break up the stalks .. pound them* >

It has been noted that among the functions of switching codes in the classroom are the maintenance of discipline and other classroom management concerns (Merritt *et al.*, 1992). In the three short extracts below, examples are given of the teacher using a mixture of Colloquial Brunei Malay (underlined) and *Bahasa Melayu* to try to get the students to answer in a louder voice, to encourage more participation from the students and to elicit responses.

Extract 9 (Primary 4: Science)

T: What do you find after a few minutes .. what happen to the paper?

S: It dries up

T: Right .. the paper dries up . **basar basar manjawap atu** < *answer loudly* > . the paper dries up . OK . could you read the next question?

Ss: What is the source of heat?

Extract 10 (Primary 4: Science)

T: Now where do we find the cockroach?

S: In dark places

T: In dark places .. **saurang ganya manjawap .. yang lain mana mulutnya . puasa jua .. inda kan puasa .. buka mulut atu** < *only one person is answering .. the rest, where are your voices . are you fasting .. it's* *not the fasting month .. open your mouths* > .. OK . where can you find the grasshopper?

Extract 11 (Primary 4: Science)

T: Now carbohydrate .. **kalau kamu makan** < *if you eat* > **mandangar tu tadi cakap** teacher < *listen to what I've just been saying* > . if you eat too much of these food . **apa maksud** teacher **sana .. apa maksud** teacher < *what's my meaning here?* > **kalau makan terlalu banyak** < *if you eat too much* >

S: **jadi lampuh** < *get fat* >

T: **apanya kata** teacher **tadi**? < *what did I say just now?* >

S: **mambari lampuh** < *get fat* >

T: it is not good for your^

Ss: teeth

T: for your .. health . for your health . not good for your health .. you will become very^

Ss: fat

It would appear that Malay (both Colloquial Brunei Malay and *Bahasa Melayu*) is important for classroom management routines. In addition, there is the pervasive use of Malay discourse particles such as *tau* 'know', ('do you know?' or '*yes, I know*'), *faham* 'understand' ('do you understand?' or '*yes, I understand*'), and *apa lagi* 'what else?'. One example will suffice.

Extract 12

T: .. what can you see . this one?

Ss: cake

T: OK . **tapi pandangan teacher . anu ani ialah** pie .. < *in my view it's a pie* > **tau** pie? < *do you know pie?* >

S: **tau** < *yes, I know* >

T: **tau** pie? < *do you know pie* >

Ss: **tau** < *yes, we know* >

T: OK . now .. **ani . apa ni**? < *this, what's this?* >

Ss: potatoes

I have already referred to a common discourse feature is the classrooms observed, that is, the cued elicitation technique used by the teacher to orchestrate choral responses (as in Extract 2 above). Two further examples are provided below. In Extract 13, the term 'infectious diseases' occurs in the textbook. The teacher begins to provide a gloss in Malay, but instead of giving the full gloss, he elicits the final morpheme of the Malay term for 'infectious', *berjangkit*. This occurs at the end of the teacher's first utterance and is indicated by [^]. Extract 14 provides a further example.

Extract 13 (Primary 5: Science)

T: .. infectious diseases .. **penyakit yang berjang**^ < *infectious diseases* >
Ss: **kit** [Ss provide the last syllable]
T: **tau penyakit**? < *do you know the word* **penyakit**? >
Ss: **tau** < *yes, we know* >

Extract 14 (Primary 4: Science)

Ss: 'These foods are necessary for us to grow healthily.'
T: OK stop .. for us to grow healthily . meaning **nya untuk kitani mambesar dengan**^ < *it [means] to grow with*^ >
Ss: **kuat** < *strong* >
T: **sihat** .. < *health* > OK . let's read again

This orchestration of choral responses, a sort of 'oral filling in the blank', referred to by Coleman (1996: 17) as the 'completion chorus phenomenon', is exemplified in Extracts 2, 11, 13 and 14. It is not only a common feature of a range of classrooms observed in Brunei, but is found in many other classroom contexts. Several studies of classroom language practices have made reference to it, or similar phenomena. In Prophet and Rowell's study of junior secondary schools in Botswana, for example, the strategy is referred to as 'the most commonly used question and answer technique' (Prophet and Rowell, 1993: 204). Chick's (1996) significant notion of 'safe-talk' is based on this feature of teacher–student collusion. In his micro-ethnographic study of a mathematics lesson in a KwaZulu classroom in apartheid South Africa, he suggests that 'the rhythmic manner in which ... participants synchronise the chorusing sequences ... serve social rather than academic functions' (Chick, 1996: 30). Such functions include reducing the possibility of loss of face, giving classroom participants a sense of accomplishment, and allowing them to 'hide their poor command of English; to obscure their inadequate understanding of academic content; and to maintain the façade of effective learning taking place' (Chick, 1996: 36). Chick's arguments are persuasive, although in the Brunei classrooms observed, it should be noted that the orchestration of choral responses occurred in both English and Malay.

In the choral responses discussed above there appears to be little choice about which language can be used by the students. Not only is the cue given when to come in, but also, following the teacher's choice of language, the language of the response. In the discussion below, I highlight switching between languages across teacher–pupil turns where there appears to be no explicit cue or prompt from the teacher about the choice of language required in the students' response.

In Extracts 15 and 16 below, the teachers put labels on display, 'island' in Extract 15 and 'furniture' in Extract 16 within the framework of a 'Wh-question'. In both cases, a student responds with a label in Malay.

Extract 15 (Primary 4: Geography)

T: what's an island?
S: **pulau** < *island* >
T: **pulau** < *island* > . beach?
S: **pantai** < *beach* >

Extract 16 (Primary 4: Geography)

T: do you know what is furniture?
S: **alat perabot** < *furniture* >
T: **alat perabot** < *furniture* > furniture like table .. chair

One teacher, after viewing the lesson transcript, referred to this type of teacher questioning strategy as a 'comprehension check', as it allowed her to check whether the pupils understood the meaning of a particular lexical item in English. By asking such a question, the teacher actually gave the students in her classroom the opportunity to put the Malay label *pulau* ('island') on display, alongside the English word. The teacher did not expect a full answer, such as 'an island is a piece of land completely surrounded by water' in response to her question, and any such response would have been marked student talk. In actual fact, the teacher was tacitly inviting a response in Malay. In both extracts, the teachers accepted the responses in Malay, and repeated them in Malay. In the second example, as well as repeating the response in Malay, she reformulated it in English, and provided two examples of types of furniture. There were very few occasions in this and other classrooms where a teacher rejected a response in Malay to a 'Wh-question'.

In the classrooms observed, then, students were given the opportunity to display their knowledge of learning that had taken place. Such displaying of knowledge was often synonymous with providing labels for vocabulary items in either English or Malay. Heath (1986) has described this genre of classroom language use, that is, where the teacher attempts of elicit a vocabulary item, as a 'label quest', and I have extended this term to include the sort of bilingual label quests which have been described above. I assert that the teachers' use of certain question types provides important signals to the students about their choice of language in such interactional sequences. In other words, there is some tacit understanding about 'what goes linguistically', so to speak, in the sequential flow between teacher and students. This understanding is based on the institutional norms and the history of interaction in the classrooms.

Before concluding the discussion of some of the bilingual practices in the classrooms, I want to focus on some of the instances where students break free from the straightjacket of filling in slots, choral reading and providing one-word responses to the teacher's initiation. It is significant that such occasions are very few indeed. It will have been noted from the extracts discussed above that student responses in the classroom are very often limited to single words, and are very often simple verbal recall statements. Students are encouraged to provide these simple recall statements but there is very little opportunity for meaningful communication. I would like to provide a number of examples where students do offer a little more than a one-word verbal response to an initiation from the teacher, as I believe that such examples are quite telling. They inform us about the possible advantages of bilingual practices in the classroom.

In Extract 17, two different students offer statements in Colloquial Brunei Malay, even though the teacher is talking about the subject in English. The first student provides an opinion that snails 'make us frightened' and the second suggests that lobsters 'can be eaten'.

Extract 17 (Primary 4: Science)

T: Ah . grasshoppers destroy our vegetables sometimes .. now what about snail .. is it harmful?

S: **mambari takut** teacher < *make us frightened* >

T: **inda pulang menakutkan tetapi** < *it's not really frightening but* > for our vegetables and plants .. it kill our plants .. make our plants .. they eat the stems . and destroy it .. now . lobster.

S: **dapat makan** < *can be eaten* >

T: Ah . it's useful . you can eat . the lobster

There is something different about the discourse here. The two students are not simply filling in slots, but are offering opinions. They are able to do this by using the language with which they are more familiar.

In Extract 18, the first student utterance is merely a slot-filling response to a teacher initiation. The second student utterance is an unusually long, unelicited statement from the student. This statement, in a standard form of Malay, is not followed up by the teacher. I would argue that many teachers are not able to break out of the straightjacket of the default mode of classroom interaction.

Extract 18 (Primary 4: Science)

T: [talking about cockroaches] Ah . **ani namaya** < *these are called* > breathing holes . **tempat apa?** < *what are they for?* >
S: **tempat bernafas** < *for breathing* >
T: **tempat bernafas** < *for breathing* > **ia inda memakai hidung** . ah < *they don't have noses* >
S: **di Pelajaran Am di Darjah Dua kami ada belajar** cockroach < *In General Studies in Primary Two, we learnt about cockroaches* >
T: OK . now . insect lay eggs to hatch their young . **semua** insects **mengeluarkan apa?** < *what do all* insects *lay?* >
Ss: **telur** < *eggs* >

One further example will suffice. In this extract from a geography lesson the teacher was going through various professions and checking whether the pupils knew what they meant within the tightly controlled initiation, response and evaluation routine. The first part of the exchange follows the usual pattern. The move by the student 'teacher *aku bercita-cita menjadi judge*' ('teacher, my ambition is to become a judge') was extremely marked, and this was signified to some extent, by the laughter from several students following this student's contribution. It was as if he had said the wrong lines or had spoken out of turn. The teacher smiled, and provided a brief evaluation of the student's statement. This evaluation gave her the opportunity to move back into the initiation-response-evaluation mode with a further initiation of '*apa* sailor?' ('what's a sailor?'). The teacher did not build on the contribution made by the pupil and she quickly resumed the default pattern of classroom discourse.

Extract 19 (Primary 4: Geography)

T: barber .. **tukang^** < *[has the job of^]* >
S: **potong rambut** < *cutting hair* >
T: driver
Ss: drive
T: cobbler .. **membuat** < *makes* >
S: **kasut** < *shoes* >
. . .
T: judge **ani apa?** < *what's a* judge? >
Ss: [inaudible]
S: **hakim** < *judge* >

T: **hakim** < *judge* >
S: teacher **aku bercita-cita menjadi** judge < *my ambition is to become a judge* > [student laughter]
T: you want to be judge . good . sailor . **apa** sailor? < *what's* a sailor? >
S: **anak kapal** < *sailor* >

The last three extracts are unusual in that they are outside the default pattern of discourse in the classrooms observed. And yet they are telling examples in that they suggest a way that students with limited competence in English might make more meaningful contributions to content lessons.

Bilingual Encounters in a Bilingual System: Some Implications

What, then, do the bilingual encounters described in this paper inform us about the way the teachers and students cope with a second language, as well as a standard variety of Malay, in content lessons? The first point to be made is that the classroom participants cannot manage content lessons in English alone and therefore need to make recourse to Malay, be it Colloquial Brunei Malay or *Bahasa Melayu*. They are not alone! Studies in many other multilingual contexts, some of which I have made reference to in this paper, demonstrate similar bilingual encounters in the classroom. For example, Cleghorn (1992), in a study of primary level science classes in Kenya, found a complex pattern of code-switching. She argues that 'important ideas were more easily conveyed when the teacher did *not* adhere strictly to the English-only language of instruction policy' (Cleghorn, 1992: 311, original emphasis). In the Brunei context, and specifically in the classrooms that were the focus of this study, use of Malay allowed a greater freedom of expression and provided more meaningful opportunities for real communication. So much of what usually goes on in these classrooms, as well as classrooms in other contexts, is slot-filling, labelling and chorusing. As Chick (1996) has pointed out, such practices can create an illusion that learning (of both content and English) is taking place.

The relationship between classroom practice and language policy is not a simple and straightforward one. In fact, it is extremely co   ^lex. In many contexts, there appears to be little recognition on the part (^hout the relationship between language policy and classroom
al. (1992) have argued that issues of language choice ir   much more complex than can be legislated for. Polic' need to consider how language is used in the classroor   teachers to 'more accurately identify communicativ tional effectiveness' (Merritt *et al.*, 1992: 105).

I wish to argue, as has Rubagumya (1990) in re] Tanzania, that switching between languages sho' abnormal at the present stage in the development of Brunei's bilingual system. The system, implemented 15 years ago, is still in its infancy, and there are still many constraints. Included among these are the shortage of teachers fully competent in both English and *Bahasa Melayu*, the low level of English language proficiency of the students at the time of the transition to English as a medium of instruction, the demands of the curriculum and the examination system, and the linguistic difficulty of the textbooks (Ahmad, 1992). Brunei is not alone in facing such constraints as these. For example, Johnson (1992) suggests that the last three are typical of the situation in Hong Kong. He reports that in Hong Kong teachers resort to code-switching as 'the best solution to the problems' (Johnson, 1992: 169).

In a separate paper (Martin, 1996b), I have questioned whether language planners and curriculum developers should endorse, or at least recognise, the use of Malay in the classroom. One reason why there may be no official recognition is the concern about the efficiency of a pedagogy that supports the switching between languages. Although models that allow some use of the first language in the content classroom are available, they are not without problems. Switching between languages is creative rather than mechanistic, so any attempt to impose strict guidelines (see, for example, Faltis, 1989) is unnatural and, probably unsustainable. A less controversial model is that provided by Drexel-Andrieu (1993). Part of her strategy for inclusion of the first language (German) in geography lessons taught in English, was the use of bilingual glossaries.

I would suggest that the way forward here is the recognition that bilingual practices in the classroom are important as a way of accomplishing lessons in multilingual contexts. A corollary of this is the need to dispel the myth that such bilingual practices are a substandard form of communication. It is the classroom participants, teachers and learners, ultimately, who make decisions about which languages are most appropriate for different events in the classroom and their views need to be heard. At present, although much has been written on bilingual educational policies, there are few studies on the potential effectiveness of bilingual practices in the classroom. There is an urgent need for studies that not only take into account the classroom participants' voices, but also provide some coherent framework for an appropriate bilingual methodology for a bilingual system.

Transcription conventions

Conventional punctuation has not been used. Full stops are used to indicate pauses, and question marks to indicate questions.

Teacher
Student

Ss: Students
Roman type: English
Bold type: Malay
< *Italics* > < *Translations into English* >
[ ] Commentary on what is happening in the classroom
'Ali is . . . ' Indicates reading from the textbook or other resource
^ Indicates raised intonation where the teacher expects students to complete a statement

References

Adendorff, R. D. (1996) The functions of code switching among high school teachers and students in KwaZulu and implications for teacher education. In K.M. Bailey and D. Nunan (eds) *Voices from the Language Classroom* (pp. 388–406). Cambridge: Cambridge University Press.

Ahmad Haji Jumat (1992) Dwibahasa (Bilingual) System of Education in Negera Brunei Darussalam. *Proceedings of the Conference on Bilingualism and National Development* (pp. 2–35). Universiti Brunei Darussalam, Bandar Seri Begawan, Brunei, December 1991.

Annual Report for the State of Brunei 1938. (1939) J. Graham Black. Singapore: Government Printing Office.

Arthur, J. (1996) Codeswitching and collusion: Classroom interaction in Botswana primary schools. *Linguistics and Education* 8 (1), 17–33.

Atkinson, D. (1987) The mother tongue in the classroom: a neglected resource. *ELT Journal* 41 (4), 241–47.

Auer, P. (1984) *Bilingual Conversation*. Amsterdam: John Benjamins.

Auer, P. (1990) A discussion paper on code alternation. *European Science Foundation Network on Code-switching and Language Contact: Papers for the Workshop on Concepts, Methodology and Data* (pp. 69–87). Strasbourg: European Science Foundation.

Baetens Beardsmore, H. (1993) Report to the Ministry of Education of Brunei Darussalam on the visit to Schools and Discussions with Ministry Officials. Unpublished document.

Baetens Beardsmore, H. (1996) Reconciling content acquisition and language acquisition in bilingual classrooms. *Journal of Multilingual and Multicultural Development* 17 (2–4), 114–17.

Braighlinn, G. (1992) *Ideological Innovation under Monarchy. Aspects of Legitimation Activity in Contemporary Brunei*. Amsterdam: VU University Press.

Camilleri, A. (1996) Language values and identities: Code-switching in secondary classrooms in Malta. *Linguistics and Education* 8 (1), 85–103

Canagarajah, S. (1995) Functions of codeswitching in ESL classrooms: Socialising bilingualism in Jaffna. *Journal of Multilingual and Multicultural Development* 16 (3), 173–95.

Canagarajah, S. (1999) *Resisting Linguistic Imperialism in English Teaching*. Oxford: Oxford University Press.

Chick, K. (1996) Safe-talk: Collusion in apartheid education. In H. Coleman (ed.) *Society and the Language Classroom* (pp. 21–39). Cambridge: Cambridge University Press.

Cleghorn, A. (1992) Primary level science in Kenya: Constructing meaning through English and indigenous languages. *International Journal of Qualitative Studies in Education* 5 (4), 311–23.

Coleman, H. (ed) (1996) *Society and the Language Classroom*. Cambridge: Cambridge University Press.

Cummins, J. (1988) Language planning in education in multilingual settings. In V. Bickley (ed.) *Languages in Education in a Bilingual or Multilingual Setting* (pp. 262–264). Hong Kong: Institute of Language in Education, Department of Education.

Das, B.K. (ed) (1987) *Patterns of Classroom Interaction in Southeast Asia*. Anthology Series 17. Singapore: SEAMEO Regional Language Centre.

Drexel-Andrieu, I. (1993) Bilingual Geography. In H. Baetens Beardsmore (ed.) *European Models of Bilingual Education* (pp. 173–82). Clevedon: Multilingual Matters.

Edwards, J. (1993) Implementing bilingualism: Brunei in perspective. *Journal of Multilingual and Multicultural Development* 14 (1&2), 25–38.

Faltis, C.J. (1989) Code-switching and bilingual schooling: An examination of Jacobson's New Concurrent Approach. *Journal of Multilingual and Multicultural Development* 10 (2), 117–27.

Fishman, J. (1977) The social science perspective. In *Bilingual Education: Current Perspectives*. Arlington, VA: Center for Applied Linguistics.

Garrett, P., Griffiths, Y., James, C. and Scholfield, P. (1994) Use of the mother-tongue in second language classrooms. *Journal of Multilingual and Multicultural Development* 15 (5), 371–383.

Gonzalez. A. (1996) Using two / three languages in Philippine classrooms: Implications for policies, strategies and practices. *Journal of Multilingual and Multicultural Development* 17 (2–4), 371–383.

Gonzalez. A. (1998) The language planning situation in the Philippines. *Journal of Multilingual and Multicultural Development* 19 (5 & 6), 487–525.

Government of Brunei Darussalam (1985) Education System of Negara Brunei Darussalam. Bandar Seri Begawan: Curriculum Development Centre, Ministry of Education.

Guthrie, L.F. (1984) Contrasts in teachers' language use in a Chinese-English bilingual classroom. In J. Handscombe, R.A. Orem and B.P. Taylor (eds) *On TESOL 1983: The Question of Control* (pp. 39–52). Washington D.C.: TESOL.

Heath, S.B. (1986) Sociocultural contexts of language development. In D. Holt (ed.) *Beyond Language: Social Change and Cultural Factors in Schooling Minority Students*. Los Angeles Evaluation, Dissemination and Assessment Center, California State University, CA.

Johnson, F.R.K. (1992) TESOL Teacher-training for content subject teachers in L2 immersion programmes. In J. Flowerdew, M. Brock and S. Hsia (eds) *Perspectives on Second Language Teacher Education* (pp. 167–185). Hong Kong: City Polytechnic of Hong Kong.

Jones, G.M. (1996) Bilingual education and syllabus design: Towards a workable blueprint. *Journal of Multilingual and Multicultural Development* 17 (2–4), 280–293.

Jones, G., Martin, P.W. and Ozóg, A.C.K. (1993) Multilingualism and bilingual education in Brunei Darussalam. *Journal of Multilingual and Multicultural Development* 14 (1 & 2), 39–58.

Kershaw, E. (1994) Final shifts: Some why's and how's of Brunei-Dusun convergence on Malay. In P.W. Martin (ed.) *Shifting Patterns of Language Communication in Borneo* (pp. 179–94). Williamsburg, VA: Borneo Research Council.

Lin, A.M.Y. (1996) Bilingualism or linguistic segregation? Symbolic domination, resistance and codeswitching in Hong Kong Schools. *Linguistics and Education* 8 (1), 49–84.

Lin, A.M.Y. (1999) Doing-English-lessons in the reproduction or transformation of social worlds. *TESOL Quarterly* 33 (3), 393–412.

Martin, P.W. (1995) Whither the indigenous languages of Brunei Darussalam? *Oceanic Linguistics* 34 (1), 27–43.

Martin, P.W. (1996a) Brunei Malay and *Bahasa Melayu*: a sociolinguistic perspective. In P.W. Martin, A.C.K Ozóg and G. Poedjosoedarmo (eds) *Language Use and Language Change in Brunei Darussalam* (pp. 27–36). Athens, Ohio: Ohio University Center for International Studies. Center for Southeast Asian Studies.

Martin, P.W. (1996b) Code-switching in the primary classroom: one response to the planned and the unplanned language environment in Brunei. *Journal of Multilingual and Multicultural Development* 17 (2–4), 128–44.

Martin, P.W. (1999) Bilingual unpacking of monolingual texts in two primary classrooms in Brunei Darussalam. *Language and Education* 13, 1, 38–58.

Martin, P.W., Ozóg, A.C.K and Poedjosoedarmo, G. (eds) (1996) *Language Use and Language Change in Brunei Darussalam*. Athens, Ohio: Ohio University Center for International Studies. Center for Southeast Asian Studies.

Martin-Jones, M. (1990) Codeswitching in the classroom: a discussion document. In *European Science Foundation. Papers for the Workshop on Impact and Consequences: Broader Considerations* (pp. 79–109). Brussels, November 1990.

Martin-Jones, M. (1995) Code-switching in the classroom: Two decades of research. In L. Milroy and P. Muyskens (eds) *One Speaker, Two Languages: Cross-Disciplinary Perspectives on Code-switching* (pp. 90–111). Cambridge: Cambridge University Press.

Mehan, H. (1981) Ethnography of bilingual children. In H. Trueba, G.P. Guthrie and K. Au (eds) *Culture and the Bilingual Classroom: Studies in Classroom Ethnography* (pp. 36–55). Rowley, MA: Newbury House.

Merritt, M., Cleghorn, A., Abagi, J.O. and Bunyi, G. (1992) Socialising multilingualism: Determinants of codeswitching in Kenyan primary classrooms. *Journal of Multilingual and Multicultural Development* 13 (1 & 2), 103–22.

Ng Seok Moi (1996) Innovation, survival and processes of change in the bilingual classroom in Brunei Darussalam. *Journal of Multilingual and Multicultural Development* 17 (2–4), 149–62.

Ozóg, A.C.K. (1996) Code-switching in peninsular Malaysia and Brunei: a study in contrastive linguistic strategies. In P.W. Martin, A.C.K Ozóg and G. Poedjosoedarmo (eds) *Language Use and Language Change in Brunei Darussalam* (pp. 173–88). Athens, Ohio: Ohio University Center for International Studies. Center for Southeast Asian Studies.

Prophet, R.B. and Rowell, P.M. (1993) Curriculum-in-action: The 'practical' dimension in Botswana classrooms. *International Journal of Educational Development* 10 (1), 17–26.

Rubagumya, C.M. (ed.) (1990) *Language in Education in Africa: A Tanzanian Perspective*. Clevedon: Multilingual Matters.

Swain, M. (1983) Bilingualism without tears. In M. Clarke and J. Handscombe (eds) *On TESOL '82: Pacific Perspectives on Language Learning and Teaching* (pp. 35–46). Washington DC: TESOL. Reprinted in J. Cummins and M. Swain (eds) *Bilingualism in Education* (pp. 99–115). London: Longman.

Tucker, R. (1996) Some thoughts concerning innovative language education programs. *Journal of Multilingual and Multicultural Development* 17 (2–4), 315–20.

Chapter 6

Language Planning: A Grounded Approach

COLIN BAKER

Introduction

While the study of bilingualism goes back to ancient times (Lewis, 1977), it was Hugo Baetens Beardsmore's 1982 (second edition 1986) book *Bilingualism: Basic Principles* that was one of the first to provide an introduction to the topic of bilingualism. Hugo took a risk in publishing with a very new company. This book was thus the starter of the Multilingual Matters Book Series, which, in 20 years, has transformed the study of bilingualism and bilingual education. The book was the launching pad for publications that, holistically, have elevated and deeply enriched the study of languages. For being this catalyst, writers and readers alike will be eternally in Hugo Baetens Beardsmore's debt, not least this author.

There are countless students from numerous countries whose baptism into bilingualism was through Hugo Baetens Beardsmore's (1982,1986) helpful and very accessible book. It provides an introduction to important distinctions and definitions, an immersion into essential conceptual tools, and the interdisciplinary foundational knowledge necessary for a wide-ranging understanding of bilingualism. In readable prose and with careful presentation, it furnishes the essential store of knowledge and understandings for students to move forward into more specialised and complex areas of bilingualism.

One of those specialised areas which has grown in scholarly writing and research since the early 1980s has been language planning. Indeed, in a new millennium, the plight of around 6000 endangered languages in the world has become a topic of global importance. It has also offered all those interested in languages the chance to translate theory into practice and contribute to an issue about the conservation of species and the protection of linguistic and cultural diversity.

This chapter is contextualised in the struggle in Wales to preserve and revitalise the Welsh language. Such contextualisation places limits on generalisation to other language minorities fighting to preserve their language and culture. However, the adoption of a language action planning approach in Wales provides a strategy based on the specification, monitoring and achieving of language planning targets, which it is possible to emulate in other contexts.

The purposes of this chapter are therefore (1) to highlight the need to prevent the current steep decline in the diversity of language and cultures in the world, (2) to briefly outline the language-planning schema that has evolved in Wales, and (3) to portray 'language action planning' whereby the theory of language planning is translated into target-based language strategies that are grounded in the realities of diminishing and dying languages.

The Challenge of the Demise of Languages of the World

A 'new millennium' concern for endangered and dying languages is symbolised in three recent challenging publications: (1) by Daniel Nettle and Suzanne Romaine (2000) hauntingly entitled _Vanishing Voices: The Extinction of the World's Languages_, (2) by David Crystal (2000) with a stark title of _Language Death_ and (3) by Tove Skutnabb-Kangas (2000) with the bluntly challenging title of _Linguistic Genocide in Education – or Worldwide Diversity and Human Rights?_ These important and timely books herald in an era where much thought and effort is required to avert the current language ecology disaster. This chapter is situated within this scenario – specifically in Wales and with the revitalisation of the Welsh language following its fast decline in the 20th century.

A language of communication dies with the last (or more exactly the last-but-one) speaker of that language. For humanity, that is great loss. It is a loss of even more importance than the dreadful destruction of animal and plant species. In Cameroon in 1994/95, a researcher, Bruce Connell, visited the last speaker of a language called Kasabe (or Luo). In 1996, he returned to research that moribund language. He was too late. The last speaker of Kasabe had died on 5th November 1995 taking the language and culture with him (Crystal, 2000). Simply stated, on 4th November 1995 Kasabe existed. On 5th November it did not. On one day, a world view particular to Kasabe existed, a small part of a colourful worldwide language mosaic. The next day, we were all the poorer.

There is little more striking than the words of those who are the last members of a dying language, or those linguists or anthropologists who meet such 'last speakers'. Marie Smith, the last speaker of the Alaskan Eyak language reveals the personal pain: 'I don't know why it's me, why I'm the one. I tell you, it hurts. It really hurts' (Nettle & Romaine, 2000, page 14). Richard Littlebear (1999), a Native American Cheyenne member, tells of his meeting with Marie Smith.

> I felt that I was sitting in the presence of a whole universe of knowledge that could be gone in one last breath. That's how fragile that linguistic universe seemed.

The number of languages in danger of extinction depends on an initial count of how many languages currently exist. Grimes (2000) lists 6809 living languages in the world, while Mackey (1991) suggests 6170 living languages. Moseley and Asher's (1994) *Atlas of the World's Languages* specifies close to 5900 discrete languages, while Bright (1992) lists 6300 living languages. The UNESCO publication *Atlas of the World's Languages in Danger of Disappearing* (Wurm, 1996) estimates 5000 to 6000 languages in existence. The variation in estimate is due, for example, to the difficulty in defining a language (e.g. as different from a dialect), and problems of gathering reliable, valid and comprehensive information about languages in large expanses such as Africa, South America and parts of Asia. The most used list of living languages (Grimes, 2000; see also http://www.sil.org/ethnologue/ethnologue.html) sometimes relies on dated evidence, guesses and estimates, with informants varying in their expertise and ideological expectations.

Thus there is no exact agreement as to the number of living languages in the world. There is, however, growing agreement that many or most are dying languages (Nettle & Romaine, 2000). Thus, there will be many language gravestones in this century. The much-quoted warnings of Michael Krauss (1992) of the Alaska Native Research Center suggest that between 20% to 50% of the world's existing languages are likely to die or become perilously close to death in the next 100 years. Wurm (1996) similarly estimates that 50% of the world's languages are endangered. The US Summer Institute of Linguistics (http://www.sil.org/ethnologue/ethnologue.html) calculated that in 1999, 51 languages in the world only had one speaker, and 500 languages had fewer than 100 speakers. In the long term: 'It is a very realistic possibility that 90 percent of mankind's languages will become extinct or doomed to extinction' (Krauss, 1995, page 4). This estimated 90% death : 10% safe ratio is based on the argument that 50% of the world's languages are no longer being reproduced among children. Krauss (1995) also suggests that an additional 40% of the world's languages are threatened or endangered. Economic, social and political change is one such threat. Assimilation, urbanisation, centralisation, political and economic pressures may well make future generations prefer majority languages.

Thus, as few as 600 languages (10%) may survive, although Krauss (1995, page 4) believes this is too optimistic and suggests that 'it does not seem unrealistic to guess on these bases that 300 languages may be deemed safe'.

Around 7.5% of mammals and 2.7% of birds are listed as 'endangered' or 'threatened', although this may be an underestimate. There are consequently enthusiastic conservation measures. If 90% of the world's languages are vulnerable, language-planning measures to maintain linguistic and cultural diversity are urgently required.

However, a 'preservation of species' approach to language survival is different from evolution of plant and animal species in mechanisms and politics (May, 2001). The biological evolutionary metaphor may suggest to some that language loss is about survival of the fittest. If a language fails to adapt to the modern world, it deserves to die. Natural selection (Social Darwinism) suggests the inevitability of weaker forms dying. This ignores the human-made reasons why languages die – often due to political assimilationist and economic acquisitive policies. Hence social and political factors, and not just 'evolution', are at work in language loss. Power, prejudice, discrimination, marginalisation and subordination are some of the causes of language decline and death. The history of Native American languages in the United States is an example of language genocide and eradication rather than language suicide or natural change. Language loss is thus not 'evolutionary' but determined by politicians, policy-makers and peoples. An evolutionary metaphor understates and undervalues why languages die (May, 2001).

As a component of the argument for the planned preservation of the languages of the world, Crystal (2000) suggests that ecological diversity is essential for long-term planetary survival. The concept of an ecosystem is that all living organisms, plants, animals, bacteria and humans survive and prosper through a network of complex and delicate relationships. Damaging one of the elements in the ecosystem will result in unforeseen consequences for the whole of the system. Nettle & Romaine (2000) maintain that cultural diversity and biological diversity are inseparable. Where biodiversity and rich ecosystems exist, so does linguistic and cultural diversity.

Evolution has been aided by genetic diversity, with species genetically adapting in order to survive in different environments. Diversity contains the potential for adaptation. Uniformity holds dangers for the long-term survival of the species. Uniformity can endanger a species by providing inflexibility and unadaptability. The range of cross fertilisation becomes less as languages and cultures die and the testimony of human intellectual achievement is lessened.

In the language of ecology, the strongest ecosystems are those that are the most diverse. That is, diversity is directly related to stability; variety is important for long-term survival. Our success on this planet has been due to an ability to adapt to different kinds of environment over thousands of years (atmospheric as well as cultural). Such an ability is born out of diversity. Thus language diversity maximises chances of human success and adaptability.

Language diversity in the world coexists with much diversity of purpose and value for each individual language. Each and every language contributes to an expression of identity, is a repository of heritage, and cumulatively world languages contain the sum of human knowledge. Inside each language is a vision of the past, present and future so that when a language dies its vision of the world dies with it. If the world's languages create a mosaic of different perspectives, one part of that rich mosaic is lost. Language not only transmits visions of the past but also contains the cement of social relationships, individual friendships, plus a wealth of organising experiences, as well as ideas about art, craft, science, poetry, song, life, death and language itself. A language contains a way of thinking and being, acting and doing. If there are 6000 living languages, then there are 6000 overlapping ways to describe the world. If Krauss, (1995) worst scenario is realised, there will be around 300 components to the world's cultural and linguistic mosaic left in around a hundred years' time, and not 6000. To avert this disaster, interventionalist grounded language planning is essential.

Language Planning

To halt this catastrophe facing most of the world's languages and cultures, language action planning needs to gain momentum and importance. The argument of this chapter is that, for such language planning to succeed, it needs to develop clear priorities and well-defined targets that fit an integrated whole. Language planning becomes a sequence of enterprises, derived from theory, translated into grounded actions and interventions, and subsequently monitored for their success (or failure). The evaluation of such practical measures should feed back into refining theory and feed forward into more effective interventions. Here the focus is language revitalisation and not theory testing. So what is language action planning and how is it related to language-planning theory?

Language planning refers to 'deliberate efforts to influence the behaviour of others with respect to the acquisition, structure, or functional allocation of their language codes' (Cooper, 1989: 45). Cooper (1989) provides a classic scheme for understanding language planning by asking a series of key questions. What actors (e.g. elites, influential people, counter elites, policy implementers) attempt to influence what behaviours (e.g. the purposes or functions for which the language is to be used) of which people (e.g. of which individuals or organisations) for what ends (e.g. overt (language-related behaviours) or latent (non-language-related behaviours, the satisfaction of interests)) under what conditions (e.g. political, economic, social, demographic, ecological, cultural) by what means (e.g. authority, force, promotion, persuasion) through what decision-making processes and means, with what effect or outcome?

Traditionally, such language planning involves three interacting, over-lapping and inter-dependent operations (Cooper, 1989; Daoust, 1997; Dogancay-Aktuna, 1997; Hornberger, 1994; Kaplan & Baldauf, 1997; Wiley, 1996): status planning (e.g. raising the social, economic and political (sometimes religious) status of a specific language across as many language domains and institutions as possible), corpus planning (e.g modernising terminology, standardisation of grammar and spelling) and acquisition planning (creating language spread by increasing the number of speakers, opportunities to use the language, and incentives to motivate use).

Acquisition language planning

Acquisition planning is particularly concerned with language reproduction in the family and language production at school. Despite receiving less attention in language planning theory (e.g. Kaplan & Baldauf,1997), nevertheless, when theory moves towards grounded action, family and education (as the institutions for intergenerational transmission) are regarded as foundational, almost quintessential (e.g. European Commission, 1996; Fishman, 1991, 1993, 2000).

Acquisition planning is crucial in saving the world's languages as there are two simple and primary reasons why languages die. First, languages die when parents who are able to speak a minority language speak (instead) a majority language in the home. When minority language transmission does not occur at family level, then there is little or no hope of future generations speaking that minority language. Second, minority languages die when education is through the majority language. When minority language production does not occur at school, there can be little expectation that the minority language will survive unless it is strongly embedded in religious practice. In grounded language action planning, intergenerational language reproduction and language production through minority language education have a very high priority. Reproduction and production of language in the young is an essential foundation but is insufficient by itself in language survival. It breeds new life and propagates; it does not provide the oxygen for language life after childhood. It provides the potential; it cannot guarantee long-term practice and purpose.

Academic theory and research is certainly helpful in expanding the meaning of these three forms of language planning, with exemplification being available from previous international efforts (e.g. Cooper, 1989). However, conceptual clarification and theory has too infrequently become translated into practical advice and evaluation of interventions. Too rarely has the theory/practice divide been crossed to suggest (on the basis of current knowledge) what interventions may be relatively more effective and efficient in language reversal and revitalisation. However, Joshua Fishman's framework for reversing language shift has become important in suggesting priorities in interventions and strategies, and it is to this we now turn.

Fishman's framework for reversing language shift

When language-planning theory is translated into grounded practice, context will be important. As Fishman's Reversing Language Shift (1991, 1993, 2000) framework and particularly the Graded Intergenerational Disruption Scale (GIDS) reveals, languages can be at widely different stages of recovery (or termination). Just as the Richter scale measures intensity of earthquakes, so Fishman's scale gives a guide to how far a minority language is threatened and disrupted (Table 6.1).

Table 6.1 Fishman's (1990, 1991) Graded Intergenerational Disruption Scale for threatened languages

Stage 8: Social isolation of the few remaining speakers of the minority language. Need to record the language for later possible reconstruction.
Stage 7: Minority language used by older and not younger generation. Need to multiply the language in the younger generation.
Stage 6: Minority language is passed on from generation to generation and used in the community. Need to support the family in intergenerational continuity (e.g. provision of minority language schools).
Stage 5: Literacy in the minority language. Need to support literacy movements in the minority language, particularly when there is no government support.
Stage 4: Formal, compulsory education available in the minority language. May need to be financially supported by the minority language community.
Stage 3: Use of the minority language in less specialised work areas involving interaction with majority language speakers.
Stage 2: Lower government services and mass media available in the minority language.
Stage 1: Some use of minority language available in higher education, central government and national media.

Fishman's scale is valuable for analysing language minority situations in a comparative international context. It indicates the priority for a threatened language at a particular stage. What it does not do is to provide a detailed plan of action for a specific language. Such action plans will need interventions at many different levels (e.g. individual, community, organisational, central and local government, mass media) creating a variety of opportunities for language reproduction and interventions that are implemented with an appealing menu of incentives. Such opportunities and incentives are particularly needed to stimulate intergenerational language transmission.

Fishman (1991, 1993, 2000) underlines the crucial importance of intergenerational transmission in language revival and revitalisation. Increasing the stock of speakers through family language reproduction is important for minority languages in all the eight stages of GIDS. Yet such intergenerational transmission does not occur in a vacuum. There have to be perceived incentives for families to raise their children in a minority language (or bilingually). Such incentives may be latent and unspoken (e.g. parents regarding transmission of a cultural and linguistic inheritance as important). Incentives can also be publicised and promoted such that parents are persuaded (e.g. the cognitive and economic advantages of a child becoming bilingual).

Persuasion through successful language marketing (see Baker & Jones, 1998) is, however, only definable within a context that accounts for the historical, social, cultural, economic and especially political circumstances and predicaments of a minority language. Each struggle for language survival is situated; its strategy for revitalisation will reflect local philosophy, politics and pragmatism.

Language action planning

If languages are dying, then conservation and preservation measures are needed. The issue becomes what political, policy, provision and practical interventions are needed to keep a dying language alive, to reverse language shift, to reach a steady maintenance level for that language, and to effect language revitalisation and revival. A Darwinian 'survival of the fittest' approach to languages can be guaranteed to lead to wide-scale language death. Therefore, for those who wish to preserve the rich language mosaic of the world, language action planning is essential.

Such language action planning may involve voluntary effort, persuading and mobilising remaining language speakers to preserve their native language. Bottom-up approaches are much to be applauded, and may lead to affirmative action among language users and not just bureaucratic and cerebral activity among language politicians and central government language planners. However, funded intervention measures (top-down) that are well funded are probably also needed in a scenario of stark reality of language decline and death. When and where language-planning bodies exist (e.g. the Basque Country, Ireland and Wales) a language intervention policy has to be formulated and implemented. Typically this policy engages all three aspects of language planning: status, corpus and acquisition.

For those who work in language-planning agencies, whose responsibility it is to effect language reversal, there is little theory-derived advice as to the priorities, practical measures, actions and strategies that have the highest chances of saving, maintaining or enhancing an endangered language. If theoretical approaches to language planning are to relate to the practical measures needed to save endangered languages, we need to develop language action planning. We need to cross the theory/applied divide with all the risks and dangers that political, policy and practical involvement holds. The essential issue becomes 'what interventions and actions can be implemented that will ensure a higher probability of success in reversing and reviving a language?'

Dissenters

Not all agree with an interventionalist stance. Ladefoged (1992) argues that it is paternalistic of linguists to believe that they know what is best for a language. A linguist, by definition, has expertise in language, but is not necessarily an expert on culture and community, politics and the pragmatics of language decision-making. Ladefoged (1992) also argues that it is dangerous for a linguist to assume that they know what is best for a language group, and what outcomes are important for their future. Such a stance goes beyond their specialist knowledge and qualifications.

Ladefoged (1992) maintains that it is self-serving and intrinsically valuable for linguists to support threatened languages. They have a vested interest and are not neutral players in the game of language salvation. But would a professor of medicine with expertise in a deadly virus not give advice to government and communities to minimise fatality? Would an academic biologist with knowledge and understanding of a particular threatened species not be prepared to add ideas to how that species may be best preserved? A discipline is strengthened when connections are made between theory and practice. 'Only connect and both will be exalted'. A position of solitude or neutrality is not only impossible. It also removes the very humanity of studying something that is so central and sacred to the soul of human existence. Linguists will not have all the answers. Their knowledge is partial, and a component of a language-planning whole. Yet they have a crucial role in language planning.

The challenge

For language planning decision-makers, a pivotal question is: if you were given *x* million dollars/pounds to spend on reviving, reversing and revitalising a specific language, how would you spend that money? It would clearly be a nonsense to spend a third each on acquisition, corpus and status planning. Issues of prioritisation, cost effectiveness, short-term and medium/long-term strategies immediately become raised. Competing ideologies that variously prioritise voluntary or centralist infrastructures, public or private organisations, community or individual user focuses, broad-brush approaches or specific target setting, for example, soon reveal that language action planning is not divorced from politics, competing disciplinary approaches and personal preferences among those with leadership responsibilities and power. In Wales, the challenge has recently been enlivened by a transfer of political power from London. Devolution has led to a new confidence in strategies to reverse language shift.

Welsh Language Revitalisation

In the first UK census to include a language question (1891), 54% of people in Wales (910,000) reported themselves as Welsh speaking. By the 1991 Census, this figure had declined to 18.7% and 530,000 people (OPCS, 1992). The decline over 100 years has been so great that language action planning became imperative (see Baker (2000) and Williams (1997) for an overview).

Welsh is one of the very few minority languages that is expected to buck the universal trend of minority language decline and extinction. One of the main reasons for this has been well-focused and clearly prioritised language planning. Through such language planning, the Welsh language has moved from a sharp decline this century to 'level maintenance'. In the last two censuses (1981, 1991) the same figure for the percentage of Welsh speakers has stabilised at 19%. At its best, language planning has led to the Welsh language becoming revitalised, to its being used in more domains, with increased Welsh-medium education, more status within institutions, and to the language becoming increasingly connected with the economy, especially in the context of sustainable development. There is now a general acceptance by most (around 85% according to opinion polls – see: http://www.bwrdd-yr-iaith.org.uk/) of the population of Wales that bilingualism is beneficial for individuals and communities. For individuals, bilingualism provides wider communication opportunities, giving access to two windows on the world by being bicultural, enabling access to two literacies, raising self-esteem, enabling a secure sense of Welsh identity, and widening employment opportunities. For communities, bilingualism provides continuity with the past, cohesiveness for the present, and a source of collaborative endeavour for building the future.

However, there is no assurance that Welsh will survive as a living language without continued and purposeful language action planning. The reasons why so many of the world's languages are predicted to die are many and varied: industrialisation, urbanisation, economic and industrial development, immigration, emigration, new trends in communication, mass media, increasing travel, affluence and the rise of the global village. All of these are contemporary threats and challenges to the heritage language in Wales.

The Welsh Language Board

The Welsh Language Board has been a vital institution in revival efforts – both the advisory Board which was set up in 1988, and the statutory Board which took its place in 1993. The Board was established in December 1993 on a statutory basis, with the principal function of promoting and facilitating the use of the Welsh language. However, a central Government agency depends on public goodwill and partnerships with constellations of public (e.g. state education), private (e.g. businesses) and voluntary (e.g. pre-school playgroups) organisations whose activities support the Welsh language in employment, wealth creation, education, language learning (e.g. adults), relations with the public (e.g. banks, shops, hotels, local and national government organisations), culture (e.g. *eisteddfodau* 'cultural festivals'), community-generated activities and individual enterprises (e.g. Welsh or bilingual websites; the development of *CySill* and *Cysgair*, the Welsh language spelling- and grammar-checking software for PCs).

Currently, funded, formal Welsh Language planning occurs mainly but not exclusively through the Welsh Language Board (see http://www.bwrdd-yr-iaith.org.uk/) and its many partners. The action planning activity can be approximately categorised under the following overlapping and interacting headings:

Acquisition planning

(1) Family Language Reproduction
(2) Bilingual Education
(3) Adult language learning and linguistic confidence building.

Opportunity, use and incentive planning

(1) Economy (e.g. employment of bilinguals in the public, private and voluntary sectors);

(2) Culture, leisure, social, community usage,

Status planning

(1)   Institutionalisation in public, private and voluntary sectors (e.g. law, government, banks, charity activities);
(2)   Modernisation (e.g. Internet, mass media).

Corpus planning

(1)   Linguistic standardisation;
(2)   Linguistic modernisation;
(3)   Public vernacular (communicative (plain) Welsh).

It is possible for the Welsh Language Board to plan politically and centrally for the status, corpus and acquisition of the Welsh language yet not directly intervene in the daily usage of ordinary people. It can attempt to influence language choice, but not control. Modern Welsh terminological dictionaries, bilingual road signs, and the right to use a minority language in court are valuable successes in Welsh corpus and status language planning. Yet these successes have relatively little impact on the daily language lives of people. None of these are foundational in affecting the everyday language of the vast majority.

At the user level, languages decline when speakers drop in numbers and their daily usage diminishes. Therefore, language planning needs to relate to everyday language life as enacted in homes, streets, communities, workplaces and leisure (sometimes religious) activities. In Wales, such planning involves interventions in the economy so that minority language speakers can function in Welsh in employment (Welsh Language Board, 1999). Such planning also involves targeting key local cultural, leisure, social and community institutions where minority language speakers will use their language, form relationships and networks using that language. Planning also needs to empower local communities directly, enabling everyday language life to be enacted through a minority language.

In language action planning there are no fail-safe remedies and no guaranteed solutions. If a minority language is to survive, there has to be permanent endeavour. The time lag in terms of policy implementation in the field of language is much longer than in other policy areas (e.g. intergenerational transmission). The quick fix is a rarity. However, in international terms, the Welsh language is currently regarded as one of the most effective models of how to plan, intervene, engineer change and reverse language shift. Examples where Welsh language planning has successfully bucked the trend of downward shift include:

- the Welsh Language Act of 1993 providing language rights;
- the funding of economic, cultural and social initiatives (*Mentrau Iaith*) in local communities;
- the spread of bilingual education at primary and secondary level;
- Welsh as a compulsory subject in the National Curriculum;
- the vitality of movements such as *Mudiad Ysgolion Meithrin* (pre-school education), *Urdd Gobaith Cymru* (youth movement), local and national *eisteddfodau* (cultural events);
- Welsh language schemes, particularly in public organisations giving, for example, the right of the public to interact with the organisation in Welsh;
- increasing use of bilingualism in business and the economy.

Nevertheless, there is still cause for concern, as research findings in Wales (see http://www.bwrdd-yr-iaith.org.uk/) reveal where language planning has yet to show success. For example:

- 40% of children who complete primary education as first-language Welsh speakers commence their secondary education as second-language Welsh speakers and take their curriculum through the medium of English;
- the Welsh Language Board's commissioned surveys show that more than 40% of Welsh-speaking adults lack confidence in using the language, and therefore use it infrequently;
- many bilingual teenagers use the language less frequently as they grow older (though this trend may be reversed in later life);
- geographically, the Welsh language has tended to decline by a westwards movement, with many communities lessening in their everyday use of the Welsh language.

Overcoming these tendencies presents a considerable challenge, and it would be unrealistic, in the coming decades, to expect a large Welsh language revival. Maintenance at current levels would be an achievement. But maintenance must not become the target: it is too limiting a vision and mission. New initiatives and targets are needed. Introduced below are some initiatives that are a selection from a large list of possibilities, and reflect the agreed prioritisation and strategy of the Welsh Language Board. This strategy is now illustrated beginning with language acquisition planning.

Welsh language acquisition planning

In all minority languages, there are families who only use the majority language with their children. In Wales, where both parents are Welsh speaking, 8% speak only English to their children. Due to perceived economic or educational advantages of speaking English, or status in the neighbourhood, herein lies a principal and direct cause of language shift in Wales. Where there is such a shortfall in language maintenance in families, education becomes the principal means of producing more language speakers. Through bilingual education, Welsh second-language learning in school and adult classes (e.g. Ulpan), the potential numbers of minority language speakers can be increased. Achieving such increases is easier to plan through bilingual education than through family intergenerational transmission.

Acquisition planning to encourage family intergenerational transmission occurs by, for example, interventions with parents, health visitors, midwives (Evans, 2000) as well as by language learning in school, adult language classes, and literacy. It is to the former (family intergenerational transmission) we now turn.

There is a significant task in persuading parents to pass on the language to their children. Such persuasion is always going to be difficult. It is not easy to reach parents, nor is it easy to influence them. However, it is vital to raise awareness of language issues among parents for intergenerational transmission to occur. Therefore, the Welsh Language Board has recently engaged in two innovative language marketing projects to overcome such difficulties. Effective intervention has occurred by (1) providing crucial information in *Bounty* packs (packs of free samples and information given via hospitals to new and expectant mothers) across Wales; and (2) training midwives and health visitors to provide information about bilingualism to parents.

Bounty packs

Parents typically do not discuss which language or languages to use with their newborn children. There is no family language planning. Hence, such families need a prompt or stimulus to begin the discussion, and need to know the advantages of bringing up their children to become bilingual. Language awareness raising is as important in the family as it is in school.

The Welsh Language Board has commenced a series of marketing campaigns targeting future parents. In order to minimise the costs of personalised marketing campaigns, the Board decided to establish direct contact by forming partnerships with 17 Welsh hospitals. An information pack providing answers to the questions raised by future parents on early bilingualism and existing pre-school organisations was distributed to health professionals, midwives and staff specialising in this area. Included in this pack are promotional goodies (nappies, ointments and so on) and it is typically distributed through maternity hospitals.

The language pack is entitled *Bringing up Bilingual Children* and enables health professionals and midwives to answer questions raised by families, often from the first meeting, on the issue of teaching children and which language they should use. Over 30,000 brochures were distributed to future parents in the first year of the project. The current pack contains several brochures, a poster, a guide listing hundreds of phrases that can be used with babies and a video. The pilot campaign was conducted in Carmarthenshire (South Wales) in 1998–99. An evaluation/impact study showed that 78% of parents remembered receiving the pack and 33% had kept the documents so that they could refer to them later on. Encouraged by the success of this pilot campaign, the Welsh Language Board is extending the campaign to other geographical areas and widening its cooperation with health professionals.

Training health workers

The Welsh Language Board became aware that there is a need to give parents the opportunity to discuss language issues before family language patterns become established. They therefore started a pilot project in West Wales, in cooperation with midwives and health visitors, in which the choice of language in the family is discussed with the mother during pregnancy and after the child's birth.

At the first meeting between a midwife and future mother (during pregnancy), the midwives are trained to raise the question of languages and supply the parents with bright, colourful leaflets that provide 'answers'. At the invitation of these professionals, leaders in charge of bilingual pre-school groups visit hospitals to give presentations aimed towards groups of new or future parents, developing a triangular relationship between the hospital, education and parents, thus raising awareness about the advantages of bilingualism for the child. Training courses that provide relevant hospital staff with information on bilingualism are now organised with partner institutions (e.g. schools of nursing; large hospitals in Welshspeaking areas).

Such projects may make valuable interventions and have laudable aims. But do they have an effect on language transmission in the home? Sometimes, the best of intentions, the most innovative of interventions, can have little real effect on language shift. Hence the Welsh Language Board has recently moved into more target-based and outcome-based language action planning. This will now be presented.

Target language planning

It is important in grounded language planning to have broad aims and to evolve clear prioritisation. But broad aims can be the ruination of the best

Table 6.2 Examples of Target

By March 2003 Forty per cent of relevant health visitors and midwives to be provided with information packs and to have attended a training session.
By March 2006 All of relevant health visitors and midwives to be provided with information packs and to have attended a training session.
By March 2002 Materials for parents of pre-school children supporting the use of Welsh in the home and providing information about the benefits of early bilingualism to be produced and distributed; such materials will focus on mixed language families and homes where the medium is mostly English.
Effectiveness of this intervention will be imperfectly and partly observed from the results of the 2011 census, with a target increase in Welsh language transmission: (1) in homes where both parents speak Welsh from a 1991 baseline of 92% to 95%; and (2) in homes where one parent speaks Welsh from a 1991 baseline of 48% to 60%.

of intentions. Aims are often lofty aspirations, towards which specific policies make varying degrees of progress. Language planning aims can sometimes be good intentions, wishes and hopes that do not relate to grounded activity nor successful interventions. Broad-brush strategies seem rational as language planning can have much variety (especially with status planning), but may result in a lack of effective and cost-efficient policies and practices. The Welsh Language Board therefore has moved towards 'target language planning'. Target language planning involves (1) a clear overall conceptualisation of language planning – (e.g. status, corpus, acquisition and opportunity/incentive planning); (2) the setting of realisable and sustainable targets that are (3) prioritised and (4) monitored for their completion, effectiveness and outcomes. Examples of target planning are given below in Table 6.2.

Welsh-medium and bilingual education

Only 6.3% of children in Wales aged three speak Welsh: nearly all of these will have acquired the language at home. So, in order to increase numbers, early years education has a vital part to play. In early childhood, a language is acquired easily and naturally, spontaneously and subconsciously. Therefore, state pre-school provision and *Mudiad Ysgolion Meithrin* (the Welsh language pre-school playgroups – 981 units throughout Wales in 2002) have a crucial role in Welsh language acquisition in young children, from both Welsh- and English-speaking homes.

Before the Second World War, almost no Welsh language learning or other curriculum use of Welsh (e.g. content teaching) was allowed in primary or secondary schools. In the 1960s to 1990s there was considerable growth in the use of Welsh in schools. In 2002, over 30% of Wales's school-children are involved in Welsh-medium or bilingual education. There are 449 Welsh-medium or bilingual primary schools out of a Wales total of 1681 schools. In the secondary sector, 49 out of a total of 229 schools are defined as Welsh-medium or bilingual schools and some 60 use Welsh as a medium of instruction for part of the curriculum. In many of these schools, the majority of pupils come from non-Welsh-speaking homes. One significant development during the past decade has been the introduction of Welsh as a subject within the curriculum of every child in Wales. By the year 2001, almost every child in Wales had been taught Welsh between the ages of 5 and 16 (i.e. for 11 years of schooling).

For all children, the essential aims of bilingual education in Wales should be (according to the Welsh Language Board): to develop communicative fluency in the Welsh and English languages; to develop biliteracy in the Welsh and English languages; to become multicultural and increasingly multilingual; and to have entitlement to an equal access to the potential economic and employment benefits of bilingualism. To achieve these four aims, the Welsh Language Board has defined various strategies: (1) increasing *continuity* in Welsh-medium/bilingual provision in order that children who complete primary education fluent in Welsh and English continue to have bilingual secondary provision; (2) establishing a *continuum* from early language learning to full fluency, and to move from the current separation of Welsh first- and second-language lessons and Welsh-medium content teaching; (3) establishing a *concurrent* use of both languages in teaching and learning contexts; evolving a bilingual approach in classrooms rather than language separation. It is important that a bilingual education strategy has clear targets that reflect priorities, time-scales and ownership of responsibility (Tables 6.3, 6.4 and 6.5).

Table 6.3 Pre-school education: Examples of targets

By March 2005 To have increased the number of parents choosing state or voluntary Welsh-medium nursery education by 10% against a 1999 baseline.
By March 2005 To have increased the number of schools/units/*cylchoedd* providing Welsh-medium education by 5% against a 1999 baseline.
By March 2005 To have increased the number of schools/units/*cylchoedd* including a bilingual provision by 50% against a 1999 baseline.

Table 6.4 Primary school education: Example of target

By March 2005 The number of children in bilingual education at the primary level to have increased by 10% from a 1999 baseline.

Primary school education

Approximately one in five children participate in bilingual education in primary education in Wales. Such primary school provision is an entitlement where there is sufficient parental demand, or a sufficient saturation of Welsh speakers from Welsh-speaking homes or from pre-school education. This provision should be within a reasonable travelling distance.

Post primary school education

A major strategic initiative is required to ensure continuity throughout the education system for children who become fluent in Welsh and are capable of taking their curriculum through the medium of Welsh. Out of every 20 children in Wales who leave the primary school capable of taking bilingual education at the secondary level, only 12 do so. That is, about 40% of children do not opt for bilingual education at secondary level even though they are capable of such dual-language education.

The idea of a continuum also makes it more rational for children who become fluent in Welsh to move to bilingual education rather than be placed in second-language Welsh classes. If the assessment of proficiency in Welsh was connected to a continuum, the movement of children from first-language Welsh classes in primary school to second-language Welsh classes in secondary school would certainly decrease.

Opportunity/incentive planning

Increasing opportunities and incentives to use Welsh needs to occur in two major areas: (1) the instrumental use of Welsh (e.g. economic use), and

Table 6.5 Post primary school education: Examples of targets

By March 2006 The percentage of children taking bilingual education at secondary level (having obtained first-language Welsh skills at primary level), to have increased by 25% from a 1999 baseline.
By March 2006 The numbers of students taking some, most or all of their further education or higher education courses bilingually to have quadrupled from a 1999 baseline.

(2) the integrative use of Welsh (that is, in all fields e.g. social, cultural, leisure and community use). There have to be convincing reasons for parents to bring up their children in Welsh, and persuasive motivations for children to become fluent in speaking Welsh and literate in the language whilst at school. The economic carrot has increasingly become important in marketing Welsh language intergenerational transmission and bilingual education, and needs to be captivatingly marketed.

The more the Welsh language has economic and employment value, the more it is likely to be attractive to parents to transmit the language to their children, and the more it is likely to be attractive to children to learn Welsh thoroughly at school. Thus, marketing the economic value of the Welsh language is increasingly regarded as essential, targeting: individuals (particularly in the younger age-groups); small and medium-sized enterprises; and all larger public and private institutions. This needs to operate in terms of both the local and national economy.

While the economic and employment value of the Welsh language is a strong motivation for learning, retaining and using Welsh, its danger is that it can be short term, pragmatic and occasionally 'doing the right thing for the wrong reason'. Therefore, more longer-term, deep-seated motivations are also needed for making Welsh a long-term living language.

The theory of minority language maintenance implies that a minority language requires reserved functions and usage. For example, when in times past Welsh had a reserved place in chapels and churches, maintenance occurred. Recently, the Welsh language has moved away from being reserved for particular domains into trying to capture language use into as many domains as possible. In doing this, the Welsh language is always

Table 6.6 Opportunity/incentive planning: Examples of targets

By March 2005 One hundred national companies providing goods and/or services to the public in Wales to have a member of staff responsible for increasing the companies' use of Welsh, in partnership with the Welsh Language Board.
By March 2005 To raise awareness about the use of Welsh in business within the business community generally, and specifically in 3000 companies providing goods and/or services to the public in Wales.
By March 2006 The numbers of students in Welsh medium vocational training to have doubled against a 1999 baseline.
By March 2006 To have increased by 10% against the 2002 survey baseline the number of workplaces operating bilingually.

going to be in competition with an all-pervading and powerful majority language (e.g. television, newspapers, Internet). Nevertheless, there is little choice except to try to maintain and increase Welsh language usage in as many areas of culture and leisure – in social and community relationships – as is possible, if we are to attract people to use the language.

It is in this context that we have seen arguably the most exciting of recent language planning developments, namely the *Mentrau Iaith* – community language initiatives (see: http://www.bwrdd-yr-iaith.org.uk/). They are becoming a highly effective means of engineering bespoke language planning, tailored to the needs of the communities they serve. They are achieving much in terms of: marketing the use of the language; providing social opportunities to use the language; and revitalising the use of the language in communities.

Status planning

Status here will be treated not only in official, infrastructural and domain terms, but also in a psychological manner so that connections are made with language users at a grounded level. This is a wider use of the term 'status planning' than has historically been the case, but is helpful to discuss language planning interventions that impact on actual users and language use.

Every aspect of Welsh language use is important to the status of the language – this holds for every event and for every occasion on which Welsh is used by institutions and individuals. The factors which confer status on the language are many and complex, and span the whole range of language use, from speaking Welsh in the National Assembly to listening to Welsh language pop music. Passions and prejudices, vested interests and deep-seated values affect judgements and prioritisation about 'what gives the Welsh language status'.

Parents are influenced by a variety of factors when deciding to raise their children in English or in Welsh or bilingually. The value which children attribute to the Welsh language in education will be much affected by such status effects. Whether children use Welsh in the playground, the street, with friends, and whether teenagers go on to use Welsh in their 20s and 30s, will be much affected by status factors. The choice by parents and children of bilingual or English-medium education will often be much influenced by the status factors attached to Welsh and English (and bilingualism).

An argument can be made for preserving (and increasing) everything that affects the status of the Welsh language. Nothing becomes unimportant. Such components of language status exist in delicate interactions and combinations and not as separate, isolatable influences. Remove a few bricks and the public may believe that the castle is beginning to crumble.

Supporting key 'status' institutions and ensuring the language has a modern status (e.g. in Information and Communications Technology) are two key criteria for judging the relative importance of different components that make up the status of the language. Language Schemes are expected of public institutions as part of the 1993 Welsh Language Act and play a major role in status planning. These are a specific statutory responsibility for the Welsh Language Board, stimulating development in the delivery of a bilingual service across Wales and across institutions. They are active across the public and Crown sectors, and also influence service planning and delivery in the voluntary and private sectors. They have stimulated much of the increase in the use of Welsh, and providing a bilingual service has become a mark of quality service in Wales. The Board's task over the next five years in this area of our work will increasingly focus on ensuring the present momentum is maintained, and that organisations are honouring their commitments. As well as the field of education and training, this will include being proactive in fields such as health and social care, justice and the law, the statutory planning process, the arts and culture, tourism and the economy.

Corpus planning

Welsh language corpus planning centres around two areas: the need for linguistic standardisation, and the need to develop a form of Welsh that is popular, used and useful. The first need has often been met by producing specialised dictionaries (e.g. for nursing, education, the law). However, 'popular' standardisation often occurs through the mass media such as Welsh language TV and radio programmes. The second need has been addressed, so far as forms and related material are concerned, by *Cymraeg Clir*, which seeks to do for written Welsh what the Plain English Campaign does for English.

Table 6.7 Status planning: Examples of targets

By March 2005 350 statutory and 70 voluntary Welsh language schemes to have been submitted to the Board for approval.
By March 2005 The number of performance reports on the implementation of Welsh language schemes received annually by the Board to increase to 260 (from 97 in 2000): 50% of those received will be scrutinised and investigated annually over the period.

Table 6.8 Corpus planning: Examples of targets

By March 2004 Specialised terminology dictionaries to be available free on the Internet from a Welsh Language Board server.
By March 2004 Multimedia modules on *Cymraeg Clir* (Plain Welsh) to be available to all institutions, public and private, and deliverable through the Internet.

All languages must develop and change, evolve new terminology and forms of expression that reflect changes in culture, ideology, relationships, and means of communication. A language that sticks rigidly to past usage becomes a moribund language. To its credit, the Welsh language has developed to reflect changes in, for example, technology and science, as well as developing terminology so that Welsh can be used in an increasing number of professions, institutions and activities. Welsh must continue to adapt, continue to spread its new terminology, and continue to gain acceptance for forms of Welsh that will make it a living language for new generations. Therefore, further initiatives and developments are needed in Welsh language corpus planning.

Conclusions

Hugo Baetens Beardsmore's (1982) book was succinctly entitled *Bilingualism: Basic Principles*. This chapter has focused on the need to preserve such bilingualism and suggested that a basic principle to achieve preservation is language action planning. For bilingualism to have a future, language minorities, in particular, have to be motivated to reproduce their language in the family, and ensure there is a further production line in bilingual schooling. Unless those foundations are secured, languages in the world will continue to die at the present alarming rate.

Language acquisition planning is the foundation of language revival. But there needs to be tiers of reasons why families should reproduce a minority language in their young, and why schools should engage in first- and second-language teaching and content learning through two languages. The tiers of reasons include religious, economic, social, cultural, community, instrumental and integrative motives.

Status and corpus planning are important, but ultimately depend on successful language acquisition planning. They provide the *raison d'être* for such acquisition planning. Thus an interactive and holistic approach to language planning is needed. Yet such holism has to be joined by clear focuses and prioritisation in language planning. Pragmatically, there has to be hard choice about what interventions are attempted and funded. Clear targets, monitored for their success, are needed to maintain a clear focus and rationalise hard choices.

There are no guarantees, no winning formula and no best bets in language action planning, as language minority contexts differ and change. Yet the plight of the majority of the minority languages of the world requires a new grounded approach to language planning. Unless grounded action occurs in language planning, future linguistics will be more centred on language death than living languages and bilingualism.

Note

Further information about the *Bounty* packs are available from the Welsh Language Board at the following address: Bwrdd yr Iaith Gymraeg, Siambrau'r Farchnad, 5–7 Heol Eglwys Fair, Cardiff, CF1 2AT, Wales (UK).

References

Baetens Beardsmore, H. (1982) *Bilingualism: Basic Principles*. Clevedon: Multilingual Matters.

Baetens Beardsmore, H. (1986, second edition) *Bilingualism: Basic Principles*. Clevedon: Multilingual Matters.

Baker, C. (2000) Three perspectives on bilingual education policy in Wales: Bilingual education as language planning, bilingual education as pedagogy and bilingual education as politics. In R. Daugherty, R. Phillips & G. Rees (eds) *Education Policy in Wales: Explorations in Devolved Governance*. Cardiff: University of Wales Press.

Baker C. & Jones, S.P. (1998) *Encyclopedia of Bilingualism and Bilingual Education*. Clevedon: Multilingual Matters.

Bright, W. (ed.) (1992) *The International Encyclopedia of Linguistics*. Oxford: Oxford University Press.

Cooper, R.L. (1989) *Language Planning and Social Change*. Cambridge: Cambridge University Press.

Crystal, D. (2000) *Language Death*. Cambridge: Cambridge University Press.

Daoust, D. (1997) Language planning and language reform. In F. Coulmas (ed.), *The Handbook of Sociolinguistics*. Oxford: Blackwell.

Dogancay-Aktuna, S. (1997) Language planning. In N. Hornberger & D. Corson (eds) *Research Methods in Language and Education*. Volume 8 of the *Encyclopedia of Language and Education*. Dordrecht: Kluwer.

European Commission (1996) *Euromosaic: The Production and Reproduction of the Minority Language Groups in the European Union*. Luxembourg: Office for Official Publications of the European Communities.

Evans, G.L. (2000), Dwy Iaith o'r Diwrnod Cyntaf: Bilingual from the beginning. *Bilingual Family Newsletter*, 17 (2), 1–2.

Fishman, J.A. (1991) *Reversing Language Shift*. Clevedon: Multilingual Matters.

Fishman, J.A. (1993) Reversing language shift: Successes, failures, doubts and dilemmas. In E.H. Jahr (ed.) *Language Conflict and Language Planning*. New York: Mouton de Gruyter.

Fishman, J.A. (2000) Why is it so hard to save a threatened language? In J.A. Fishman (ed.) *Can Threatened Languages be Saved?* Clevedon: Multilingual Matters.

Grimes, B.F. (2000) *Ethnologue – Languages of the World* (14th Edition; 2 volumes). Dallas,Texas: SIL International.

Hornberger, N.H. (1994) Literacy and language planning. *Language and Education*, 8 (1&2), 75–86.

Kaplan, R.B. & Baldauf, R.B. (1997) *Language Planning from Practice to Theory.* Clevedon: Multilingual Matters.

Krauss, M. (1992) The World's Languages in Crisis. *Language*, 68, 6–10.

Krauss, M. (1995) Language Loss in Alaska, the United States and the World. *Frame of Reference (Alaska Humanities Forum)*, 6 (1), 2–5.

Ladefoged, P. (1992) Another view of endangered languages. *Language*, 68 (4), 810–11.

Lewis, E.G. (1977) Bilingualism and bilingual education: The ancient world of the Renaissance. In B. Spolsky and R.L. Cooper (eds) *Frontiers of Bilingual Education.* Rowley, MA: Newbury House.

Littlebear, R. (1999) Some rare and radical ideas for keeping indigenous languages alive. In J. Reyhner *et al.*, *Revitalizing Indigenous Languages.* Flagstaff, Arizona: Northern Arizona University.

Mackey, W.F. (1991) Language diversity, language policy and the sovereign state. *History of European Ideas*, 13, 51–61.

May, S. (2001) *Language and Minority Rights.* London: Longman.

Moseley, C. & Asher, R.E. (1994) *Atlas of the World's Languages.* London: Routledge.

Nettle, D. & Romaine, S. (2000) *Vanishing Voices: The Extinction of the World's Languages.* Oxford: Oxford University Press.

Office of Population Censuses and Surveys (OPCS) (1992) *The 1991 Census of Great Britain.* HMSO: Office of Population Censuses and Surveys.

Skutnabb-Kangas, T. (2000) *Linguistic Genocide in Education – or Worldwide Diversity and Human Rights?* London: Erlbaum.

Welsh Language Board (1999) *A Strategy for the Welsh Language: Targets for 2000–2005.* Cardiff: Welsh Language Board.

Wiley, T.G. (1996) Language planning and policy. In S.L. McKay & N.H. Hornberger (eds) (1996) *Sociolinguistics and Language Teaching.* Cambridge: Cambridge University Press.

Williams, C.H. (1997) Language contacts in northwestern Europe: English-Welsh. In H. Goebl, P. Nelde, Z. Stary & W. Wölck (ed.) *Contact Linguistics.* Berlin: Walter de Gruyter.

Wurm, S.A. (ed.) (1996) *Atlas of the World's Languages in Danger of Disappearing.* Paris: UNESCO Publishing.

Chapter 7

Accepting Bilingualism as a Language Policy: An Unfolding Southeast Asian Story

GARY M. JONES

Introduction

In his seminal publication *Bilingualism: Basic Principles* (1982) Hugo Baetens Beardsmore probably frightened us all with his many definitions of bilingualism. As he made clear, what might seem like a simple notion to the layman, the ability to use two languages, is actually a minefield for the unwary. I have had both the misfortune and fortune of finding myself in that minefield. Through circumstance I found myself working in a country that had just adopted a bilingual education system, and through further circumstance researching and advising on that system.

This paper examines how a better understanding of bilingual education has been achieved in Brunei, tracing key decisions from the time that a bilingual education system was introduced in the country, in 1985, up to the present. This section of the paper draws greatly on a paper that was prepared for a recent conference in Hong Kong (Jones, 2000). The paper then examines three other Southeast Asian countries, Singapore, Malaysia and the Philippines, noting particularly how similar the language needs are and how English-speaking bilingualism has become the goal of most of the region's countries.

Bilingual Education in Brunei

Brunei adopted a bilingual education system in 1985, shortly before the University of Brunei Darussalam was opened. Brunei did not enjoy the luxury of being able to plan the system before actually implementing it: the system arose as a result of a number of circumstances, many of them unforeseen. These circumstances have been documented in earlier publications

(Jones, 1997; Jones *et al.*, 1993). Suffice to say, Brunei has a bilingual education system that uses both English and Malay as mediums of instruction. Some subjects are taught in English, others in Malay, a system that has been described as 'bi-monolingualism' (Dodson, 1985: 325).

With little planning having taken place prior to implementation it was very much a case in Brunei of 'learn as you go'. Part of this learning process has involved international conferences on bilingualism held in Brunei. These have provided the opportunity for Brunei to learn from the experiences of others (and latterly, for other countries to learn from Brunei's experiences).

Conferences

At the first of these conferences, *Bilingualism and National Development* (BAND91), John Edwards warned of a number of issues that should concern language planners in Brunei. First, he mentioned 'legislative tension' (Edwards, 1992: 49) that might occur in Brunei given that an educational role for Malay is a constitutional requirement while in reality English plays the dominant role in the education system. He went on to warn against relying too heavily on schools as the sole agent of change: 'The second generality involves the reliance, the over-reliance, upon school as an agent of change. This problem is especially clear when the school is asked to lead, to take society in a direction not wholly endorsed by that larger body' (1992: 60–1). His final concern was about domains and perceived elitism. He noted:

> The problem is that some domains may be seen as more important than others and may, in fact, come to be the preserve of a social elite. Could this be a feature in Brunei, particularly since (as we've seen) most of the 'modernised' and 'modernisable' subjects at school are associated with English? Everyone goes to school; everyone gets a thin wash of English; but not everyone has equal opportunity to deepen this fluency, or to practise it in rewarding ways. (1992: 62–3)

While John Edwards' advice was heeded and representation made to the relevant authorities in Brunei, principally the ministry of education, action has not always followed. One question, that of social elites, is not just an issue in Brunei and is discussed later in this paper.

Another theme at the BAND91 conference was the perceived tension between competing languages in Brunei's education system and in the society as a whole – a social rather than legislative tension. Although rarely explicitly stated, misunderstanding and a certain amount of jealousy resulted in English being adopted as a school language. For some this was regarded as a Malay versus English issue, with sides withdrawing into their respective camps. Colleagues at UBD, past and present, have commented on this. Conrad Ozog (1993: 70) compared the situation with that in Malaysia where 'it is not wise to praise English without at the same time praising Malay'. McLellan (1997: 158) quotes Wan Mohd Zain (1991: 26–7) who denies 'that English and Malay constitute a "zero-sum game" in which more of one implies less of the other'.

Wherever two or more languages are used in a community some form of rivalry and tension is almost bound to exist. Prior to BAND91 this tension was palpable and the conference was used as a platform to discuss some of the issues – on the assumption that it is better to talk about such issues openly rather than let misunderstandings fester. BAND91 helped to bridge the differences and subsequent conferences have continued to try to involve language practitioners from both mediums. I am sure that the present relative language harmony at UBD and in Brunei has been helped by these conferences.

Following the success of BAND91 a second conference on bilingualism was held in 1995. This was entitled *Bilingualism Through the Classroom: Strategies and Practices*. This conference looked specifically at the bilingual classroom and how teaching could be improved. More than half the papers at this conference were specifically on Brunei. The papers were published as a special edition of *The Journal of Multilingual and Multicultural Development*, 17: 2–4, 1996.

A paper that examined one of the most pressing issues at that time, and which is still an important issue, was *Code-Switching in the Primary Classroom: One Response to the Planned and the Unplanned Language Environment in Brunei* by Peter Martin. That code-switching exists in Brunei classrooms is clear to everyone; that it is frowned upon by school inspectors is also well known. The paper attempted to explain a role for code-switching and for a greater appreciation of the processes of becoming bilingual. This paper was important because it brought the topic out into the open – for too long the subject had been avoided, I think because nobody wanted to admit that what was actually happening in the classroom was different from what was officially prescribed. A paper of my own, *Bilingual Education and Syllabus Design: Towards a Workable Blueprint*, attempted to take what was currently known about language acquisition and bilingualism and match this to the needs of the Bruneian school syllabus. The idea of a *blueprint* suggests that an education syllabus designed for one country might have wider applications. Of course, a system developed for a particular country cannot be adopted wholesale by any other country, but assuming similar underlying characteristics from country to country then it is only natural to assume that solutions to similar problems might also be transferable.

Hugo Baetens Beardsmore was present at both these conferences and also visited Brunei again during July and August 1993. He subsequently produced a report entitled *Visits to Schools and Discussions with Ministry Officials*. This report analysed Brunei's current education system and offered suggestions for its future orientation. Baetens Beardsmore made a further visit and produced a second report for the Ministry of Education in Brunei in 1998. These visits, reports and the various seminars that have ensued have been enormously helpful in developing a much better understanding of the problems facing Brunei and the possible solutions it might employ.

Other Influences

As well as the conferences that were held in Brunei and the consultative visits by Baetens Beardsmore, much was being learned from research conducted in the country as well as from the considerable literature that has developed around the field of bilingualism. *Bilingualism: Basic Principles* provided a start (as it has done, I would think, for a great many other researchers) and is still required reading. Multilingual Matters' *Journal of Multilingual and Multicultural Development* has provided a constant source of support, as has its more recent *International Journal of Bilingual Education and Bilingualism*. Other journals that are subscribed to and on the reading lists of students at UBD are *Multilingua* and *Language Problems and Language Planning*.

Other publications that have had immediate relevance to questions of language acquisition and which have helped to clarify research priorities include Leslie Milroy's (1987) *Language and Social Networks*; the work of Howard Giles (1973) and Giles and Coupland (1991) on accommodation theory, and Schumann's work (1978 and 1986) on acculturation. Core texts particularly on bilingualism, in addition to *Basic Principles*, have been Romaine's (1989) *Bilingualism*; Colin Baker's (1988) *Key Issues in Bilingualism and Bilingual Education* and (1993) *Foundations of Bilingual Education and Bilingualism*, and John Edwards' (1994) *Multilingualism*.

Language planning has also been a priority. An early reference, and one still frequently referred to, is Baldauf and Luke's (1990) *Language Planning and Education in Australasia and the South Pacific*. Other early references which have helped to formulate plans are Rubin and Jernudd (1971) *Can Language be Planned?*; Cooper (1989) *Language Planning and Social Change*; Appel and Muysken (1987) *Language Contact and Bilingualism*; Baetens Beardsmore's (1993) *European Models of Bilingual Education*, and the work of Joshua Fishman (1974 and 1993, among others) has obviously been influential. More recently Kaplan and Baldauf (1997) *Language Planning from Practice to Theory* has helped bring issues up to date.

Classroom applications have been enormously influenced by the work done in Canada, particularly by Jim Cummins (1984, 2000 and, with Swain, 1986, among others), Merrill Swain (1983, 1985, and 1993) and Fred Genesee (1987 and, with Jasone Cenoz, 1998).

In addition to the references already mentioned, the current reading list for students studying bilingualism at UBD includes Li Wei's (2000) *The Bilingualism Reader*, and publications specifically about language in Brunei: Martin *et al.* (1996) *Language Use and Language Change in Brunei Darussalam*, and Jones and Ozog (1993) *Bilingualism and National Development*.

Of course, new articles, ideas and research are constantly being added to the arsenal of understanding that we have about bilingualism and related subjects. This theoretical knowledge and insights into the experiences of others working in similar fields means that researchers in Brunei now have a much clearer understanding of the implications of the bilingual education system and its ramifications. Needless to add, much research is still needed and there is obviously still much to learn, but there is also time to reflect.

What Has Been Learned?

Introducing the bilingual system of education, especially since this was followed very soon afterwards by the establishment of a university, raised the question of what is a language. This question was asked in relation to the languages of Brunei. Until the establishment of the university there was a widely held assumption that the country's various languages were all dialects of Malay. Work by Nothofer (1991) quickly dispelled this notion and today the differences between dialects and languages in Brunei are much better understood and appreciated.

A greater understanding of the country's language mosaic made it possible to appreciate constraints affecting the education system. For instance, assuming that people speak various dialects of the same language also assumes much commonality between languages and, especially for education purposes, that the school language, Standard Malay, is similar to or even the same as the pupils' home languages. The research dispelled this notion: Bruneians are not just multidialectal, they are also multilingual. This has enormous implications for the schools. Whether working in a mono, bi or multilingual system there is usually the assumption that one of the school's languages, usually the first and most important language of the school, is also the language of the pupil's home. This is not the case in Brunei: for the majority of children Standard Malay is a new language first encountered when they enter school. Nevertheless, given the multilingual nature of the society, and given the impracticalities of trying to use Brunei

Malay as a school language, Standard Malay must remain as a medium within the schools.

Attitude

It was always assumed that attitude would be an important factor in determining the success of the education system. For this reason a survey was conducted across the country to determine attitudes towards bilingual education and bilingualism in general. The survey was prepared at UBD and conducted with the assistance of the Ministry of Education. It was comprehensive and designed to reach a large representative cross-section of the Brunei population. A major consideration was confidentiality and to develop the trust of the respondents. This was achieved and the result was a truly comprehensive national analysis of attitudes towards languages used in the education system.

Prior to conducting the survey there was an assumption that the Brunei population might actually be opposed to bilingual education and to the use of English in the school system. This concern reflected the many statements that were being made at the time about nationalism and the use of the Malay language. As it turned out, however, it was revealed that while many individuals were saying one thing their actions were very different. Overwhelmingly the population showed itself to be in favour of neither Malay nor English education systems, but rather a bilingual education system using both Malay and English. In other words, the population showed itself to be hugely supportive of exactly the sort of education system that the country had introduced.

Problems

In his report to the Bruneian Ministry of Education in 1993, Hugo Baetens Beardsmore highlighted the relation of Jim Cummins's BICS/CALP division of language and its relation to Brunei. Cummins (1984) BICS/CALP division has been well documented and discussion of the subject has been brought up-to-date by Cummins himself (2000). The basic assumption of the division is that BICS-type skills (Basic Interpersonal Communication) must be acquired before a learner is ready for CALP-type skills (Cognitive Academic Language Proficiency). Moreover, CALP involves some universal underlying proficiency that is shared across languages. Thus CALP is transferable – skills learned in one language could be transferred to another and vice versa. When planning a school curriculum, therefore, the obvious thing to do would be to first encourage the development of BICS before proceeding with subjects that require CALP skills. In a monolingual school system this progress would occur quite naturally. In a bilingual system, however, this progression cannot be assumed.

When planning the school curriculum and the order and medium in which subjects would be introduced the first consideration in Brunei was the final school examinations and the language mediums in which they would be taken. Thus it was decided that those subjects that are examined in English when the pupils are sixteen years of age (the final year of compulsory schooling) should be taught as early as possible in English while those that would eventually be examined in Malay would be taught in Malay. In practice, however, this means that many subjects requiring CALP are introduced in English before the pupils have fully mastered BICS in that language. Teachers therefore find themselves in the impossible situation of having to teach academically demanding subjects to pupils in a language that the pupils do not properly understand.

Teachers

As has been suggested, the introduction of the bilingual system was done with little planning. There was no time to retrain teachers or explain objectives. As a result many teachers found themselves teaching in a medium in which they were not particularly comfortable. An important criteria for any bilingual education programme is that teachers should be proficient in the target language. This was not the case for all teachers in Brunei in 1985. Since then the local teacher training institute within the University of Brunei Darussalam has been graduating as many teachers as it can. All must be proficient in English, although the accepted level of proficiency means that some graduates still fall short of being good role models for their pupils.

A problem that has been realised with expatriate rather than local teachers in Brunei is that they very often lack an appreciation of the problems faced by pupils in a bilingual as opposed to a monolingual education system. This is particularly true of teachers who are themselves monolingual and who come from monolingual countries and whose previous teaching experience has only been with monolingual children. They are recruited to teach English-medium subjects and many of these teachers unfortunately have the attitude that the pupils should adjust to them rather than that they make changes to their own teaching methods.

A Problem Shared?

The experience of three other Southeast Asian countries

In a recent paper examining language planning questions in Southeast Asia (Jones, 2000) I attempted to draw comparisons between Brunei and its near Southeast Asian neighbours, Singapore, Malaysia and the Philippines. These four countries have many features in common: they had all been colonised or protected by English-speaking Western powers and all have retained some use of English in their school systems. In addition to this, however, it is now apparent that some form of bilingual education has become the preferred medium of instruction.

A study in Singapore on 'Trends of English Use Among Chinese Singaporeans' conducted in 1996 by Xu Daming and Tan Pek Ling sought to discover what attitudes the Chinese Singaporeans have towards English in comparison to Chinese. In many respects, therefore, this allows for a close comparison of attitudes towards the English Language between Singaporeans and Bruneians. The Brunei attitude survey dealt with all sections of the community, while the Singaporean survey only studied the Chinese. Nevertheless, the Chinese do make up over 77% of the Singaporean population.

Xu and Tan discovered, perhaps not surprisingly, that among the living generations of Chinese Singaporeans there has been a dramatic shift from Chinese to English. From the grandparents' generation of 90% using Chinese to only 53% of the children's generation using Chinese as the solely predominant language at home (Xu & Tan, 1996: 10). Most notable is the shift to some form of Chinese/English bilingualism rather than one or other of the languages being dominant.

The study showed that, as in Brunei, English is used mainly in the instrumental domains of work and in public, particularly in conjunction with Chinese (Malay in Brunei). Chinese is clearly the most used language, with less than a third of the sample using both English and Chinese regularly. The research suggests a high community regard for Mandarin and an instrumental one for English.

In summing up their research, Xu and Tan came to the following conclusion:

> In spite of a dramatic language shift from Chinese to English which has taken place in the two youngest generations of contemporary Chinese Singaporeans, the Chinese population in Singapore as a whole is still predominantly Chinese-speaking. To this population, English is important chiefly because it is the language of dealing with the authorities. At the same time Mandarin is also regarded as important as it is identified as the language of the community. Although at least half of the population is bilingual, the balanced bilinguals are a minority. At the same time, the majority of the population has a high regard for bilingualism, much higher than their bilingual abilities. The general trends for the population seem to be a movement towards bilingualism rather than a shift to monolingually English. (Xu & Tan, 1996: 20–1)

In other words, and matching the Bruneian results very closely, Singapore is looking to maintain *two* languages, to create a bilingual population.

Malaysia inherited English as a result of its colonial heritage, and precisely because of this colonial heritage it was a vestige of its past that it wanted to discard on independence. However, the English language never went away. Despite introducing an education system that relegated the teaching of English, the language continued to be used in the country, especially in the influential urban districts in and around Kuala Lumpur.

After independence, and as reflected in government policy, the use and teaching of English in Malaysia declined. However, throughout this period the worldwide use of English, and its importance in commerce and business, grew. Even in Malaysia, big businesses, including those owned by Malays, used English as their main working language (Asmah Omar, 1996, refers to Mani Le Vasan, 1996). Conflict between national ideology and the linguistic demands of a country aiming to achieve full industrial development by the year 2020 was inevitable.

Recent developments in education have helped to promote the wider use of English. Many private institutions of higher education have opened while the country's established universities have experienced a proliferation of twinning programmes with overseas English-speaking universities. In December 1993 the Prime Minister announced a policy allowing for the use of English in universities and colleges. In fact, English had always been used as a medium of instruction for various academic disciplines, no matter what the official policy may have been. Asmah Omar notes that 'in the University of Malaya English is used for the teaching of certain courses at the undergraduate level in various faculties, such as the Faculties of Medicine, Dentistry, Science, Engineering and Law. At the post graduate level, many of the faculties teach their courses in English' (Asmah Omar, 1996: 7). However, the Prime Minister's announcement was seen to legitimise the use of English and to remove some of the misunderstanding surrounding the language and its use in education.

It may be assumed that language planning is a function of government, especially a ministry of education. However, government merely responds to the needs of industry and markets. In Malaysia it is the desire to achieve full industrialisation by the year 2020 that is determining the needs of industry, and at the moment industry needs, among other skills, employees who are competent in the English language. However, to fulfil the needs of nationhood, Malaysia also wants to promote the national language. Malaysia therefore finds itself in the same position as Brunei and Singapore – having a need for both the national language and English.

The Philippines is really a different proposition from the other three countries in so far that it has so many languages, ten of which are considered major languages (Gonzalez, 1998: 489). It is a polyglot society with a number of languages vying if not for national supremacy at least for regional supremacy. In this sense, therefore, the Philippines has more in common linguistically with parts of Africa and India than it does with other Southeast Asian countries. Gonzalez has argued for some time now (Gonzalez, 1993) that the choice of a national language has been divisive rather than unitive. While English has a role as a LWC, the role of the national language and vernacular languages has caused some tension. This must give rise to greater language planning problems, and problems of a different nature, than are faced in the other countries.

Like Brunei, Singapore and Malaysia, however, there is an assured role for English in the Philippines together with the country's national and, to some extent, regional languages. Like the other Southeast Asian nations this need is principally an instrumental one. And like the other countries there is a wide range of ability in how well the language is understood and used.

Social Elite

Common to all four countries is that knowledge of English brings with it economic advantage. Elite groups have always realised this and in each of the four countries, often now for generations, the elite has ensured that their own children have a good command of English. Indeed, English may be the only language that their children know, especially if these children are sent overseas for their education in English-speaking countries.

Although there is a social disadvantage in not knowing the national language, many families obviously feel that this is of little consequence: their social circle is English speaking and they may not have a need, or a desire, to communicate outside this circle. While such families have to face the cultural loss of not knowing their own national language there is the economic advantage of not only knowing English, but knowing it well, using it regularly and being proficient in its use. Most Southeast Asian children only have exposure to English at school, especially those from economically disadvantaged backgrounds. For such children English really is a foreign language and one, due to the lack of opportunity to practise its use, that often remains so.

The comparative economic advantage that elite groups have enjoyed in the past through access to English is now, however, being eroded. In the not too distant past access to English was limited to a few. Today, however, through universal schooling, the language is available to virtually everyone (although obviously not on an equal footing). This universal teaching removes the language's exclusivity. While in the past access to the language almost guaranteed material benefit, today this is no longer the case. It is still true that good communication skills, particularly in English, are in demand from employers, but it must also be realised that as more people become proficient in English so this particular skill will be assumed and on its own will not guarantee any sort of job security. In economic terms, the marginal benefit of knowing English is decreasing.

Planning

Deciding which languages should be taught in schools is both a political and economic question. Discussion of language inevitably involves the question of cultural and national identity and therefore a national language (regardless of whether it is nationally known and used) must for political reasons be included on any agenda. The language of wider communication, in this case English, is included for economic reasons and often only after overt pressure from industry.

Although more than one language has been introduced in the education systems of each of the four countries in question there is very little equality between the languages themselves. While Malay has many speakers and is widely used throughout Malaysia, Indonesia and Brunei the same is not true of Filipino, which does not appear to have been completely accepted even by all Filipinos. These languages find themselves competing with English, a language that is truly global and one that has enormous clout in terms of its use, usefulness and prestige. Although everything should be done to ensure a place for all a nation's languages at the table, the reality is that there is a lot of competition between languages and the battle between the various national languages and English is an unequal one.

In terms of their standardisation, intellectualisation and, to a lesser extent, modernisation, the national languages of Southeast Asia are in a permanent state of having to play catch up with English. To a great extent the situation has been exacerbated by the revolution in communication. It is now just as easy to communicate with someone on the other side of the world as it is with someone in the next town. As a result the need and use for regional and national languages has diminished.

There is no obvious solution to this problem of language inequality. Possibly there does not have to be. It may be sufficient for a language to play a symbolic rather than an actual role in the affairs of a nation. Malay is the national language of Singapore, but its actual use is largely restricted to the minority Malay community. Gonzalez has noted that Filipino is a symbol of unity and linguistic identity (Gonzalez, 1998: 520), which is not the same as saying that it should be used in the sciences or in technology. It can, but these are domains, and they are obviously not the only ones, in which it is probably always going to be at a disadvantage compared with English. I would not like to suggest that the drive to intellectualise other languages be conceded, rather that there is little point in trying to compete head on with a language that is already so well developed in this domain and whose dominance is likely to continue to be enhanced rather than diminished.

Classroom

It is schools and the classroom teacher that bear the brunt of actually implementing language policy. The decision to implement such a policy may be determined by the needs of industry and made by politicians, but it is school teachers that actually have to implement policy. It is a huge responsibility and one faced every day by the teachers in Brunei, Singapore, Malaysia and the Philippines. A perennial problem, and one regularly written about in the press, is that of perceived deteriorating educational standards, particularly English language standards. Even in Singapore the apparent erosion of English language standards makes headline news (e.g. *Straits Times*, 29 October 1999). There is particular concern in Singapore that while 'Singlish' (the local variety of English) is increasingly understood and used Standard English is not. Certainly in Brunei there is concern about the quality and quantity of newly recruited teachers. As a small country it has always suffered a chronic shortage of local teachers and it is now trying to train as many of its own teachers as possible. The concern is that in trying to do this quickly quality might suffer. Malaysia's English language teaching standards suffered as a result of the years when the language was little used in education, thus diminishing the pool from which potential teachers could be drawn. In the Philippines Gonzalez (1996: 214) has noted that 'the quality of recruits and teachers of certain age brackets leaves much to be desired'.

What is certainly happening in the classrooms is that pupils are behaving in a way that is perfectly natural for bilinguals: they are mixing their languages. In both the Philippines and Brunei it has been observed that it is something of a misnomer to describe lessons as 'English medium'. What actually takes place is code-switching. This has been observed by Baetens Beardsmore (1998) and Martin (1997) in Brunei and by Sibayan (1982) in the Philippines. It is only natural for bilinguals to code-switch; thus it could be argued that code-switching in class merely reflects what happens in the real world. However, with so few other occasions to actually use the target language classroom code-switching can be pernicious. Martin (1997) has estimated that Bruneian school children may only actually speak four hours of English in school over a whole year.

A further potential problem once code-switching becomes established is that a new non-standard variety of English might emerge, as has happened with Singlish. While there may be some pride in having a kind of English that is obviously a national variety such a language is clearly of little use when the avowed aim of education is to teach a language of wider communication. Educated speakers who know both the local and standard variety of English are in a privileged position, those who know only the local variety are almost as disadvantaged as those who know no variety at all. Gonzalez fears that a Philippine-English pidgin and subsequently a creole could emerge in the Philippines (Gonzalez, 1998: 519) in much the same way that Chabacano developed from a Philippine-Hispanic pidgin.

There has been discussion about Brunei English and Manglish (Malay and English). For the most part the examples of borrowings from Malay, together with Malay and Chinese structure used in English sentences, is a source for some amusement. An obvious local and simplified variety of English is present in both Brunei and Malaysia, but its presence has not yet caused any concern. Given that as in Singapore and the Philippines it is proficiency in standard English that the education systems of both countries wish to achieve then perhaps more attention should be given to the emergence of local varieties of English in these two countries.

Conclusion

As I hope this paper has demonstrated, Southeast Asian is undergoing something of a language revolution – developing forms of bilingualism that include both English and the national languages. The acceptance of this type of bilingualism marks a significant political change. Until recently national aspirations were linked with the promotion of a national language. National languages and local cultures are still being promoted, but increasingly with the acknowledgement that a country's development involves access to and involvement in global markets, and such involvement is improved by use of a common language, most usually English.

It should be appreciated that 'global markets' does not simply refer to selling products. Globalisation involves producing and selling in many different countries, and the companies involved are not all major multinationals. With e-trade it is possible for the smallest companies to sell their products globally, and such transactions are normally done in English. Larger companies may have a head office in Japan or the United States but factories are located wherever the best conditions (for the company) exist. The need for local suppliers, schools for employees' children and clerical and local technical support all involves some need for English. Thus, to use a term from economics, a multiplier effect exists and even a small local investment may result in a large demand for English.

Given the need of a role for more than one language within a society the quantum leap is in trying to introduce a school system that meets the needs of both nationism and nationalism. Establishing the necessary school courses, preparing both teachers and textbooks takes time. Gonzalez (1996: 215) suggests ' . . . a decade time frame is too short . . . The length differs from one sociolinguistic situation to another, but I am more and more convinced that a generation of 40 years is a minimum'. In Brunei we are 15 years into this process. Having reached this point it might be said that the system has now bedded down, but we are still very far from reaching a point where we might be satisfied, so Brother Andrew's forty year time frame makes very good sense from a Bruneian perspective.

Development of the role of language and national aspirations continues to be a fascinating process in Southeast Asia in general and in Brunei in particular. This is an unfolding story and one that still has a long run ahead of it.

References

Appel, R. and Muysken, P. (1987) *Language Contact and Bilingualism.* London: Edward Arnold.

Asmah Haji Omar (1996) English in public and community use: a question of status and goals. Paper presented at the First English in Southeast Asia Conference, Singapore, 21–3 November, 1996.

Baetens Beardsmore, H. (1982) *Bilingualism: Basic Principles.* Clevedon: Multilingual Matters.

Baetens Beardsmore, H. (ed.) (1993) *European Models of Bilingual Education.* Clevedon: Multilingual Matters.

Baker, C. (1988) *Key Issues in Bilingualism and Bilingual Education.* Clevedon: Multilingual Matters.

Baker, C. (1993) *Foundations of Bilingual Education and Bilingualism.* Clevedon: Multilingual Matters.

Baldauf, R. and Luke, A. (1990) *Language Planning and Education in Australasia and the South Pacific.* Clevedon: Multilingual Matters.

Cenoz, J. and Genesee, F. (eds) (1998) *Beyond Bilingualism.* Clevedon: Multilingual Matters.

Cooper, R.L. (1989) *Language Planning and Social Change.* Cambridge: Cambridge University Press.

Cummins, J. (1984) *Bilingualism and Special Education: Issues in Assessment and Pedagogy.* Clevedon: Multilingual Matters.

Cummins, J. (2000) *Language, Power and Pedagogy.* Clevedon: Multilingual Matters.

Cummins, J. and Swain, M. (1986) *Bilingualism in Education.* London: Longman.

Dodson, C.J. (1985) Second language acquisition and bilingual development: a theoretical framework. *Journal of Multilingual and Multicultural Development* 6, 325–46.

Bilingualism: Beyond Basic Principles

Edwards, J.R. (1992) Implementing bilingualism: Brunei in perspective. In G. Jones and C. Ozog (eds), *Collected Papers from the Conference on Bilingualism and National Development* (Volume 1) (pp. 39–69). Bandar Seri Begawan: Universiti Brunei Darussalam.

Edwards, J.R. (1994) *Multilingualism.* London: Routledge.

Fishman, J. (ed.) (1974) *Advances in Language Planning.* The Hague: Mouton.

Fishman, J. (ed.) (1993) *The Earliest Stage of Language Planning.* The Hague: Mouton.

Genesee, F. (1987) *Learning Through Two Languages.* Cambridge, MA: Newbury House.

Giles, H. (1973) Accent Mobility: A model and some data. *Anthropological Linguistics* (15), 87–105.

Giles, H. and Coupland, N. (1991) *Language Contexts and Consequences.* Buckingham: Open University Press.

Gonzalez, A. (1993) An overview of language and development. *Journal of Multilingual and Multicultural Development* 14 (1, 2), 5–24.

Gonzalez, A. (1996) Using two/three languages in Philippine classrooms: The implications for policies, strategies and practices. *Journal of Multilingual and Multicultural Development* 17 (2–4), 210–19.

Gonzalez, A. (1998) The language planning situation in the Philippines. *Journal of Multilingual and Multicultural Development* 19 (5, 6), 487–525.

Jones, G.M. (1996) Bilingual education and syllabus design: Towards a workable blueprint. *Journal of Multilingual and Multicultural Development* 17 (2–4), 280–93.

Jones, G.M. (1997) The evolution of a language plan. *The International Journal of Language Problems and Language Planning* 21 (3), 197–215.

Jones, G.M. (2000) Some language planning questions facing Brunei Darussalam, Singapore, Malaysia and the Philippines. In M.L.S Bautista, T.A. Llamzon and B.P. Sibayan (eds) *Parangalcang Brother Andrew* (pp. 226–38). Manila: Linguistic Society of the Philippines.

Jones, G.M., Martin, P.W. and Ozog, A.C.K. (1993) Multilingualism and bilingual education in Brunei Darussalam. In G.M. Jones and A.C.K. Ozog (eds) *Bilingualism and National Development* (pp. 39–58). Clevedon: Multilingual Matters.

Kaplan, R.B. and Baldauf, R.B. (1997) *Language Planning from Practice to Theory.* Clevedon: Multilingual Matters.

Le Vasan, M. (1996) System and process in computer mediated discourse: A case study of business communication in a Malaysian corporation. PhD thesis submitted to the Faculty of Languages and Linguistics, University of Malaya, Kuala Lumpur, 1996.

Li Wei (ed.) (2000) *The Bilingualism Reader.* London: Routledge.

Martin, P. (1996) Code-switching in the primary classroom: One response to the planned and the unplanned language environment in Brunei. *Journal of Multilingual and Multicultural Development* 17 (2–4), 128–44.

Martin, P.W. (1997) Accomplishing lessons bilingually in three primary classrooms in Negara Brunei Darussalam: Insights into the dwibahasa programme. PhD thesis, University of Lancaster.

Martin, P.W., Ozog, A.C.K. and Poedjosoedarmo, G. (eds) (1996) *Language Use and Language Change in Brunei Darussalam.* Ohio: Ohio University Press.

McLellan, J. (1997) Linguistic imperialism and the cultural politics of EIL in the context of Southeast Asia: Outsiders' and insiders' perspectives on the role of English. In Brown, A. (ed.) *English in Southeast Asia 96* (pp. 156–65). Singapore: National Institute of Education.

Milroy, L. (1987) *Language and Social Networks*. Oxford: Blackwell.

Nothofer, B. (1991) The languages of Brunei Darussalam. In H. Steinhauer (ed.) *Papers in Austronesian Linguistics. Pacific Linguistics, A-81* (pp. 151–76). Canberrra: Australian National University.

Ozog, A.C.K. (1993) Bilingualism and National Development in Malaysia. *Journal of Multilingual and Multicultural Development* 14 (1, 2), 59–72.

Romaine, S. (1989) *Bilingualism*. Oxford: Basil Blackwell.

Rubin, J. and Jernudd, B.H. (eds) (1971) *Can Language be Planned?* Hawai'i: University Press of Hawai'i.

Schumann, J. (1978) The acculturation model for second language acquisition. In Gringas, R. (ed.) *Second Language Acquisition and Foreign Language Teaching* (pp. 27–50). Washington: Center for Applied Linguistics.

Schumann, J. (1986) Research on the acculturation model for second language acquisition. *Journal of Multilingual and Multicultural Development* 7 (5), 379–92.

Sibayan, B.P. (1982) Teaching children in two or three languages. Paper read at the seminar on Interlanguage Processes in Language Learning and Communication in Multilingual Societies. Singapore: SEAMEO Regional Language Centre.

Straits Times (29 October 1999) Moves to prevent erosion of English. Singapore.

Swain, M. (1983) Bilingualism without tears. In M. Clark and J. Handscombe (eds) *On TESOL '82: Pacific Perspectives on Language and Teaching* (pp. 35–46). Washington DC: TESOL.

Swain, M. (1985) Communicative competence: Some roles of comprehensible input and output in its development. In S. Gass and C. Madden (eds) *Input in Second Language Acquisition* (pp. 235–53). Rowley, MA: Newbury House.

Swain, M. (1993) The output hypothesis: Just speaking and writing aren't enough. *Canadian Modern Language Review.* 50 (1).

Xu Daming and Tan Peck Ling (1996) Trends of English use among Chinese Singaporeans. Paper presented at the First English in Southeast Asia Conference, Singapore, 21–3 November 1996.

Chapter 8

Markets, Hierarchies and Networks in Language Maintenance and Language Shift

LI WEI and LESLEY MILROY

Introduction

In reviewing over 30 years of research on societal multilingualism, Fishman (1991) suggests that there are three key aspects which an 'informed evaluation' of language maintenance and language shift should consider: habitual language use, behaviour towards language, and socio-cultural change processes. He argues that most progress has been made in conjunction with the measurement of habitual language use, or in his famous question 'Who Speaks What Language to Whom and When', and least in conjunction with socio-cultural change processes. This, in Fishman's opinion, 'reflects the greater precision of scholarly work with language as a result of the more highly systematic nature of language and language behaviour', while the 'social sciences in general and sociology in particular simply have not reached the same level of precise and systematic analysis' (1989: 253). Fishman's own model of *domain analysis* focuses on the habitual language use of individual speakers and has been widely used in the study of language maintenance and language shift. In contrast, no similarly coherent model is available for analysing the socio-cultural processes associated with language maintenance and language shift.

Research to date has been concerned primarily with isolating those factors which accelerate language shift from those which inhibit it and favour maintenance. While such lists of factors may help clarify what contributes to language maintenance and language shift, they have little to say about the relative importance of the various factors, or about how individual speakers and their communities respond to macro-level societal pressures. What seems to be needed is an integrated approach that addresses the social, political and economic change processes at large as well

128

as the ways in which individual speakers deal with the changes in everyday interaction.

In this chapter, we discuss a model which attempts to understand the process of language maintenance and language shift in relation to the concomitant processes of socio-cultural changes of the society, and furthermore to evaluate the effect and effectiveness of language policies. This model is based on the work of political economists and is known as the Market, Hierarchy and Network model (Frances *et al.*, 1991). We shall discuss the applicability of the model with reference to the sociolinguistic situation of Singapore.

The Market, Hierarchy and Network Model

The Market, Hierarchy and Network model has been developed by social and political scientists to address the question of how society is co-ordinated and indeed if it is coordinated (Frances *et al.*, 1991). When applied to multilingual and multicultural societies, such questions cannot be fully answered without considering the issue of language and its role in social life. It has been argued that language is a form of cultural, or more generally, symbolic, capital, which is exchangeable in the marketplace of social interaction. One's ability to use the appropriate language in the appropriate manner (i.e. according to conventions established in the interests of the groups that dominate the interaction) affects one's chances of gaining access to situations where valuable resources are produced and distributed, and once there, to participate in the processes of production and distribution, indeed to benefit from them. As a result, linguistic and cultural capitals acquire a value of their own, and become sources of power and prestige in their own right (Heller, 1989, 1994). In multilingual societies, therefore, language planning (i.e. how the use of language is managed at the societal level) becomes a vital issue in the overall control of recourses and opportunities as well as in the co-ordination of individuals' everyday life. Social scientists, especially political economists, have identified three agencies which are central to the contemporary societal structures and which seem to have important implications for language planning and management in multilingual and multicultural societies. These three key agencies are: markets, hierarchies, and networks.

Market

The market is characterised by a process of selection and change. We normally think of the market as consisting of a large number of buyers and sellers, voluntarily exchanging goods and services at an agreed price. This, however, is an extreme case – perfect, free competition where no single party is large or powerful enough, relative to the market overall, to have any direct control over the value of the goods that are exchanged is in fact rare. There are usually a range of market conditions that economists call 'monopolistic competition'. Here, a number of competitive enterprises have at least some control over the market price, though not total control, while others, although allowed to exchange their goods, have virtually no say on the market price. In the meantime, the market system overall, which is often regulated by the government and government-sponsored institutions, acts as a kind of social auctioneer, providing unseen but vital links between the buyers and sellers and helping to set the market price. A possible long-term outcome of the market is monopoly where a single party sets the market price.

When applied to language, we can take multilingualism as the symbolic market where different speech communities, or competitors, negotiate and exchange their own languages, the linguistic capital. While different groups will have differing goals in mind (e.g. simply maintaining a presence or share in the marketplace, or gaining some quick profit), their ultimate aim is to gain overall control of the market price, in this case to set the social conventions of language use. Language planning can be seen as 'auctioneering', which does not fix the conventions of language use, but declares what these conventions are and encourages the competition. For a variety of historical, social and political reasons, the market value of the different languages will not normally be the same, and there is little opportunity for truly equal exchange. The market force determines that there will be winners and losers, each having to calculate their short- and long-term costs and benefits. Eckert (2000) provides a relevant discussion of different kinds of material and symbolic market, in relation to linguistic practices of groups and individuals.

Hierarchy

Although the market is clearly a key component of modern society, individuals and groups working in a highly competitive market framework have to organise their activities internally and this is likely to be done in a manner that evokes the attributes of a hierarchy in one way or another. Indeed, the market requires individuals and groups to have more sophisticated organisational systems to enhance their competitiveness.

The term hierarchy immediately conjures up the ideas of tradition and bureaucracy. This is because hierarchies invoke a stratification of authority and the following of rules. Thus each level of a hierarchy directs the action of those 'lower down', ultimate authority residing with those at the 'top', and at each level those involved carrying out more narrowly defined tasks with less and less autonomy. What is particularly important, however, is that hierarchy also presupposes an already determined outcome or purpose. Planning and management, language or otherwise, can therefore be more effective when hierarchies are utilised, usually by breaking down the ultimate outcome into a set of sub-processes for the different layers. So hierarchy depends upon ideas of organisation, task specialisation and rationality. Social scientists have suggested therefore that despite its problems, hierarchy remains the most efficient mechanism for integrating the activities of large groups of people and for making large organisations work effectively.

For language policies to be effective, then, hierarchies need to be utilised. The various levels of social structure, profession organisation, school, neighbourhood, family, etc. will all have to be co-ordinated. This implies not only identifying the influential agencies (i.e. individuals and groups, or even organisations) but also the organisational and administrative apparatuses, the decision-making routes, and most importantly perhaps the specified functions and capacities (or task specialisation) of each level of the hierarchy.

Network

It might be tempting to think that market and hierarchy exhaust the possible mechanisms of social co-ordination and so long as they are 'under control', the expected outcome is guaranteed. The reality is that individuals operate on a day-to-day basis in their immediate, localised networks. The informal relationships people develop through social interaction form a web of ties, with distinctive patterns and features. Network members share a common ethic and outlook and can discuss and decide policy informally between themselves. Networks therefore not only act as norms of enforcement mechanism to their members, but also build up resistance to external pressure. In this way, members create alternative markets, which are capable of operating in opposition to the dominant market (see further Milroy & Milroy, 1992). Yet, the very informality of networks makes it difficult for the outsider, including government and other formal institutions, to monitor and control their activities. Most networks are highly exclusive of outsiders, and they are not subject to any obvious or external accountability.

Sociolinguistic research to date has confirmed that localised, close-knit networks facilitate language maintenance (e.g. Milroy, 1987). They give their members a sense of belonging. Local norms of language behaviour can be developed, in opposition to the standard norms, within such networks. In a discussion on the so-called 'reversing language shift' efforts by some communities whose languages are at risk, Fishman (1991: 4) comments that:

> Societally based RLS [reversing language shift] cannot be accomplished at all if it is not accomplished at the immediate family and local community levels . . . Indeed, for RLS to 'take hold' these 'lower levels' constituting face-to-face, small-scale social life must be pursued in their own right and focused upon directly, rather than merely being thought of as obvious and inevitable by-products of 'higher level' (more complex, more encompassing, more power-related) processes and institutions.

Let us now turn to the case of Singapore and illustrate how the forces of market, hierarchy and networks compete with each other in language maintenance and language shift in a multilingual society.

Societal Multilingualism in Singapore

Singapore is a city-state of 226 sq. miles with a population of 3 million: 78% of the population are ethnic Chinese, 14% Malay and 7% Indian. Each of these three main ethnic groups can be further distinguished into sub-communities according to place of origin and the so-called 'dialect' they speak. The Chinese group, for example, comprises Hokkien (43.1%), Teochew (22.1%), Cantonese (16.4%), Hakka (7.4%), Hainanese (7.1%) and smaller communities of Foochow, Henghua, Shanghainese, and Hokchia. Each of these sub-communities has its own 'dialect', some being more closely related to each other (in linguistic structural terms) than others. The official languages of Singapore are English, Mandarin Chinese, Malay, and Tamil.

Until the mid-20th century, a resident of Singapore could sustain a lifestyle which operated largely in a mono-ethnic enclave. It was even possible to live and work within a community that was virtually mono-dialectal (Gupta, 1994). This was particularly true in the Chinese community, where different 'dialect' groups had their own identifiable settlements in various parts of the country. The early Teochews, for example, settled in Sembawang, Upper Thompson and Punggol areas, all in the north of Singapore, while the Hokkiens lived in the southern areas, along the Singapore River. Members of the Malay community whose ancestors had emigrated from what is now Indonesia also lived in communities that were almost exclusively Beginese or Javanese.

Such geographical compartmentalisation was reinforced in the nineteenth century by a policy of segregation, which was laid down by Stamford Raffles in his original plan for Singapore. This gave rise to areas such as Chinatown and Little India, which were intensely urban, and the *kampongs* (from the Malay *kampung*, 'village'), which had a more rural character. There were some mixed areas too, but they tended to be English-oriented, in the sense that the English language was used as the lingua franca for communication among people of different ethnicities. Clarke (1992), for example, described some neighbourhoods in which Eurasians and Jews lived side by side and where major English-medium schools congregated.

For the Chinese at least, the segregated settlement reinforced their 'bang', or clan, consciousness. Members of a 'bang' usually had the same surname and place of origin and spoke the same dialect. They grouped themselves together to maintain their ethnic tradition and promote their group culture. An important offshoot of the 'bangs' were the language schools, which served not only as a place to educate their children but also as a centre for mutual support, exchange of information and organisation of community activities among their members. Admission to these schools was strictly according to dialect divisions. The 'bang' structure was institutionalised in 1889 with the establishment of the Chinese Advisory Board and further strengthened in 1906 with the setting up of the Singapore Chinese Chamber of Commerce and Industry. Among the various 'bangs', the Hokkiens were by far the most powerful economically and consequently played a leading role in the Chamber as well as within the Chinese community generally. Second in position were the Teochews (see Cheng, 1985 for a historical view of the Chinese communities in Singapore).

Over the course of the twentieth century, mono-ethnic living has become progressively harder. Now virtually all Singaporeans live in ethnically mixed areas. According to the 1990 census, 86% of all households live in HDB flats, flats built and controlled by the Housing Development Board. The policy in these vast estates is, as it has been since the 1960s, to mix the racial groups, preventing the formation of ethnic ghettos (Gupta, 1994). Limits have been placed on the percentage representation of the races in each neighbourhood, which presumably reflect the ethnic ratio of the country as a whole (87% Chinese, 25% Malay and 10% Indian and others). Multi-ethnic living provided the opportunity for extensive contacts between different groups, which in turn led to bilingualism and multi-lingualism.

Yet, bilingualism and multilingualism have different meanings for different ethnic groups in Singapore. A bilingual speaker of the Malay or Tamil community, for instance, is normally proficient in English and either Malay or Tamil, all of which are official languages of Singapore. A typical bilingual speaker of the Chinese community, on the other hand, would be someone who speaks his/her ethnic 'dialect' (e.g. Hokkien,

Table 8.1 Predominant household language, 1980 and 1990

Language	Per cent	
	1980	*1990*
Total	100.0	100.0
English	11.6	20.3
Mandarin	10.2	26.0
Chinese dialects	59.5	36.7
Malay	13.9	13.4
Tamil	3.1	2.9
Others	1.7	0.7

Source: Department of Statistics, Singapore: Advance Data Release (1991: 17)

Teochew, Cantonese, etc.) and either Mandarin, the officially sanctioned Chinese language, or English, while a typical multilingual Chinese would speak one or more 'dialects' and *both* Mandarin and English. As in mainland China, the notion of 'dialect' in Singapore is not based on any sound linguistic ground. Rather, it is a status symbol, i.e. only Mandarin Chinese is recognised officially as the national language and languages other than Mandarin are assigned the status of 'dialects' whose use is discouraged in public domains. We shall see shortly the government policies towards languages and language varieties in Singapore. Before that, let us look at some facts and figures of the recent changes in language use in Singapore.

Over the past two decades, Singapore has undergone phenomenal socio-economic changes, rising to become a major international economic power. Parallel to the socio-economic changes has been a massive language shift from ethnic to national and international languages. Table 8.1 is taken from the 1990 Census of Population, which illustrates the changes in predominant household language in Singapore between 1980 and 1990.

As we can see, the percentage of households in Singapore with predominant use of 'Chinese dialects' declined from 60% in 1980 to 37% in 1990, while the percentage of households speaking Mandarin more than doubled from 10% to 26%. In the meantime, the percentage of households speaking English at home increased from 12% to 20%.

This set of data also suggests that the changes in household language use have been more significant for the Chinese and Indians than for the Malays. Further details of the differential language shift are given in Table 8.2.

While all three communities have increased their use of English, the Malays have maintained their overall language use pattern. The Chinese

Table 8.2 Predominant household language by ethnic group 1980 and 1990

Language	Per cent	
	1980	*1990*
Chinese households		
English	10.2	20.6
Mandarin	13.1	32.8
Chinese dialects	76.2	46.2
Others	0.5	0.4
Malay households		
English	2.3	5.5
Malay	96.7	94.3
Others	1.0	0.2
Indian households		
English	24.3	34.8
Malay	8.6	13.5
Tamil	52.2	43.7
Others	14.9	8.0

Source: Department of Statistics, Singapore: Advanced data release (1991: 18)

have shifted significantly from 'dialects' to Mandarin, and the use of Malay has apparently increased in the Indian community.

Within each of the three main ethnic groups, there are some interesting variations in the extent of language shift in different sub-communities. In the Malay population, for example, the native speakers of the Polynesian languages (e.g. Javanese, Boyanese) have shifted to English more significantly than the Bahasa Malay speakers. The extent to which different subgroups of the Chinese community have been affected by language shift is illustrated in Table 8.3.

Bearing in mind that there has been no significant in-migration to Singapore since the early 1960s, such large-scale, complex changes in the sociolinguistic patterns in Singapore can be attributed largely to the deliberate and often forcefully implemented government policies towards language and language varieties.

Language Policy in Singapore

Language planning in Singapore is characterised by the direct intervention of the government. In reviewing the language policy initiatives of the Singaporean government since the country's independence, Gopinathan

Table 8.3 Language shift among the Singaporean Chinese

	Language claimed as principal language to spouse (% of Chinese living in same household as spouse)	
	1980	*1990*
Hokkien	34	26
Teochew	17	11
Cantonese	15	10
English	12	20
Mandarin	13	28
Other Chinese dialects	9	5

Source: Department of Statistics, Release No. 8 (1991), and Statistical Release No. 3 (1990)

(1988) points out two key factors that seem to have influenced the government's thinking: the first is the need for social and political stability in a highly multi-racial society, and the second is the need for rapid economic growth.

It is clear from the literature that in many multilingual societies, language-bred hostility is a major source of social tension. During Singapore's colonial years, there was already some awareness among the ordinary people as well as the government that some means for linguistic interaction must be found, given the multi-ethnic and multilingual nature of the Singapore society. It was assumed that English had the most potential as a link language. However, the colonial authorities were not prepared to expand English-medium schooling, and after 1920 a sizeable proportion of the Chinese population demanded Chinese-medium education. The government then faced building Chinese schools, training teachers and the like.

Since independence, the Singaporean government has successfully transformed English from a colonial language and an object of suspicion among ordinary citizens into a *de facto* national language. This transformation has been achieved by identifying English not simply as a 'neutral' link language between the various ethnic groups, but as a major source of economically valuable knowledge and technology. The discourse of the governmental language policies was one that was more commonly heard in discussions of the market economy. From the early 1970s to the late 1980s, the Singaporean Prime Minister Lee Kuan Yew repeatedly argued that knowledge of an international language such as English would give the nation access to world markets and the people better living standards. Over the years, the government has sought to shape a vision of Singapore as a rational, modernising society. Rapid economic growth since the 1980s seems to have helped convince the vast majority of the population that knowledge of English provides better opportunities for them as individuals, as well as for the country as a whole. There is now remarkable acceptance of English as a national language of Singapore.

As Singapore moves towards a more centralised administrative structure, with an economy dominated by multinationals and power in the hands of an English-educated technocratic elite, traditional power brokers such as family businesses, clan associations, and trade unions are likely to feel alienated. The government is fully aware that the retention and promotion of ethnic heritage, including ethnic language, at this time is likely to ensure, as Gopinathan (1988: 397) puts it, 'that these groups will have something to hold on to and, if not support, at least acquiesce in large-scale social engineering'. Language is thus seen as a valuable tool for managing the effects of social dislocation brought about by modernisation.

What is particularly interesting, however, is that, with regards to the Chinese population, the government has chosen to promote Mandarin, which is not spoken as a native language by any of the Chinese groups in Singapore, instead of the various ethnic Chinese languages native to the country's population. In 1978, the Singaporean government launched the well-known 'Speak Mandarin Campaign'. Once again, the need for ethnic unity and the need for economic development combined in influencing the government policy. It was argued that using the so-called 'dialects' would fragment the Chinese community and prevent the nation from accessing the growing, potentially huge market of mainland China. (It is interesting to note that the Speak Mandarin Campaign coincided with the Open Door Policy in China in 1978.) The government has repeatedly emphasised Singapore's fundamental nature as an Asian society and the importance of playing a leading role in the developing economies of Asia. To be able to speak Mandarin, as the then Prime Minister Lee put it, would give 'confidence to a people to face up to and overcome great changes and challenges' (as quoted in *The Straits Times*, 22 September 1984). The Speak Mandarin Campaign has since been an annual event and has become more forceful over the years. Among the measures taken have been public campaigns which aimed at service personnel (e.g. postmen, government office clerks), as well as the more ordinary workers and private employees (e.g. taxi drivers and hawkers), the organisation of public forums, panel discussions, seminars on the Speak Mandarin theme, and eradication of television and radio programmes and commercials in 'dialects' and dubbing popular Cantonese programmes from Hong Kong into Mandarin. Mandarin is now widely spoken in domains which were once reserved for 'dialects' (e.g. family) or English (e.g. schools).

In sum, the linguistic market of Singapore can be characterised by the co-existence of four languages – English, Mandarin-Chinese, Malay and Tamil, each having its specific market value. There are many other ethnic and community languages and dialects which, although they do not compete directly on the national market, are popularly used and have their own special symbolic value, thus constituting localised alternative markets. As with other types of market, the linguistic market is in a process of constant selection, competition and change, but the direction of change is influenced by the strength of specific alternative markets. Recent accounts of the sociolinguistic patterns in Singapore have described a 'post-diglossia' situation, in which the functional distribution of languages and language varieties becomes less distinctive and a new generation of speakers have begun to take on a positive attitude towards code-switching indiscriminately between different languages and language varieties (Xu *et al.*, 1998). Such a situation is clearly a result of the market competition.

To regulate the market, language planning and language policies have been initiated, usually through a number of interrelated, complex hierarchies, including government agencies, educational institutions, and community organisations. It is not entirely clear at the moment how effective language planning has been in Singapore. No evaluative research has been carried out to date.

In the meantime, there are units of society that may work against the hierarchies that in turn work against the market. Such units tend to be the informal, localised, personal networks. It is the networks that ultimately decide whether a language is maintained or relinquished and whether a particular policy towards language use and language education is implemented (see Li Wei *et al.*, 1997 for an example). It may be the case therefore that for language planning to be effective, focus needs to be redirected to such informal, localised, personal networks.

Summary and Conclusion

Since Fishman's seminal paper in 1964, language maintenance and language shift has become a pivotal topic in sociolinguistic research. There now exists a large body of literature documenting the linguistic fortunes of a range of communities in different parts of the world. Much of this literature, however, focuses on the experiences of minority groups, especially immigrants who may also be socially and / or economically disadvantaged. Although considerable progress has been made from that vantage point, a different perspective which examines ongoing variations and change in the patterns of language use of the majority and the socially and economically powerful groups may provide interesting insights into the socio-cultural processes of language maintenance and language shift. In this regard, Singapore presents a particularly interesting case, as bi- or multi-lingualism in Singapore is not associated with minority groups, nor with immigrants. The vast majority of Singaporeans are bilingual or multilingual, and the most multilingual individuals are likely to be from the dominant Chinese community who make up over 78% of the population.

In this chapter we have outlined a model, based on political economists' analyses of social coordination, which examines the process of language maintenance and language shift in relation to the concomitant processes of socio-cultural changes of the society. In essence, the model examines the competing forces in social coordination at three different but interrelated levels: forces of the market, of traditional hierarchies, and of personal social networks. When applied to the study of language maintenance and language shift, the Market, Hierarchy and Network model has a further capacity of evaluating the effectiveness and effect of language policies in multilingual societies. We have attempted to describe the Singapore case using this model. We hope it can be used and extended in future studies of language maintenance and language shift in other multilingual societies.

Acknowledgements

In preparing this paper, we have benefited from discussions with our colleagues in Newcastle, Ann Arbor and Singapore. In particular, discussions with S. Gopinathan, Vanitha Saravanan (both of the National Institute of Education, Singapore) and Xu Daming (previously with the Nanyang Technological University of Singapore, now of the University of California) deepened our understanding of the socio-linguistic situation and language policies of Singapore. Rod Rhodes, Professor of Politics at Newcastle, led us to the Market, Hierarchy and Network model we have used in this paper. We are most grateful to all of them.

References

Cheng, L.-K. (1985) *Social Change and the Chinese in Singapore.* Singapore: Singapore University Press.

Clarke, L. (1992) Within a stone's throw: Eurasian enclaves. In M. Braga-Blake, *Singapore Eurasians* (pp. 51–65). Singapore: Times Editions

Eckert, P. (2000) *Linguistic Variation as Social Practice.* Oxford: Blackwell.

Fishman, J. (1964) Language maintenance and language shift as a field of inquiry. *Linguistics* 9: 32–70. Reprinted in Li Wei (ed.) *The Bilingualism Reader.* London: Routledge.

Fishman, J. (1989) *Language and Ethnicity in Minority Sociolinguistic Perspective.* Clevedon: Multilingual Matters.

Fishman, J. (1991) *Reversing Language Shift*. Clevedon: Multilingual Matters.

Frances, J., Levacic, R., Mitchell, J. and Thompson, G. (eds) (1991) *Markets, Hierarchies and Networks: The Co-ordination of Social Life*. London: Sage.

Gopinathan, S. (1988) Bilingualism and bilingual education in Singapore. In C. Bratt Paulston (ed.) *International Handbook of Bilingualism and Bilingual Education* (pp. 391–404). New York: Greenwood Press.

Gupta, A.F. (1994) *The Step-Tongue: Children's English in Singapore*. Clevedon: Multilingual Matters.

Heller, M. (1989) Communicative resources and local configurations. *Multilingua* 8: 357–96.

Heller, M. (1994) *Crosswords: Language, Education and Ethnicity in French Ontario*. New York: Mouton.

Li, W., Saravanan, V. and Hoon, J.N.L. (1997) Language shift in the Teochew community in Singapore: A family domain analysis. *Journal of Multilingual and Multicultural Development* 18: 364–84.

Milroy, L. (1987) *Language and Social Networks* (2nd edn) Oxford: Blackwell.

Milroy, L. and Milroy, J. (1992) Social network and social class: Towards an integrated sociolinguistic model. *Language in Society* 21 (1): 1–26.

The Straits Times, 22 September 1984.

Xu, D., Chew, C.H. and Chen, S. (1998) Language use and language attitudes in the Singapore Chinese community. In S. Gopinathan, A. Pakir, H.W. Kam and V. Saravanan (eds) *Language, Society and Education in Singapore* (pp. 133–54) (2nd edn) Singapore: Times Academic Press.

Chapter 9

The Imagined Learner of Malay

ANTHEA FRASER GUPTA

Introduction

The use of bilingual dialogues in books intended to teach a language has a long pedigree. These 'dialogues' are constructed conversations in parallel text whose purpose may be to teach a set of vocabulary (e.g. sailing terms, numbers), or to develop some grammatical structure (e.g. interrogatives, commands), or to model plausible conversational settings for the learner (e.g. at the market, giving instructions to servants), or (usually) a combination of these. The dialogues place learners in an imaginary setting, often one in which the textbook writer believes learners may actually find themselves. Learners are intended to match the text in the new language against the text in the language they already know, and, usually in conjunction with a glossary, and often in conjunction with a grammar, are expected to be able to work out the nature of the equivalence of the two texts.

I have selected seven books which were designed for self-study of Malay by English speakers, and will be showing how the dialogues create an imagined learner whose social context reflects the history and conceptualisation of the Malay region (see Appendix for representative examples). All are general works, not aimed at a specific group (such as tourists or soldiers). Two of the books (Bowrey, 1701; Spalding, 1614) can be described as *pre-colonial*, as they come from the first phase of British involvement with the region, when British traders (alongside Portuguese and Dutch rivals) organised trading ventures and 'factories' in the emporiums of the Malay region. The Portuguese and the Dutch were well ahead of the British in their political involvement during this period. Three books (Keasberry, 1862; Lewis, 1947; Swettenham, 1881) are *colonial*, dating from a period when the British had established rule in parts of the region. And two (Liaw, 1988 and Zaharah & Sutanto, 1995) are *post-colonial*, written at a time when European colonial control had ended.

All the works seem to be relatively original, with the exception of Spalding, which is an acknowledged English version of Arthus (1613). Arthus is in turn an unacknowledged Latin edition of Houtman (1603). Arthus and Spalding both omit Houtman's prefatory and explanatory material, and his glossary, at considerable loss to pedagogic usefulness. Although my reference shall be to Spalding's English version of 1614, it must be remembered that Houtman was the true author of the Malay dialogues, which are in Houtman's Romanisation, based on Dutch orthographic tradition.

Bowrey developed his own romanisation, and the quality of his treatment of Malay was such that he was plagiarised by Howison (1801), grudgingly praised by Marsden (1812b: xlif.) and is still of use to modern scholars of Malay (Benjamin, 1997). Three of his dialogues are new versions of three of Houtman's, keeping the same outline narrative, but making many changes in language and content, as well as totally changing the orthography. Swettenham (1881) appears to have based three of his dialogues on topics from Keasberry (1862).

The number and length of the dialogues varies, the books with fewer dialogues tending to have longer ones. Five of the dialogues in Lewis (1947) were intended to be used as translation exercises. As the answers were supplied in end pages, I have treated these dialogues along with the exemplary dialogues. Most dialogues in the colonial and post-colonial books have only two speakers, but in the two pre-colonial books some dialogues have a large cast list, and a concomitantly complex dramatic structure (Table 9.1).

In the analysis, both the English and Malay texts are used to make inferences about the social context. The pattern of personal and gender reference being noticeably different in the two languages, this increases the information given by the text.

Table 9.1 Number of characters in dialogues

	Number of dialogues	*Dialogues with two speakers*	*Dialogues with three speakers*	*Dialogues with more than three speakers*
Spalding, 1614	12	3	5	4
Bowrey, 1701	10	6	1	3
Keasberry, 1862	5	3	2	
Swettenham, 1881	21	10	7	4
Lewis, 1947	20	20		
Liaw, 1988	20	18	2	
Zaharah & Sutanto, 1995	34	31	1	2

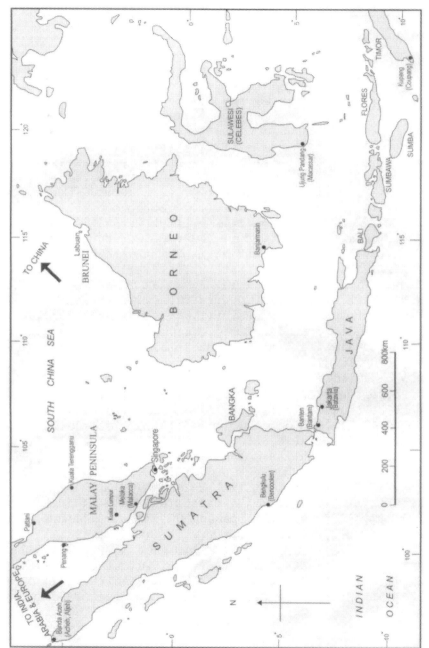

Figure 9.1 The core of the 'Malay region'

Where is the Learner?

When examining an issue of bilingualism over a period of 400 years a number of political and linguistic issues arise. The first issue relates to the naming of places whose boundaries and rulers have been liable to change. I have, wherever possible, had recourse to the modern geographical rather than political terms (Figure 9.1). Singapore's elder statesman, Lee Kuan Yew, ends the first volume of his autobiography (Lee, 1998: 667) with a map of this region, to which the caption is 'We were a Chinese island in a Malay sea. How could we survive in such a hostile environment?' Bowrey (1701) has a very attractive map of the region. Most of the region that I am calling the *Malay region* is now distributed between five independent countries: Indonesia, Malaysia, Singapore, Brunei Darussalam and East Timor. However, the boundaries of the region are potentially very wide, stretching from what is now southern Thailand to the north, to the Philippines to the east, and northern Australasia to the south. The texts used in this study do not make any explicit reference to areas beyond my map.

In the 17th century this Malay region was ruled by a complex of linked kingdoms and other polities (Turnbull, 1980 has a very clear and readable account). People we may loosely call 'Malays' (the ethnic terms of the region are, and have long been, complex) dominated regional trade and littoral settlement, and Malay was the major lingua franca in the cosmopolitan trading centres of the area. Applied to the language, the term *Malay* has also always been used as an umbrella term for a whole range of varieties, regional, social and functional (Benjamin, 1993: 352f.; 1997: 2f. outlines this complex situation in synchronic and diachronic terms). Many of the authors of books on Malay (Bowrey, 1701; Houtman, 1603; Lewis, 1947; Liaw, 1988; Marsden, 1812a; Shellabear, 1899) make an effort to characterise some of this variation in their treatment of Malay, as do many of the general discussions of the region (e.g. Crawfurd 1856: 207f.; Hamilton, 1815: 444, 542f.; Swettenham, 1907: 156f.). Swettenham (1881) makes several references to geographical variation in the dialects of the peninsula. The other texts (Keasberry 1862; Spalding, 1614; Zaharah & Sutanto, 1995) have little or no discussion of variation.

Many writers deplore the varieties of Malay used by and to foreigners, and refer to the 'true' Malay to be found among Malays. Every treatment of Malay in the 18th and 19th centuries makes a distinction between the 'pure' or 'best' Malay (usually associated with the Malay of peninsula Malaya or with the Rhio archipelago) and the Malay used as a lingua franca:

> Whereas in all the Islands of [the Archipelago] . . . the *Malayo* Language is received and generally used in all the Trading Parts of those *Islands*

having a peculiar Language of their own: Nay on some of the greater *Islands*, (as particularly on *Borneo*) there is several different Nations and Languages, with several of which I have conversed. But I must tell you, that the *Malayo* Language spoken in the *Islands*, is somewhat different from the true *Malayo* spoken in the *Malayo* Country, altho not so much, but to be easily understood by each other. The Malayo spoken in the *Islands* is called *Basadagang* [in Modern Malay this would be *bahasa dagang* = 'the language of (foreign) trade'], that is to say, the Merchants' or Trading Language, and is not so well esteemed as the true *Malayo*. (Bowrey, 1701)[1]

These varieties of Malay could appear to facilitate the learning of Malay, but their prevalence also hampered the learning of the 'pure' Malay:

It generally happens . . . that Europeans in India[2] acquire from each other in the first instance, rather than from the natives, their knowledge of the language; by which means the imperfections of expression are propagated, and the difficulties of correcting them are increased by the proneness of servants and other dependent connexions to conform to the idiom of their masters, in order that they may be the more readily understood. (Marsden, 1812a: viif.)

Swettenham (1881: x) also divides responsibility between Europeans and Malays, because 'every Malay, when introduced to a white face, takes it for granted that the stranger's knowledge of Malay is very halting and imperfect, and will try always, through politeness, to talk down to the standard of his white friends'. This lingua franca was recognised in the nineteenth century, however, to the extent of being officially recommended as the medium through which English should be taught (Gupta, 1994: 42; Hullett, 1887).

By the mid-20th century two major standard varieties had emerged from Malay, which are now often called *Bahasa Indonesia* ('the Indonesian language', Indonesian) and *Bahasa Melayu* ('the Malay language', Malay – also called *Bahasa Malaysia*, 'the Malaysian language', in Malaysia). The three twentieth-century books are based on modern standard Malay (an official language in Malaysia, Singapore and Brunei), although Liaw (1988) adds appendices on the differences between 'Bahasa Melayu and Bahasa Indonesia'. The blurb of Liaw claims that the book 'will enable you to read and write Standard Malay language in a couple of months and have a comprehensive grasp of Bahasa Indonesia'. Sutanto has authored a companion volume to Zaharah and Sutanto (1995) on Indonesian (Sutanto, 1994), reflecting the partial separation of these two modern standard languages in the 20th century.

The linguistic features of the varieties of Malay used in these books (like any discussion of the pedagogical implications of the works) is outside the scope of this paper, but the social complexity of Malay is certainly relevant.

From the 16th century to the 20th century the Malay world experienced colonial activity of various sorts from the Portuguese, the Dutch, and the British, with some areas (such as Malacca) experiencing colonisation by all three colonial powers, others (such as Bencoolen) by two of the three, and others (such as Singapore) by only one. Different parts of the region were also variably affected by a range of types of contact with India and with China, including substantial migration from China and (to a lesser extent) from India, especially in the 19th and 20th centuries.

The pre-colonial and colonial books under examination are all written by British people with some knowledge of the region. Claims of experience in the region may be made in the introductory materials (as they are by Houtman, Spalding, and Bowrey). Bowrey (1701) refers to his 19 years (for documentation see Temple, 1925: xviif.) in the East Indies, when:

> I did Furnish my self with so much of the *Malayo* Language as did enable me to Negociate my Affairs, and Converse with those people without the assistance of a Prevaricating Interpreter, as they commonly are.

For these two pre-colonial writers, the main arena for European activity is in the sea ports and trading centres of Sumatra and Java, although few of their dialogues are specific about location. Seven of Spalding's dialogues appear to be located in the region, two of them in or near Acheh (in one dialogue two men arrive in Acheh on horseback and anticipate hitting the bars), and two of them at an unspecified sea port en route to Acheh or Bantam. Four of Spalding's dialogues are apparently located in the Low Countries (presumably in a Dutch-speaking environment, although in one of them a character unexpectedly explains that she hasn't contributed much to the conversation because 'I cannot speake French well') and the remaining one could be anywhere. Lombard (1970:7f.) refers to Houtman's choice to place his ninth dialogue so firmly in the Low Countries as giving an interesting insight into his mentality. Certainly there is a stark contrast between some of the strongly located early dialogues, where sea captains from Gujarat, Holland and Flanders are greeted with pomp, elephants and dancing girls by Malay kings, and the later texts involving Northern European domestic scenes (and food) and trading of English wool with people from Ghent. The placing of these dialogues in the imagined learner's own culture is inexplicable.

A century later, Bowrey is still centred in Java and Sumatra, with Bantam being the only named place where a dialogue is set. Five of the dialogues are set in or near unspecified trading ports in the Malay region, where English merchants are rivals for trade (mostly in spices) with Dutch merchants. Bowrey's eighth dialogue is clearly based on the same source as Spalding's (and Houtman's) twelfth, with a similar narrative of a landlubber approaching a boat for passage, going on a sea voyage, having a storm, and arriving at the destination. However, while the Houtman–Spalding ship sails from an unspecified port in the Low Countries to Lisbon, Bowrey's sails (in great detail) from Bantam to Persia.

In contrast to the archipelagic setting of the dialogues, Bowrey's very full preface situates the 'true Malayo language' in the peninsula, and two of his dialogues portray an encounter, in a place outside the region, between two travellers, one English and one from the Peninsula. In his ninth dialogue the Englishman answers questions about Christianity (this involves reproducing the Creed, the Lord's Prayer, and the Ten Commandments). In the tenth, however, the Englishman interrogates the Malay about the Malay region from *Patani* in the north (tributary to *Siam*) through the peninsula, to Sumatra, Java, and Borneo, with detailed information on all the major coastal trading cities (including three pages on *Banjarmasseen*). In the early 18th century, the Dutch controlled major trading centres in the region, especially Batavia (a threat to the Malay-run Bantam), and Malacca. The main British interest was a modest fort in Bencoolen, rather out of the main routes, and Bowrey's whole aim is expressed by the English traveller in this dialogue. The two hope to meet again:

> I had rather that meeting could be in those South-Sea Countries, where the *English* might gain great profits by Trade, if they would settle Factories in proper places.

Over the course of the 19th century British interests transferred to the peninsula, where British control was first established in the offshore islands of Penang (from 1786) and Singapore (from 1819), and, to a lesser extent, Borneo, while Dutch and Portugese interests remained in other parts of the archipelago.

At this crucial period, when British colonial interests can be said to have really begun, appeared Marsden's grammar and dictionary (1812a, 1812b), which was to be the standard treatment of Malay until Winstedt (1913). Marsden proudly uses real texts, not constructed dialogues, but it is worth mentioning that he situates the learner very differently from any of the books I am examining in this paper. His 21 texts range widely, but despite Marsden's attachment to Sumatra as the source of the best Malay, there is a domination by the peninsula that was not present in the earlier texts. Two of Marsden's texts are translations of the Bible. Of the rest, 11 are letters from members of peninsula royal families (10 of them to Francis Light, the founder of British Penang, and one to the 'Governour General of Bengal'), five are literary texts, and two are historical documents from Sumatra. Marsden's imagined learner is apparently a reader and writer of Malay as well as a speaker, and his scholarly treatment and exemplary texts show his imagined learner to be someone operating at the highest social and linguistic level.

Keasberry's book has no preface, but is published in Singapore by an author who was a long-term resident (Abdullah, 1843, transl. A.H. Hill, in Hill (ed.) 1969: 289f.). Keasberry had spent most of his life in the Malay region, mostly in Singapore, but also in Batavia. After a period studying in America, he returned to Singapore as a Malay teacher and missionary. He was a pupil of Abdullah bin Abdul Kadir, usually known as Munshi ('Teacher') Abdullah. Born in 1797, Abdullah was a Malaccan of mixed Tamil, Yemeni and Malay background, coming from a highly educated family of religious teachers (his father had taught Marsden). Abdullah's autobiography has become a classic of Malay literature and in the twentieth century his style came to be seen as a model for a modern but 'pure' type of Malay (Hill, 1969: 28).

Given the length and depth of Keasberry's Malayan experience, it is surprising that his dialogues are (as we will see) so homogeneous. All five place the learner firmly in the urban parts of the Peninsula. One is specifically set in Singapore.

Swettenham's book (1881) was written explicitly for those in the Straits Settlements. When he wrote the *Vocabulary* he was the 'Assistant Secretary for Native Affairs', and was later to become Governor. He explains why he has chosen the topics and locations for his dialogues:

> Some of the conversations, such as those with the Cook, Gardener, Syce, &c., are for the help of persons living in the Colony, and would naturally be held with Chinese or Tamils, Javanese and Boyanese. Others, such as the dialogues on a River, in the Jungle, during Disturbances, &c, may prove of use to those whose duties or pleasure take them into the Malay States. (Swettenham, 1881: viii)

The places mentioned in Swettenham's dialogues include a number of very precise locations on the island of Singapore, Penang, and places in the (then) wilder parts of the Peninsula. Shellabear (1899) unfortunately does not have dialogues that lend themselves to my method of analysis (he has carefully graded exemplary sentences), but his sentences suggest similar contexts to Swettenham's.

Lewis (1947) acknowledges help from British scholars of Malay. She also identifies two men with Malay names (both barristers with degrees from Cambridge), and two women with Malay names, as having made 'contributions to the conversations' (Lewis, 1947: viii). The blurb of the second (post-colonial) edition of Lewis (1968) refers to the use in the book of 'the romanised script authorised for Government publications in Malaysia'. Lewis does not reveal much about herself (not even her gender), but her sources of authority are all peninsular and she firmly situates her learner in Malaya, and in a Malay environment, not in the trading littoral of the wider region:

> People will tell you that it is possible to 'pick up' Malay in a couple of months. So it is, if you are going to be content with the 'bazaar' Malay of the sea-ports. But if you are interested in language and wish really to know and understand the Malays, you will find that the initial confidence which such a method gives you will prove illusory and will be succeeded by a feeling of frustration. (Lewis, 1947/1968: xi)

Her book is aimed at someone who is beginning their study of Malay 'before they reach Malaya'. Of those of her dialogues which can be located, one is set in Kuala Lumpur, and five in rural parts of the Peninsula.

The two post-colonial books are written by people with non-European names. Liaw (an ethnic Chinese) is identified in the preface as being in the Department of Malay at the National University of Singapore. No biographies or affiliations, most unusually, are supplied for Zaharah or Sutanto, and there is no preface. One of the authors has a Malay name, and the other an Indonesian name. The locals have learnt English, so that they can directly introduce the target language through the medium of English.

The two post-colonial books locate their imagined learner in the urban world of Singapore and of the Peninsula. Of those dialogues which can be more precisely located, five of Liaw's dialogues are located in Singapore, and a sixth, which relates a road accident in Malaysia, appears to be located in Singapore. Zaharah and Sutanto's 10 locally located dialogues are all in Peninsula Malaysia (of these, two are in Kuala Lumpur, one in Penang, and one on the East Coast of Malaysia). Two of their dialogues are overseas (one in London, one in Washington, DC).

Over the 400 years of self-teaching books on Malay, we see a geographical narrowing. The earliest books place the imagined learner in the coastal trading centres, especially those of Java and Sumatra. In the colonial period the learner is situated in the Peninsula, and its urbanised islands, while the two post-colonial texts firmly locate the learner in one of the two independent countries of the Peninsula, Malaysia or Singapore. Malaysia locations appear to be entirely Peninsular ('West Malaysia'), rather than including

Table 9.2 Gender of characters in dialogues

	Number of characters identifiable as male	Number of characters identifiable as female	Percentage of gendered characters male
Spalding, 1614	46	3	94
Bowrey, 1701	25		100
Keasberry, 1862	6		100
Swettenham, 1881	45		100
Lewis, 1947	21	16	57
Liaw, 1988	19	10	66
Zaharah & Sutanto, 1995	31	35	47

those parts of Malaysia on Borneo. With the exception of Swettenham (1881) and Lewis (1947) the imagined learner operates in a heavily urban environment. Spalding (1614). Bowrey (1701) and Zaharah and Sutanto (1995) do have one or two dialogues in rural settings, but the characters are on horses or in cars en route to an urban centre.

The changing focus of location of the dialogues reflects the development of British colonial interest in the region, which began in the trading ports across the whole region, but came to be centred on the Peninsula. The post-colonial texts reflect the post-1946 separation of the region into independent states with their own socio-political and linguistic traditions.

Who is the Learner?

The characters of the dialogues are usually gendered and are sometimes named or characterised in a way that allows their geographical or ethnic origin to be established. Surprisingly few of these books include characters who appear in more than one dialogue. Where a character is clearly the same person in more than one dialogue (such as Liaw's Tan Ah Lek, a Singaporean Chinese learning Malay, who appears in five of the dialogues, including the example in the Appendix) I have classified that character only once. However, if a character is not characterised much, and if there is no continuation of narrative from one dialogue to another, we cannot assume continuity of person even if there is a continuity of name. For example, Lewis has two characters with the name of 'Ahmad', one a child who appears with his mother in two dialogues (in one of which she is named as 'Aminah') and one of whom is an adult, the husband of 'Fatimah'. The only book in which this difficulty may give rise to misrepresentation is Keasberry's, as his dialogues all contain a character identified as M[*aster*] and one or two others identified as *S*. The S character is a *servant* in three instances, but also a *shopkeeper*, a *washerman*, a *shoemaker*, and a *poultry seller*. In my calculations I have assumed that the M character is a single person, and that his servant is also one individual, but that the shoe-makers, shopkeepers and so on are separate individuals. As the example in the Appendix illustrates, Swettenham's dialogues degenerate into topic-linked lists of phrases, but all begin with a dialogic section.

Gender

Characters may be gendered by a pronominal reference in the English text (e.g. he, she), or by reference with a gendered term in either English, or Malay, or both (e.g. a *man, washerman, Sir, Lord, lady medical officer, housewife, Mr, headman, mother, the girls, tuan, Mak, misi, saudara, saudari*). Sometimes common sense allows identification (it's likely that the captains and sailors of a 17th-century ship, whether an East Indiaman or a 'country ship', would have been largely or wholly male). At times only the name gives gender information (e.g. Fatimah, Asma, Mahmud).

Using all this information we can see that it is only in the later texts women become potential learners of Malay (Table 9.2).

The placement of the imagined learner in a very male world indeed seems reasonable in the two earliest texts, at a time when it is unlikely many British women would have been moving around the region. Two of the females in Spalding are in the Dutch domestic scene of his ninth dialogue, while the third is a woman who briefly speaks to the king in the first dialogue (about a Gujarati sea captain encountering the local king). Even so, these dialogues are supposed to place imagined learners in a situation where they might wish to speak the language, and presumably the captains and traders of Spalding and Bowrey's world might have wanted to have conversation of one sort or another with local women at times – certainly some of the exemplary sentences in Bowrey (e.g. 'He nipt the nipple of her breast') suggest this. The absence of women from Keasberry and Swettenham is more surprising, as by this time European women, including Keasberry's own American wife (Abdullah, 1843, transl. A.H. Hill, in Hill (ed.) 1969: 290), were certainly learning Malay. Liaw's relatively low proportion of females probably reflects the norm of gendered characters in books of this type (Gupta & Lee, 1990). All the authors except Lewis and Zaharah are male.

The Learner in the Dialogue

The imagined learner often appears in dialogues as a character with whom the actual user of the book might identify – the foreigner or the outsider who wants to learn Malay. Such characters appear in many of the dialogues from all periods, but the identifying character can be a little hard to tease out. A speaker's national or ethnic group is often explicitly identified by the author. Spalding (1614) and Lewis (1947) sometimes make explicit comments in introductory material or in notes. For example, Spalding normally introduces characters in headings (see Appendix), where, as in this example, we need to understand terms like *Germane* and *Indian* in their 17th-century sense, and to use the Malay text for clarification when necessary (*orang Hollande*, 'a Holland person').

Lewis includes a number of cultural comments in footnotes on dialogues. For example, in her thirteenth dialogue, 'An Invitation', Che'Hawa comes to Che'Rakiah's house to invite her to a wedding feast. 'Makan-lah sireh' says Che'Rakiah, which is glossed in English as 'Help yourself to sireh', and footnoted as follows (Lewis, 1947: 270):

> By this time the two women would be seated on the ground, on the creamy-green *mêngkuang* matting of the inner room. Che'Rakiah pushes the betel-nut box (*bêkas sireh*) across to Che' Hawa, and there is a pause while they prepare their 'quids' for chewing. The ingredients of a quid are: lime, gambier, tobacco, betel-nut and sireh leaf.
>
> Malays are never effusive in their manner of greeting, and in their conversations are usually quiet and leisurely, with few words and long pauses.

This is a very clear contextualisation. It is equally clear when characters identify themselves. In many of the dialogues of all the books, characters make self-revelation. For example, Liaw's first dialogue (1988: 3, 'About oneself') sees Ahmad and Tan exchanging names, dates of birth, place of birth and nationality, thus identifying Tan as Singaporean and Ahmad as Malaysian.

When characters are given names (except in the two pre-colonial books, where names seem to be ethnically meaningless) they can predict a likely ethnicity – a *Mary Tan* can be assumed to be an ethnic Chinese, and a *Mrs Brown* can be expected to be European. I also make the assumption that everyone with a Muslim name of a type that might be carried by a 'Malay' is a Malay (Fatimah, Jamilah). I fully recognise (as I of all people, an ethnic European with an Indian surname, should) that names can mislead or be ambivalent: I have consistently gone for the obvious, on the assumption that the writer is working with stereotypes rather than with oddities (though Zaharah & Sutanto seem to be especially keen on names that give little away, such as *Anthony, Sony, Susan*). At other times identification must be inferential, and, as can be seen from Table 9.3, many dialogues do not allow for any inference. It seems reasonable to assume that a king is

Table 9.3 Ethnic and national mix in dialogues

	Number of dialogues with identifiable foreigner³	Number of dialogues involving 'locals' only, but of mixed ethnicity/nationality	Number of dialogues involving only 'Malays'
Spalding, 1614	6		
Bowrey, 1701	6		
Keasberry, 1862	5		
Swettenham, 1881	21		
Lewis, 1947	6	2	12
Liaw, 1988		17	3
Zaharah & Sutanto, 1995	9	7	11

likely to be (in the widest sense of the word) 'Malay', and that shopkeepers and service providers are likely to be 'local', while in 1947 a district officer was bound to be British. A dialogue with only 'Malays' in it would have no potential learners, but a dialogue with locals of mixed ethnicity potentially does, as (more obviously) does a dialogue with a foreigner.

Foreigners (of whom two are identified as Dutch, one as Flemish, and one as Gujarati) appear in all but one of the Spalding dialogues that are located in the Malay region. Most of Bowrey's foreigners are generic Europeans, though two are identified as English, and one is clearly not Dutch, as he is in competition for nutmegs with the Dutch captain. Keasberry's *master* is 'an European and a gentleman' (Keasberry, 1862: 71, fifth dialogue) of unknown nationality. Swettenham's dialogues all have an identifiable male master-type, who can safely be assumed to be the potential learner and a European. In many dialogues this character places himself as an outsider by asking about local conditions, and in some cases comparing them to conditions in Europe (as in the discussion about the weather). Names are actually suppressed by Swettenham (*Tûan – –*).

Lewis's district officer must be British, and the others all have Anglo-Celtic surnames (*White, Black, Brown* and, anomalously, *McNeill* and *Smith*). All but one of Lewis's foreign characters are in the passages intended for the learner to translate from English to Malay, where presumably the identification of the learner with a character is intended to be stronger than where only reading is involved. No one in Liaw's book comes from outside the Malay region. Three of Zaharah and Sutanto's foreigners are identified as English or British, two as American, and one more has an Anglo-Celtic surname (*Smith!*). Although both Lewis and Zaharah and Sutanto have a reasonable number of female characters, only one of Lewis's foreigners (Mrs Brown, who gives commands to her gardener) is female, and while six of Zaharah's foreigners can be identified as male, only two can be identified as female (one of the tourists, and Sue, a student in London, who explains a Trafalgar Square demonstration to the Malaysian Anthony) – the business visitors and residents are all male.

In the pre-colonial and colonial books the learner is clearly imagined as a 'European' foreigner. This character is still around in the post-colonial period, at least in Zaharah and Sutanto (1995), published outside the region. Liaw, published within the region, concentrates on a different imagined learner, one whom we also see in Zaharah and Sutanto's multi-cultural Malaysian dialogues. Apart from a handful of dialogues in which an educated guess at ethnicity of speakers is impossible, all the mixed-local dialogues in these books include at least one character who is identifiable as a Malay. So this imagined learner is a non-Malay local, using Malay in the company of Malays. In the earlier periods it would have been unthinkable that a local would have been learning Malay through the medium of English – the acceptance of this in Liaw's book especially is a clear reflection of the impact of the spread of English in the post-colonial period.

Malay as the major regional lingua franca has, since the mid-twentieth century, been threatened by the encroachment of English as an intra-national, as well as an international lingua franca (Gupta, 1997). In a post-colonial context, where proficiency in English is a marker of prestige, it may be seen as offensive to speak Malay cross-ethnically – the choice of Malay by an English speaker may be seen as an implication that the hearer is unable to speak English (and is therefore uneducated). Because Malay is the national language of Malaysia in a very real sense, Malay is much more available as a lingua franca in Malaysia than it is in Singapore, where Malay is the national language only *de jure*. The rare use of Malay as a lingua franca in post-1980s Singapore makes some of Liaw's dialogues difficult to parallel in real life Singapore. In modern Singapore it is unlikely that (as happens in dialogue six) a Chinese man coming to an office to visit another Chinese man would address an ethnic Indian office worker in Malay. Many of Liaw's dialogues, perhaps responding to his own sense of implausibility in some of his settings, clearly position one participant as a learner, whose use of Malay is pedagogically motivated.

Equality

This is one of the hardest aspects of the dialogues to analyse. In order to consider the power relations between the learner and the speakers of Malay,

I have examined the dialogues in an effort to determine what proportion of them show characters engaged in relatively egalitarian relationships, and what proportion show characters one of whom is noticeably superior to the other.

I have classified the dialogues (with some caution) on the basis of both situational inegality and the pattern of social deixis (Levinson, 1983: 89f.) revealing linguistic inegality.

- Some relationships are inherently hierarchical. The relationship of employee and employer is hierarchically determined, as is (in a different way) the relationship of a parent and a child. On the other hand, if characters are described as *friends* or *colleagues*, the relationship is being portrayed as equal.
- An asymmetry of style of address and reference reveals an unequal relationship.

Usually the asymmetry of a known relationship is reflected in the language, as, for example, when a business executive, Asmah, addresses her secretary as *Maznah*, while Maznah addresses Asmah as *Puan Asmah*, where 'Puan' is a title (Zaharah & Sutanto, 1995: 152). But sometimes the language is the only evidence of an unequal relationship, the information being present in either both the English and the Malay text, or (rarely) in just the English text, or (more commonly) in just the Malay text. This is the case when, in a conversation about the customs connected with getting rice from the barn, Che'Wan calls his companion *Aminah* and *'Minah*, but Aminah uses *Che'Wan*, where *Che'* is a title. Where kinship terms are used these may reflect hierarchically ranked relationships (e.g. use of a kinship term for an elder sibling, terms of address for parents). The relationship of husband and wife where it occurs in these texts is linguistically egalitarian, and I have classed it as such.

The Malay text is especially helpful in determining the symmetry of the relationship, as, in first and second person singular reference especially, most varieties of Malay situate the relationship between speaker and addressee rather precisely by the use of pronominal, quasi-pronominal, and nominal self and addressee reference. The range of choice is extensive, with many options of great subtlety. Modern colloquial Malay even includes the possibility of using pronouns drawn from English (*I* and *you*).

The four most recent books have extensive and explicit discussion of this aspect of Malay and many of the dialogues in all books but Spalding (1614) allow for a straightforward identification of hierarchy. For example the extracts (Appendix) show the speakers using the following first and second person terms:

Bowery		1st person	2nd person
A		kitta	
B		kitta	tuan

[incomplete information, but *tuan* likely to have been mutual, as it is between two friends in second dialogue.]

Keasberry		1st person	2nd person
	Master	aku, sahya	angkau
	Servant	sahya	tuan

[social deixis evident in 1st and 2nd person – Master superior to Servant]

Swettenham		**1st** person	**2nd** person
	Master	sahya	angkau
	Servants		Tûan

[social deixis evident in 2nd person – Master superior to Servant]

Lewis		1st person	2nd person
	Aminah	'mak	dia
	Ahmad	Mat	'mak

[social deixis evident in both persons. Speakers use for 1st person reference the term the addressee would use in 2nd person address ('*mak* = 'mother', *Mat* = variant of 'Ahmad'). *Dia* is a third person pronoun here used in 2nd person reference.]

Liaw		1st person	2nd person
	Tan	saya	saudara
	Hadi	saya	saudara

[Symmetrical. *Saudara* = 'friend (m)'.]

Zaharah & Sutanto		1st person	2nd person
	Fatimah		kau
	Chong	saya	

[incomplete evidence.]

As we see from the example texts, a whole range of nominals may be used in the first person and second person. Some of these books (including Houtman, the writer of Spalding's texts) identify some of the words as *pronouns* (Table 9.4).

The Imagined Learner of Malay

Table 9.4 Pronouns identified in the books (those identified as 'informal' or similar in italics; those identified as especially elevated underlined; all ungendered except where shown)

	1 sg	*2 sg*	*3 sg*	*1 pl*	*2 pl*	*3 pl*
Houtman, 1603 (p. 183f.)	amba, beta, ako	tun, tuan	dya	kyta	kamoe	orangdia
Bowrey, 1701	aako, kitta	*joo,* <u>tuan,</u> *packa-ne-ra*	dea	caamee	kaamoo	deóran
Keasberry, 1862	*aku,* sahya, hamba	angkau, tuan, inchi	iya, dia	kita, kami, kita orang	kamu, kamu orang	dia orang, marika orang
Swettenham, 1881	sahya, âku (+ regional variations, & info. on royal forms and written forms)	Tûan (M) angkau, *awak* (+ regional variations, & info. on royal forms)	dia	kita, kami		
Lewis, 1947 (p. 119f.)	*aku,* sahaya / saya	*engkau / hang / kau, awak, kamu,* <u>tuan,</u> (M) <u>puan</u> (F), <u>enchek / enche',</u> mika, *sahabat beta,* <u>engku (M),</u> <u>tengku (M),</u> <u>tuanku (M),</u> <u>taukeh (M)</u> <u>nonya (F)</u>	ia, dia	kita, kami, sa(hay)a (sakalian / semua)	same as sg	same as sg, also dia orang (oral), mereka (itu), orang itu
Liaw, 1988 (p. 54f.)	saya, *aku*	*awak, engkau, kamu,* anda	ia, dia, <u>beliau</u>	kita, kami	awak sekalian, engkau sekalian, kamu sekalian	mereka
Zaharah & Sutanto, 1995 (pp. 13, 37f.)	saya, *aku*	anda, *kamu, engkau*	dia	kami, kita		mereka

Table 9.4 obviously cannot reflect in full the sophistication of some of the treatments of personal reference in Malay in the more recent books, especially Lewis's (1947: 119f.). Nor does it reflect the even greater complexity of what actually happens in the dialogues (let alone real life). Obviously, even in Spalding, something is going on in the first person and second person singular which isn't happening elsewhere. Bowrey states:

Table 9.5 Comparison of social deixis in Spalding's eighth dialogue and Bowrey's fourth

	1 sg		2 sg	
	Houtman/ Spalding	*Bowrey*	*Houtman/ Spalding*	*Bowrey*
Merchant to Partner	beta	kitta, saya	tun	joo
Merchant to King	hamba	saya	tuanko	tuan
King to Merchant	ako	aako	kamoe	tuan

> The Second Person has several Words to express it by, according to the quality of the Person spoken to; as to a Person of Quality or Superiour, tis proper to say [*Tuan*] Thou or You, to an Equal [*Joo*] Thou or You, to a Servant or Inferiour, [*Packa-ne-ra*] Thou or You.[4]

We know then that Bowrey was aware of social deixis, at least in the second person, and his dialogues are amenable to analysis in this respect. In some of the more complex dialogues we see speakers varying in both the first and second person depending on addressee. However, when we come to Spalding it is much harder to see any pattern of social deixis (nor is Houtman of any help). Spalding's eighth dialogue corresponds to Bowrey's fourth, and personal reference is one of the (many) linguistic changes made by Bowrey in his adaptation of the same text (Table 9.5).

In this example there does seem to be social deixis in Spalding's text, but these patterns are not clearly sustained in the book as a whole. In the first person singular, speakers use, apparently indiscriminately, *aku, beta, (h)amba/(h)amma* and in the second, equally randomly, *tu(a)(')n* (and once *tuanna* to a female), *kamoe, angkou/en(g)(c)ko* and *kita*.[5] *Tuanko(e)* does seem to be used only to kings, but otherwise it is hard to understand any overriding system given the rapid shifts between addresses, as for example when a character asks another (in the third dialogue) who he is and where he is from:

Orang appa **enkou**?   derri manna **tun** datan?
person what **2ps**   from where **2ps** come

Note the contrast with the first line of the extract in the Appendix, where the speaker uses *kamoe* in the same question. But what does the contrast mean? The same term can be used in a startling range of relationships. For example, *tun* is used in many very different relationships, including by a mother to her son (she also uses *kamoe* to him), and by a shepherd to a more socially elevated horseman (alongside *kita*). Spalding's English text (like

Table 9.6 Number of dialogues showing egality in relationships of characters

	Equal relationship	*Unequal relationship*
Spalding, 1614	7	2
Bowrey, 1701	7	
Keasberry, 1862		5
Swettenham, 1881	1	22
Lewis, 1947	5	15
Liaw, 1988	22	1
Zaharah & Sutanto, 1995	23	12

Bowrey's) never uses *thou*, so that the only indication of status in the English is the occasional *My Lord*. Once again, it is necessary to bear in mind these uncertainties, which do not really affect the overall picture (Table 9.6). Where a dialogue has only three characters or fewer, I have classified the relationships between the dyads created in the discourse. I have not classified the very complex dialogues found in Spalding and Bowrey, in which a number of types of relationship are embodied, and this has the effect of slightly overstating the egalitarian.

This is a satisfyingly sandwich pattern, with the unequal discourses centred in the colonial period. The pre-colonial books centre on European traders who engage in trade and friendship with their local equivalents on an equal basis. They introduce their local equivalents to tobacco, while their local equivalents reassure them about the dangers of tigers.

In the two 19th-century texts, the European is undoubted master, and every text but one in these two books includes a European giving orders to locals. The exception is Swettenham's first dialogue, a discussion comparing the climates of Penang, Europe and China, in which the characters address each other as *Tûan*.

Most of Lewis's texts deal mainly with hierarchical relationships among Malays (e.g. parent/child) but it is interesting that if we look at the six texts with an identifiable foreigner, all embody unequal relationships, and in four of them the local addresses the European as *tuan* (in one the local uses *ênche*, while in one the European is female, and is addressed by the statusful *mem*) – no European addresses a local by *tuan* (they did in the pre-colonial texts). Lewis glosses *tuan* as 'master, lord, owner' (p. 362). *Tuan* isn't used at all in Liaw (1988) or Zaharah and Sutanto (1995), set in the new egalitarian world of modern Singapore and Malaysia. In Liaw the only dialogue in which address forms are asymmetrical is one in a bookshop, where the bookseller uses a respectful (by 1988 standards) *encik* in Malay and *Sir* in English. There are no 'Europeans' in Liaw's book. Zaharah and Sutanto have a number of unequal workplace relationships (e.g. headteacher/ senior teacher, boss/secretary) and family relationships. The Europeans participate only in equal relationships – they are sometimes tourists seeking information from friendly tourist offices or policemen, and making friends with locals when hitchhiking (not in fact a common activity in Malaysia), but more often they are residents who are involved in business activities in Malaysia. Rather as in the pre-colonial period they are doing business on an equal basis with locals, and making friends with them.

Some of these dialogues have a light touch (especially Spalding, Bowrey, Keasberry, and Zaharah and Sutanto), drawing on various literary and cultural stereotypes. Keasberry's S characters are servitors in the tradition of Figaro – the Master has great difficulty getting his shirt collars starched, faces unreasonable difficulty getting fresh food, and is obviously paying over the odds for his shoes (this humour is largely lost in Swettenham's rewrites). Some of Spalding's and Bowrey's dialogues are almost stageworthy – Spalding's Dutch domestic dialogue presents complexities of life in an extended family full of rivalries and complex relationships (some of the family members are too fond of the bottle), and the characters in the dialogues from Bowrey (as in the example in the Appendix) clearly have a complex life beyond the pages of the book. In Zaharah and Sutanto characters tell tall stories, gossip maliciously, and chat each other up.

The balance of egalitarian and ranked relationships in these books, and especially the placement of foreigners in them, very clearly reflects the colonial interlude, when hierarchy dominated, and when Europeans were high in that hierarchy. The pre-colonial texts portray a world in which notions of white superiority had not yet emerged, while the post-colonial texts reflect the modern ideals of social and racial equity.

What Does the Learner Want to Do?

Many of the dialogues are located in a specific environment (Table 9.7 shows the general picture). Of all the authors, Liaw is the least likely to give his dialogues a specific setting, but the anomalously low score for domestic setting is a real difference, linked to Liaw's imagined learner being the local non-Malay, whose interaction with Malays is in the public rather than private domain. Conversely, the dominance of the domestic environment in Lewis is linked to her concentration on Malay among the Malays, in dialogues in which a potential learner rarely appears. The palatial and maritime settings of the pre-colonial texts, set against the educational and

Table 9.7 The setting of the dialogues

	1614	*1701*	*1862*	*1881*	*1947*	*1988*	*1995*
Home	3	3	5	9	9		6
Social gathering						1	2
School or university						3	1
Clinic/hospital					2		2
Business place	2	1		1	3	2	7
Tourist office							1
Public place (including in or on modes of land transport)	7	2		6	2		7
Palace	2	1		1			
On ship (sea & river)	1	1		2			

medical institutions of the later books, reflect the change in the times (although Spalding's sea captains in two dialogues seek medical help for their crew members, along with the meat and fruit). In 19th century Singapore it appears (Keasberry and Swettenham) that vendors of various sorts were often summoned to the house – their dialogues are dominated by the obtaining of goods and services in a domestic setting. Although Keasberry includes no maritime settings, he does include a list of 'Nautical words'. If these settings are compared to the settings of modern books aimed at teaching English speakers French, or Dutch, or Italian, it will be seen that the tourist environment usually dominates in those texts, whereas here it is rare – a single tourist office in Zaharah and Sutanto, but no hotels or restaurants, or car hire offices. The imagined learner of Malay is not a tourist.

It can be hard to reduce the function of the conversation to something that can be displayed in tabular form (Table 9.8). There are no clear categories for this, and characters can mix business and pleasure in one dialogue, for example (especially in Spalding, 1614, Bowrey, 1701, and Zaharah and Sutanto, 1995). However, Table 9.8 shows the general purpose of talk which these authors are presenting.

The three twentieth-century texts illustrate a much wider range of contexts than the three earlier ones, with Lewis's concentration on the domestic being again reflected in a great deal of personal talk. The earlier texts are functionally oriented, reflecting once again the pre-colonial traveller engaged in trade and some social activity, while Keasberry's imagined learner is interested only in getting goods and services from menials, also a main concern for Swettenham's, whose rather wider concerns included negotiating with local royalty, attacking a rebel fort, and setting up a

Table 9.8 Types of talk

	1614	*1701*	*1862*	*1881*	*1947*	*1988*	*1995*
Sharing bio-data						14	5
Personal talk, news, invitations, domestic plans	3	4		2	9	2	14
Education					2	3	1
Socio-political issues						4	3
Malay culture		1			2	1	3
English culture		1					2
Rural topics / tasks					4		
Transacting goods & services (including medicine & war)	10	4	5	19	7	1	10

plantation. Those who used Lewis's book also were expected to need Malay to address domestic staff. Only in Liaw (1988) is the obtaining of goods and services unimportant – represented by one bookshop where a Malay dictionary is bought. The types of transactions to be undertaken in the medium of Malay include especially the purchase of foodstuffs (Spalding, Bowrey, Keasberry, Swettenham, and Lewis), medical care (Spalding, Swettenham, Lewis, Zaharah & Sutanto) and business meetings (Spalding, Bowrey, Swettenham, Zaharah & Sutanto). Only the two post-colonial texts have dialogues in which the main focus is the sharing of biodata (as in the example from Liaw in the Appendix). Other texts (including those in Spalding and Keasberry) include introductions and greetings, but do not focus on them. This is a common trope of modern language learning, in which the first lesson is typically to enable the imagined learner to give information about name and background to an interlocutor. The 20th-century books also include a certain amount of information on local culture, the focus being Malay rural culture in Lewis, Malay high culture in Liaw, and Malaysian culture and politics in Zaharah and Sutanto.

Conclusion

The way in which these books imagine the learner of Malay echoes the way in which the Malay region and the Malay language have been seen, and have been needed, by English readers. It is striking that over 400 years of books for self-teaching of Malay, the imagined context of the learner has been so predominantly in the cosmopolitan world of work in the Malay littoral. Of these books, only Lewis devotes any substantial part of her dialogues to life among Malays, while, even in the recent books, the tourist, familiar from self-help books on European languages, is also almost entirely absent. Very few of the possible psychological, social and integrational motivations of the learner (Gardner & Lambert, 1972, Schumann, 1979) are exploited in these seven books.

Despite the rhetoric of the earlier books against anything looking like a contact variety, we can see that the dialogues in all periods imagine the learner as someone who reasonably could be expected to participate in this interethnic contact, and for whom the deplored contact varieties might be appropriate. Shellabear (1899) explicitly addresses this dilemma. He warns the learner against 'those corruptions of the language which have come into use among the mixed populations of the large towns' (p. iii), singling out the use of *kaseh* as an auxiliary verb, and the 'continual use of the possessive particle *punya*'. He identifies both of these as 'Chinese constructions, and in the Malay language they are quite unnecessary and very clumsy'. However, the needs of his students oblige him to teach aspects of this despised kind of Malay. For example:

> The Straits-born Chinese use the Chinese pronouns, *goa*, I, and *lu*, you, when conversing among themselves; and it has become common among Europeans in the Straits to use the pronoun *lu* when addressing the Chinese and Tamils. A Malay should never be addressed by this pronoun *lu*, which would be considered an affront. (Shellabear 1899: 6)

Benjamin (1993) accounts for how the complex patterns of Malay for insiders and for outsiders have given rise to a situation which is problematical for the linguist. It is also problematical for the language teacher if the outsider is associated with certain linguistic varieties. The 20th-century books can escape the issue completely because they have inherited a standard language which *is* seen as suitable for non-Malays. Analysis of the dialogues shows that only in Lewis is Malay presented as the language of the Malays – rather in these books the Malay that is presented across the centuries is a regional lingua franca.

The boundaries of the region shrink in the colonial period to the central area of British involvement, which is the same region as that of the two post-colonial books – the peninsula and Singapore (not Borneo, for some reason). To gain access to the rest of the region the modern learner must turn to books on *Indonesian*, although the two post-colonial books both reflect (in authorship and explicitly) the continued closeness of the two modern languages, even making reference, for example, to the increasing use in Malay of the pronoun *anda*, under Indonesian influence.

The colonial experience is clearly reflected in the way in which the colonial dialogues place the imagined learner in a superior role, while the pre-colonial and post-colonial dialogues reflect a shared assumption that the learner needs to function across a range of hierarchical relationships with interlocutors.

Acknowledgements

I have benefited from comments on this paper, both when it was in draft form, and during discussion when it was presented orally. I would especially like to thank John Barnard, Geoffrey Benjamin, Michael Brennan, Avijit Gupta, Clive Upton, and Katie Wales.

Notes

1. Bowrey's pages are unnumbered.
2. It must be remembered that at this period the region referred to as *India* was much more extensive than the subcontinent. Marsden is of course referring to the Malay region here, which was very much part of *India*.
3   'Foreigner' presented as a non-local in the Malay region. Spalding's dialogues with a Low Country setting are not being counted here.
4. Square brackets are in original.
5. The two 20th-century books identify *kita* as 1 pl inclusive, contrasting with *kami* exclusive. Keasberry and Swettenham have it as 1 pl, Bowrey has it as 1 sg, and Spalding as 1 pl and 2 ps sg.

Appendix

This Appendix contains representative texts (or extracts from them) of the seven books.

Spalding 1614: Extract from the second dialogue (p. 10f.)

THE SECOND DI-ALOGVE FOR THE BVY-ing of victuals and diuvers proui-sion, when you come to a strange count-rey. And the persons talking together are a certaine Germane, and In-dian, and a King.	IANG DVA BAR-CATTA SAMMA TATCAL-la moela sampey dálam satoe ne-gri dagang, ken bly maccanan-satoe orang Hollande, satoe orang Indiaen, deng'an rayia di'a.
. . .	. . .
I. But who are ye? & whence come you?	I. Orang appa kamoe? derri manna datan kamoe?
G. Wee are good men, and brought from farre countries.	D. Kyta orang baick, datan dérri negry iáou.
I. What is your countries name?	I. Appannama negry kamoe.
G. Our countrey is called Holland.	D. Negry kyta namma Hollanda.
I. But wherefore came you hither?	I. Appa bowat engkou de siny?
G. Wee came hither driuen by contrary tempest, to buy some fresh victuals, for we haue been long tossed in the sea.	D. Kyta datan siny carna angin sallach, iang mau bly maccánan, carna kyta adda lamma de láoet.
I. It is well. I will declare vnto the King, that strange ships are come.	I. Baick beta pegy somba ken Sultan, iang cappal dagang adda datan.
G. If you please, I will send two men with you to the King.	D. Iicka túan mau, beta soeroh dúa órang sarta moe pada rayia.
I. Goe to, doe as you please.	I. Baick beta káboel.
G. What meaneth so great a multitude of armed men comming hither? what sound of trumpets and cornets doe I heare?	D. Boat appa datan bagytoe órang banta sammoenia tanggong siniatá? lagy beta deng'ar boenij namfierri deng'an seroney.
I. The King commeth there with all his princely traine.	I. Itoe Sultaen deng'an rayat di'a.
G. If this be so, I my selfe will go to meete him, that I may giue him honour and reuerence.	D. Bagítoe? beta pegi díri hambaken somba áken día.
I. Goe to, let vs go together.	I. Baick. pégy dúa kyta.

Bowrey 1701: first dialogue

A Dialogue Between Two Friends.	*Tootoorawn antāra sóbat dua óran.*
Relate to me the matter you would have told me of yesterday.	*Chéritra can pada ko hāl étoo éang cālam arree maoo bree taoo pada ko,*
I received a letter which advertizes that our friend *Joseph* after a long melancholy jumpt into a well and drowned himself.	*Kitta sooda tāréma soorat éang bree taoo cāmee poonea sóbat Joesoof cómādéan dea lāma dooca chéta de bāloompat ca dālam prejee daen mātee lémas dirree nea.*
Truly I am sorry, for every body counted him a sober and wise man.	*Soóngoo kitta berchinta, carna ségāla óran sanca dea óran sédang daen berboodee lāgee.*
And very rich, besides his house furnished with very rich ornaments.	*Lāgee sangat cāya, mélāin can rooma nea mengayassee dungan pāriahsan māhā gārib.*
Has he any children.	*Adda anak pada nea.*
Only one son.	*Sātoo anak lakkee saja.*
How long has his wife been dead.	*Brāpa lāma binnee nea mātee.*
Seven years.	*Toojoo tawon.*
Will you drink a cup of wine.	*Maoo minnoon angoor sa chāwan.*
Yes if mingled with water.	*Éa jéka champoor dungan āyer.*
Will you smoak tobacco.	*Maoo mengísap toombācoo.*
I am not yet used to it.	*Sampee sācāran booloom kitta bēasa.*
Will you walk in the plain lands.	*Maoo bajālan de Pādang.*
What in the heat of the day.	*Bootapa pada pānas māta arree.*
We can walk under the shade of the trees, besides the wind is cool.	*Cāmee bólee berjālan de tédoh póhone, angin lāgee séjoo.*
Il'e accompany you.	*Kitta écot pada tuan.*

Keasberry 1862: Extract from the first dialogue (p. 49f.)

M: Master; S. Servant

CONVERSATION WITH A SERVANT ...

M. Now take all the things out of the room and put them in the sun.

Skarang kluarkan sagala barang barang deri dalam bilek, jumorkan.

S. What things, Sir?

Apa apa barangnya tuan?

M. Get every thing out, for I want to have the room washed.

Samuanya kluarkan, kurna aku handak basoh bilek itu.

S. Very well, Sir.

Sahya tuan.

M. Make haste in taking out the things, do not be so long about it.

Angkatlah lukas sagala barang barang itu. jangan angkau bugiru lambat.

S. They are all out, Sir.

Samuanya sudah habis tuan.

M. Have you counted all the things?

Adakah angkau bilang samua barang itu?

S. Yes Sir, there are 7 tables, and 12 chairs.

Sudah tuan, meja ada tujoh, krosi dua-blas buah.

M. How many cloths are there?

Kain kain brapa ada?

S. There are in all 32 pieces of cloths.

Kain kain samuanya ada tiga puloh dua lei.

M. Well, stay here, and if it should rain take them in quick.

Baiklah, tunggu angkau disana, barangkali hujan kulak lukas angkat.

S. Very well, Sir.

Baiklah tuan.

M. Where have you been, just now it rained, and the cloths are quite wet?

Dimana angkau purgi, hujan tadi, samua barang barang habis basah?

S. I only went home to my meal, Sir.

Sahya pulang makan sa'buntar, tuan.

M. Why! did not you see it was going to rain? do not let me find you do so again.

Mungapa! angkau ta'lihatkah hari handak hujan, jangan aku dapat lagi skali bugitu.

S. I will take care another time, Sir.

Lagi skali sahya ingat, tuan.

Swettenham 1881: seventh dialogue (p. 26f.)

CONVERSATIONS WITH A GARDENER

The gardener is waiting, Sir.	*Tukang kabûn âda nanti, Tûan.*
To-night there are some people dineing here, get a good many flowers and arrange them on the dinner table.	*Mâlam sekârang âda ôrang mâkan disîni, chôba châri bûnga bâniak bâniak sedîkit, mengâturkan diâtas mêja mâkan.*
What kind of flowers would you like?	*Bûnga mâna mâcham Tûan sûka?*
Whatever you can get will do.	*Âpa yang âda jâdilah.*
Go to the gardens and ask the gardener, he will give you some; take a basket to put them in.	*Pergi ka'bûkit bûnga minta sâma Tûan yang jâga disîtu, dîa bûlik bâgi; bawa bâkul sâma, bûlih si'îsinya.*
There are no red flowers, Sir.	*Bûnga mêrah t'âda, Tûan.*
Never mind, get some pretty leaves.	*Tîd'apa châri daun daun kayu, mâna mâna yang elok.*
The garden is like a jungle.	*Kabûn ini seperti ûtan rûpanya.*
I think you are lazy.	*Sahya fikir angkau mâlas.*
I have no implements, Sir, how can I work properly?	*Perkâkas t'âda, Tûan, mâna bûlih kerja betûl?*
What tools do you want?	*Âpa perkâkas angkau mau?*
I will give you money and you can buy.	*Nanti sahya bâgi duit angkau bûlih bli âp'âpa yang kûrang.*
You had better buy about twenty flower pots, and put the flowers into them.	*Baik angkau bli bârang dûa pûloh pasu mâsokkan bûnga didâlamnya.*
This road is very bad, mend it.	*Jâlan ini ta'baik skâli, chôba betûlkan.*
Break some stones small and put them on the road, and then lay sand on the top.	*Hanchorkan bâtu târoh di jâlan, kemdîan bûboh pasir diâtasnya.*
The grass in the garden is very high, cut it shorter.	*Rumput di kabûn sudah terlâlu tinggi, chôba pôtong pendek lâgi.*
That is not enough it must be shorter than that.	*T'âda chûkup, mau pendek dêripâda itu.*

Lewis, 1947: sixth dialogue (p. 146f.)

Emak dengan Anak

Aminah: Mat! Chepat-lah minum kopi. Matahari 'dah tinggi. Bila lagi 'nak
            bergerak ka sekolah?

Ahmad: 'Mak, minta duit lima sen.

Aminah: Hai! 'nak jadi apa budak ini! Tadi sudah di-beri ayah lima-belas sen,
            sekarang dia minta lagi.

Ahmad: Jangan-lah lokek, 'mak. Duit yang ayah beri tadi itu 'nak belanja beli
            pensel, batang pen, kertas tulis. Kalau mau ta' tolong beri lima sen
            lagi, kebulor-lah Mat waktu rehat.

Aminah: Nah! Lima sen. 'Tapi ingat esok jangan minta duit 'nak beli kertas,
            batang pen, pensel lagi. Chepat masok baju. Kalau tidak, nanti lewat
            sampai ka-sekolah.

Ahmad: Kalau 'mak 'nak ka-kedai petang 'karang tunggu-lah sampai saya
            lepas sekolah ugama, boleh saya ikut sama.

Aminah: 'Mak ta' jadi ka-kedai petang 'karang. Petang esok kita pergi sama.

Ahmad: Baik-lah, 'mak.

Mother and Child

Aminah: Mat! Come and have your breakfast quickly. It's late. When in the
            world are you going to start for school?

Ahmad: Mother, give me five cents, will you?

Aminah: What a boy you are! Just now your father gave you fifteen cents and
            now you are asking for more.

Ahmad: Don't be mean Mother! The money that Father gave me I am going
            to spend on a pencil, and a pen, and some paper. If you won't give
            me another five cents I shall go hungry when play-time comes.

Aminah: Well, here you are. Here's five cents. But remember, don't come
            asking for money tomorrow, to buy them over again. Hurry up and
            put your *baju* on, or you'll be late for school.

Ahmad: If you are going shopping this afternoon, wait until I come out of
            Koran school, then I can come with you,

Aminah: I shan't be going this afternoon. Tomorrow afternoon, we'll go
            together.

Ahmad: Good!

Liaw, 1988: seventh dialogue (p. 93f.)

Berkenalan
(Acquaintaince)

Tan: *Maaf, siapa nama saudara?*
       (Excuse me, what is your name?)

Hadi: *Nama saya Hadi. Siapa nama saudara?*
       (My name is Hadi. What is yours?)

Tan: *Nama saya Tan. Apa pekerjaan saudara?*
       (My name is Tan. What is your occupation?)

Hadi: *Saya pelajar.*
       (I am a student.)

Tan: *Oh, saudara masih belajar? Di mana saudara belajar?*
       (Oh, you are still studying? Where do you study?)

Hadi: *Saya belajar di Sekolah Menegah Serangoon.*
       (I study at Serangoon Secondary School.)

Tan: *Saudara orang Singapurakah?*
       (Are you a Singaporean?)

Hadi: *Bukan. Saya bukan orang Singapura. Saya orang Indonesia.*
       (No. I am not a Singaporean. I am an Indonesian.)

Tan: *Patutlah saudara pandai bercakap bahasa Melayu. Mengapa saudara tidak belajar di Indonesia?*
       (No wonder you can speak Malay very well. Why didn't you study in Indonesia?)

Hadi: *Bapa saya menghantar saya belajar di Singapura. Dia mahu saya pandai bercakap bahasa Inggeris.*
       (My father sent me to study in Singapore. He wants me to be able to speak good English.)

Tan: *Sudahkah saudara pandai bercakap bahasa Inggeris?*
       (Can you speak English fluently?)

Hadi: *Bolehlah, sedikit-sedikit.*
       (Yes, a bit.)

Zaharah and Sutanto: seventeenth dialogue (p. 92f.)

Pukul berapa mesyuarat?

Chong has a reputation for turning up late at meetings and he is forever missing appointments. Fatimah, his colleague, is anxious that he should turn up to a crucial board meeting on time, as it is rumoured that his promotion is on the agenda. Fatimah tries to persuade her laid-back colleague to be more organised.

FATIMAH: Pukul berapa mesyuarat esok?
CHONG: Tak tahulah. Mungkin petang.
FATIMAH: Kau mesti tahu masa yang tepat. Kalau tidak, terlambat pula!
CHONG: Oh, ya menurut surat ini, **pukul 3.15 (pukul tiga suku)**.
FATIMAH: Semua dokumen-dokumen sudah siap?
CHONG: Belum, tapi masih ada banyak masa lagi. Bila saya sampai pejabat pada **pukul 8.30 (pukul lapan setengah)**, saya harus berjumpa Ketua Kerani, kemudian bolehlah saya habiskan surat-surat itu.
FATIMAH: Bukankah kau mesti berjumpa Encik Rama pula pada pukul **12.45 (pukul dua belas tiga suku)**? Mana ada masa untuk membuat kerja itu? Habiskanlah hari ini sebelum kau pulang!
CHONG: Tak boleh. Sekarang sudahpun **kurang lima minit pukul 5.00**. Kawan saya akan datang jemput saya pada pukul **5.15 (pukul lima suku)**.
FATIMAH: Kalau kau tak selesaikan kerja itu sebulum mesyuarat kau akan lambat lagi dan semua orang tertunggu-tunggu nanti! Bawalah kerja itu balik dan habiskan di rumah!
CHONG: Itu satu canangan yang baik. Selepas pulang dari berdansa malam ini, saya akan habiskan! Saya pasti habis **dalam masa dua jam**.

What time is the meeting?

FATIMAH: *What time is the meeting tomorrow?*
CHONG: *Don't know. Perhaps in the afternoon.*
FATIMAH: *You must know the exact time. If not you'll be late again!*
CHONG: *Oh yes, according to this letter, (it is at) 3.15 (a quarter past three).*
FATIMAH: *Are all the documents ready?*
CHONG: *Not yet, but there's still plenty of time. When I reach the office at 8.30 (half past eight), I have to meet the Chief Clerk, only after that can I finish those letters.*
FATIMAH: *Aren't you meeting Mr. Rama too at 12.45 (three quarter of an hour past twelve)? Where is the time for you to do the work? Finish them today before you go home!*
CHONG: *(I) can't. It's already five minutes to five. A friend is fetching me at 5.15 (a quarter past five).*
FATIMAH: *If you don't finish the work before the meeting, you'll be late again and everyone will be kept waiting! Bring home the work and finish it at home!*
CHONG: *A good idea. I'll finish it after the dance tonight. I'll be sure to finish it in two hours.*

References

Arthus, G. (M. Gotardi Arthusii) (1613) *Colloquia Latino-Malaica seu Vulgares Quaedam Loquendi Formulae, Latina, Malaica et Madagascarica linguis...* Frankfurt: Matthiae Beckerii.

Benjamin, G. (1993) Grammar and polity: The cultural and political background to Standard Malay. In W.A. Foley (ed.) *The Role of Theory in Language Description* (pp. 341–92). Berlin: Mouton de Gruyter.

Benjamin, G. (1997) Affixes, Austronesian and Iconicity in Malay. National University of Singapore, Department of Sociology Working Paper 132 [to appear in volume from Monograph Series on Asian Linguistics, edited by D. Gil and J.T. Collins. London: Curzon Press.]

Bowrey, T. (1701) *A Dictionary of English and Malayo, Malayo and English*. London: for the author.

Crawfurd, J. (1856) *A Descriptive Dictionary of the Indian Isles and Adjacent Countries*. London: Bradbury & Evans.

Gardner, R.C. and Lambert, W.E. (1972). *Attitudes and Motivation in Second-language Learning*. Rowley, MA: Newbury House.

Gupta, A.F. (1994) *The Step-tongue: Children's English in Singapore*. Clevedon: Multilingual Matters.

Gupta, A.F. (1997) When mother-tongue education is *not* preferred. *Journal of Multilingual and Multicultural Development* 18 (6), 496–506.

Gupta, A.F. and A. Lee Su Yin (1990) Gender representation in English Language textbooks used in the Singapore Primary Schools. *Language and Education* 4 (1), 29–50.

Hamilton, W. (1815). *The East Indian Gazeteer*. London: John Murray.

Hill, A.H. (translator and editor) (1969) Abdullah bin Abdul Kadir, *The Hikayat Abdullah*. Kuala Lumpur: Oxford University Press.

Howison, J. (1801) *A Dictionary of the Malay Tongue*. London: for John Sewell, etc.

de Houtman van Gouda, F. (1603) *Spraekende woord-boeck Inde Maleysche ende Madgaskarische Talen*. Amsterdam: Jan Ebertsz.

Hullett, R.W. (1887) *English Sentences with Equivalents in Colloquial Malay*. Singapore.

Keasberry, B.P. (1862, 3rd edn). *A Vocabulary of the English and Malay Languages*. Singapore: The Mission Press.

Lee Kuan Yew (1998) *The Singapore Story: Memoirs of Lee Kuan Yew*. Singapore: Times.

Levinson, S. C. (1983) *Pragmatics*. Cambridge: Cambridge University Press.

Lewis, M.B. (1947) (2nd edn 1968). *Malay*. London: English Universities Press/ Teach Yourself Books.

Liaw Yock Fang (1988) *Standard Malay Made Simple*. Singapore: Times Books International.

Lombard, Denys (with Winarsih Arifin and Minnie Wibisono) (1970) *Le 'Spraek ende Woord-Boek de Frederick de Houtman: Première Méthode de Malais Parlé (Fin de XVIe s.)*. Publications de l'École Française d'extrême-orient Volume LXXIV. Paris: École Française d'extrême-orient.

Marsden, W. (1812a) *A Dictionary of the Malayan Language*. London: for the author.

Marsden, W. (1812b) *A Grammar of the Malayan Language*. London: Longman.

Schumann, J. (1979) *Second Language Acquisition*. Ann Arbor: University of Michigan Press.

Shellabear, W.G. (1899) *A Practical Malay Grammar*. Singapore: American Mission Press.
Spalding, A. (1614) *Dialogues in the English and Malaiane Languages or Certaine Common Forms of Speech*. London: for William Welby [translation from Latin version by Gothard Arthus].
Sutanto Amosumarto (1994) *Colloquial Indonesian: a Complete Language Course*. London/New York: Routledge.
Swettenham, F.A. (1881) *Vocabulary of the English and Malay Languages*. Singapore: Government Printing Office.
Swettenham, F. (1907) *British Malaya: An Account of the Origin and Progress of British Influence in Malaya*. London/New York: John Lane, The Bodley Head.
Temple, R.C. (ed.) (1925) *The Papers of Thomas Bowrey 1669–1713*. The Hakluyt Society Second Series LVIII. London: The Hakluyt Society.
Turnbull, C.M. (1980) *A Short History of Malaysia, Singapore and Brunei*. Singapore: Graham Brash.
Winstedt, R.O. (1913) *Malay Grammar*. Oxford: Clarendon.
Zaharah Othman and Sutanto Atmosumarto (1995) *Colloquial Malay: A Complete Language Course*. London/New York: Routledge.

Chapter 10

Code-switching and Unbalanced Bilingualism

GEORGES LÜDI

Code-switching Versus Translinguistic Wording

Most specialists of bilingualism do agree that code-switching is a characteristic feature of fluent bilinguals' speech. In their groundbreaking work, Sankoff and Poplack (1979) established the bases of a first 'grammar of code-switching'. It has been completed and partially replaced by more recent publications (cf. Romaine, 1989: 110ff. for an overview and Myers Scotton [1993] 1997). As for the 'functions of code-switching', seminal papers by Gumperz (1967, 1982) and others have been taken up and integrated into more sophisticated systems (see Auer, 1998 for an overview).

The speaker in Example 1 is a Portuguese–French bilingual girl; she attends High School in France and is writing an essay in a bilingual classroom about holidays she spent in Portugal. The function of the code-switching is salient: it marks the geographical distance between the writer's two cultures.

Example 1

Je suis parti à la gare et je suis arrivée le lendemain à neuf heures *na estação de Pombal. I left the station [sc. in Paris] and arrived the next day at nine o'clock at Pombal station [in Lisbon]* (Araujo, 1990).

Since Grosjean (1985), this form of language behaviour has been attributed to a *bilingual mode* of speaking. We may represent the possibilities bilinguals have to define a situation as a continuum going from 'monolingual mode' to 'bilingual mode'. The nearer to the 'bilingual pole' they see (or define) the situation, the more likely they will 'mix', i.e. activate both languages in their repertoire (see also Grosjean, 2001). In Lüdi and Py (1986) we spoke more generally of 'bilingual speech' (see Figure 10.1).

Figure 10.1

Let's admit for a moment with Bernard Pottier (1992) that the intermediate steps from experience to utterance are: (1) construction of a coherent representation (what Dan Slobin (1991) calls 'thinking for speaking'), and (2) putting it into words by choosing among the possibilities the language offers. And let's assume secondly that formulation processes are lexically driven. In Willem Levelt's framework, this reads as follows:

> The preverbal message triggers lexical items into activity. The syntactic, morphological, and phonological properties of an activated lexical item trigger, in turn, the grammatical, morphological, and phonological encoding procedures underlying the generation of an utterance. The assumption that the lexicon is an essential mediator between conceptualisation and grammatical and phonological encoding will be called the lexical hypothesis. (Levelt, 1989: 181)

Bilingual speech can then be defined as a mode of speaking where rules and norms are activated that overlap single languages and govern the harmonic, i.e. the 'grammatical' mixing of elements from different languages. Myers Scotton ([1993] 1997) argues very convincingly that the matrix language chosen for various reasons (level of competence of the speaker, presumable level of competence of the audience, conformity to the situation) is normally dominant and provides the cognitive scaffolding for the semiotic organisation of a representation. However, searching for the appropriate words for what s/he wants to say, the bilingual speaker scans both of his or her lexicons (or both subsets of a global bilingual lexicon). To perform a series of pragmatic functions, to find the 'right word' (the orthonym) or to fill the gap of words s/he doesn't know, that are momentarily not accessible or that may not even exist in the matrix language, s/he will switch to the embedded language. This can be done on a single word basis (sometimes called 'nonce borrowing' e.g. Poplack & Sankoff, 1984) only if the lemma of the embedded language word matches the slot provided by the matrix language. On the contrary, if the syntactic properties triggered by the lexical unit (or the 'projections' of this unit) are not compatible with the syntactic structure of the matrix language, the speaker will choose to switch to the embedded language for a larger stretch and produce an 'embedded language island'. He might even change the matrix language. Thus, a model of bilingual speech must provide control procedures for the local matching of both language systems (Jake & Myers Scotton, 1997; Myers Scotton & Jake, 1995).

However, mixing phenomena also occur in rather monolingual settings. A well-known communicative strategy used by non-native speakers consists in relying on their L1 (or on any other language) to override communicative stumbling blocks (Broeder *et al.*, 1988; Faerch & Kasper, 1983a,b; Siguán, 1987: 211; Tarone, 1983, etc.). We have called this phenomenon *translinguistic wording* ('formulation transcodique', 'transkodische Formulierung'; Lüdi, 1996). It may be defined as a communicative strategy for getting oneself out of a predicament caused by limited lexical resources in L2. The strategy consists in the conscious use of single words or longer sequences of L1 (or any other language likely to be understood by the native speaker of L2) as a form of rescue device. Example 2 illustrates this technique, but also the way the other participants in the interaction react to it in a collaborative search for the right word. NNS1 (non-native speaker) and NNS2 are two 18-year-old German-speaking apprentices who discuss with NS, a French-speaking peer, during an exchange experience:

Example 2

NNS1: mhm. mais il y a un.. [to NNS2, in German] *was heisst Witz*?
             yeah but there is a .. how do you say 'witz'?
NNS2: [in English] a joke
NNS1: [believes that 'joke' is a French word and repeats] un joque une
NS: comment? [doesn't understand]
             what?
NNS1: [repeats the German word] Witz
NS: [takes up the German word in a French pronounciation] ah un witz
             oh a joke   (corpus Victor Saudan)

Generally speaking, translinguistic wording is an exolingual strategy. One might assume that this type of behaviour is typical for non-native speakers at the beginning of their learning process, when they need to communicate, but neither know the proper word nor are able to paraphrase their communicative intention in the target language. It may also depend on language representations induced by more or less formal learning of L2 (cf. Dewaele, 1998). Differentiated means for approximate formulation other than translinguistic wording stand for a higher developed level of interlanguage indeed. The nearer to the 'endolingual pole' (i.e. to symmet-

Figure 10.2

rical interaction between two equally competent native speakers) the interlocutors are, the less likely they will 'mix' (see Figure 10.2).

However, there is no clear correlation between this strategy and the level of competence of the speaker because balanced bilinguals may use this strategy too and because the way non-native speakers perceive the situation (monolingual vs. bilingual, formal vs. informal) has an influence on their choice of translinguistic strategies (Dewaele, 2001; Lüdi, 1997). In other terms, we need to combine both axes in a kind of co-ordinated system. We can then attribute prototypically code-switching and translinguistic wording to the bilingual-endolingual and monolingual-exolingual mode respectively (see Figure 10.3).

Do Learners Code-switch?

In the preceding paragraph, we seemed to assume that the distinction between 'learners' and 'bilinguals' is an evident one. This assumption is based on a mythical conception of bilingualism. Bloomfield (1933) defined bilingualism as 'native-like control of two or more languages'. For Ducrot and Todorov (1972), an individual may be called bilingual if s/he masters two languages, both acquired as mother tongues; the bilingual speaks two languages 'perfectly well' (p. 83). Such a definition of bilingualism excludes most persons with competencies in several languages. In order to cover the real phenomenon, we need a functional definition of plurilingualism. Therefore, any person will be called plurilingual who uses

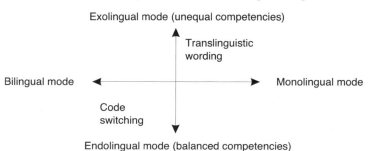

Figure 10.3

regularly two or more varieties in his / her daily life and is able to switch from one to the other when it is necessary, independently of the balance between the competencies, the modalities of acquisition and the distance between the varieties (Lüdi & Py, 1986). According to this definition, a migrant worker from Sicily in Zurich, having acquired enough Swiss German dialect for working purposes in addition to his original Sicilian dialect, is 'bilingual', as is a translator at the United Nations who developed her early childhood English–French bilingualism by systematic training. They represent two poles on a scale that covers all possible types of plurilingualism.

Such a definition of plurilingualism challenges severely the distinction between code-switching and translinguistic wording. First, most plurilinguals have in some way gaps in their (lexical) knowledge of all their languages. Even in rather monolingual situations, they might have a faster access to a word in the 'other' language. Shall we call this phenomenon code-switching (because they are bilinguals) or translinguistic wording (because of their lexical gaps)? And from which stage in their learning do we accept the use of L1 (or any other language) by learners as code-switching?

Let's first examine the hypothesis that there are formal criteria for this distinction. Myers Scotton and Jake (Jake, 1998; Jake & Myers Scotton, 1997) argue convincingly that the rules for combining elements from different languages are not to be learnt separately, after having built up a plurilingual repertoire, but are universal, present from the very beginning of language learning. Example 3 illustrates the entwining of a grammatical frame in one language (French) and lexical elements furnished by another. The matrix language is French; the rule for a compound word (object + de + material) is French, even when most of the technical terms are German. *Mast* has, by the way, no German plural mark (the French one would be inaudible):

Example 3

NNS: et il y a un petit moteur oui oui qui tire le cocon il y a la *vorrichtung*
          and there is a little motor yes that pulls the cocoon and there is the device
          [in German]
          il y a de grands *mast* de *stahl*
          there are tall masts [German] of steel [German]

                                                        (corpus Victor Saudan)

The example is totally compatible with the general rules for code-switching. However, it was not produced by a balanced bilingual, but by a learner with a quite restricted competence in the matrix language French. Nevertheless, he competently switches to German and back to French. Examples like this one support the hypothesis that there is no clear formal criteria for the distinction between code-switching and translinguistic wording.

As for the functions of code-switching, Vasseur (1990) observed a continuity between the functions of Spanish (L1) words by Latin-American women in Paris from the very first stages of learning until more advanced levels of competence: they tend to use French words when speaking for example about their children's school experiences whilst 'les mots qui restent attachés à ces expériences passées [sc. souvenirs du Chili ou de Colombie] restent des mots espagnols' (words that are linked to past experiences (memories of Chile or Colombia) remain Spanish).

Example 4

NS: ... est-ce qu'il y a une sécurité sociale? ou comment ça se passe?
      ... is there a social security? or how does it happen?

NNS: ++bon:eh:le il y a un (filiasjon) *afiliación* (se di) + un
      well uhm there is a [lexical invention] [in Spanish] affiliation they call it
      +a
      bureau pareil (ke) la sécurité sociale (ke se + se) appelle
      sermena ...
      similar office as the social security whose name is Sermena

                                                  (BE34A)

Vasseur concludes that from very early on in these exchanges certain linguistic practices get established which could be a first step towards the kind of linguistic behaviour displayed by advanced bilinguals in favourable circumstances. And Henning Wode adds: '[code-switching] is not limited to any specific level of competence, nor to any specific stage of development provided the languages between which switching is to occur are developed in the individual speaker to such an extent that s/he can be said to have two linguistic codes at her/his disposal' (1990: 37).

This leads to the conclusion that learners *can* code-switch. But this conclusion does not entail, of course, that *every use* of material of L1 or any other than the target language is functional in the sense of code-switching. We claim, on the contrary, that balanced bilinguals do make use of translinguistic wording too. If there is no clear formal distinction and if the criterion of language competence doesn't hold, how can we then differentiate between code-switching and translinguistic wording?

An Interactive Approach for Distinguishing Bilingual Speech from Exolingual Techniques

In order to find an appropriate answer, let us briefly go back to Example 3, but this time with more context.

Example 3a

NNS: et il y a un petit moteur oui. oui. qui tire le cocon il y a la *vorrichtung*
         and there is a little motor yes that pulls the cocoon and there is the device
         [in German]
         il y a de grands *mast* de *stahl*
         there are tall masts [German] of steel [German]
NS: oui donc/
         yes
NNS: avec de des . . . bottes *oder eine Schiene*
         with . . . boots [manifestly wrong word, self-correction in German:], isn't
         it, a rail
NS: un rail
         a rail
NNS: un rail. et le cocon a une petite roulette
         a rail. and the cocoon has a little wheel
NS: oui
         yes
NNS: et la roulette est dans le rail
         and the wheel is in the rail   (corpus Victor Saudan)

NS reacts to the turn 'il y a la *vorrichtung*. il y a de grands *mast* de *stahl*'
with a positive minimal feedback. There is neither the slightest sign of hesitation in NNS's code-switching behaviour nor any indication that NS
doesn't accept it as an appropriate form of speech. In other words, they interactively define the utterance as a stretch of bilingual speech – and the
situation as appropriate to the bilingual mode of speaking despite the inequality of competencies of which both are well aware.

But already in the next turn, NNS gets into trouble because he doesn't
find the word 'rail' in his mental lexicon. Interestingly, he does not continue smoothly in German as in the first turn, but hesitates by repeating the
partitive article ('de des'), makes a large pause, utters a totally inappropri-
ate word as a kind of place-holder ('bottes'), switches to German starting
with a reformulation marker ('oder') and formulates then the intended
meaning in German ('eine Schiene'). NS reacts in a totally different way this
time, providing the orthonym in French ('un rail'); and NNS repeats the
orthonym before continuing with his utterance. This is a very typical sequence of lexical work in an exolingual situation (see Lüdi, 1991a). Thus,
in opposition to the preceding turns, the use of German is interpreted this
time by both NS and NNS, as a call for help, as an indicator for a lexical
gap. The exolinguality of the situation is mutually manifested. This is to
say that the factual asymmetry between NS's and NNS's competencies

doesn't *automatically* entail specific ways of behaviour, but that the interacting partners have a considerable margin of freedom in resolving the communicative task and defining the situation. This applies particularly if we swap a perspective that is centred on modelling the behaviour of speakers or hearers for an interactive perspective. Interactivity means a reciprocal definition of the situation of communication by all interacting partners (Schütz, 1967). Based upon Schegloff's definition of 'discourse as an interactional achievement' (Schegloff, 1982), we claim that the meaning and status of translinguistic markers are *locally* negotiated and defined by the partners – in the compass of systems of social values, but sometimes with the explicit intention of questioning and reshaping these systems.

Nobody can deny that external conditions exert an influence on the speakers' behaviour. It is true that interaction takes place in a social environment only partially controlled by the affected persons. In the present case for example, the code-switching in turn 1 as well as the translinguistic wording in turn 3 are possible only because NS has a rather good competence of German as well. Similarly, long-term Swiss experiences in language use in French–German intercommunity communication ('everyone speaks his or her language and understands the other') contributed to the construction of a communication culture which certainly entails a higher acceptance of 'mixed' speech than in neighbouring countries. Thus, an existing system of linguistic values determines which 'linguistic capital' the knowledge and use of one or the other variety convey (Bourdieu, 1982; Gumperz, 1982). But despite these facts, we are not just determined in the way we use our repertoires. Schematically, these phenomena can be represented as shown in Figure 10.4.

the situation and the social structure

determine

contributes to constructing

language use

Figure 10.4

Another important point is that the interpretation of the situation may change quickly, from one turn to the other. In Example 3, it glides from a more bilingual to a more exolingual interpretation. The opposite holds true for Example 5 where a 14-year-old German-speaking girl talks about her hobbies to a French native speaker in a near-to-school context (face-to-face conversation in a room adjacent to the classroom).

Example 5

9) **I:**   tes loisirs   mhm tu fais quoi   quand tu as congé
10) **E:**   oui   mh   mh
your leisure time ehm what do you do in your leisure time?
Yes   uhm   uhm

11) **E:**   je vais à Oberwil mh dans un < Tanzsty / dio >
12) **I:**   dans un
I go to Oberwil in a dance school (German) and I yes
in a

13) **I:**   studio de danse   mhm
14) **E:**   et je oui je fais du < Jazztanz >   et je joue du piano
dance school (French)
and I yes I'm practising jazz dance (German) and I'm playing piano

15) **E:**   (rire)   mh oui ça va (rire)
16) **I:**   ah tu fais beaucoup   tu peux
yes, I can manage it
oh you're doing a lot   can you

17) **I:**   combiner mh la musique avec la danse puisque tu prends des
combine   the music   with the dance because you take

18) **I:**   leçons de piano   pas tellement tu sais jouer du jazz
19) **E:**   non
piano lessons   not really?   can you play jazz?
no

20) **E:**   non non pas encore. mais ah alors je = je joue pas du piano
no no   not yet   but   well   I don't play piano

21) **E:**   et je danse mh < Jazzmusik > X X
22) **I:**   mhm   mais mh tu joues plutôt
and I dance jazz music (German)
mhm   but what do you rather play?

23) **I:** quoi alors depuis combien de temps tu joues du piano
24) **E:**   mh
so, since when have you been playing piano?

25) **E:** deux = deux ans   oui deux ans
26) **I:**   ah deux ans   [c'est pas beaucoup]
two two years>   yes two years
*   oh two years   it's not much*

27) **E:** deux ans alors   oui
28) **I:**   mhm   c'est pas vraiment la musique
two years   yes
*   mhm   it's not really modern music*

29) **I:** moderne c'est plutôt classique encore mais peut-être
30) **E:** non   non   oui   oui
modern it's rather still classical music . . . but perhaps

31) **I:** plus tard tu pourrais quand même   parce que
32) **E:**   oui peut-être
later on you could nevertheless   because
*   yes perhaps*

33) **I:** c'est assez marrant   et puis pour le < Jazztanz >
34) **E:**   oui (laughs)
it's quite funny   and for the jazz dance (German)
*   yes*

35) **I:** vous êtes beaucoup ou bien
36) **E:**   nous sommes un groupe à dix personnes
are you numerous? or
*   we're a group of ten persons*
*   (corpus Monique Lü [3T11M])*

Lines 11–13 show the typical exolingual format again: Element in L1 followed by reformulation in the target language by NS followed by acceptance (here by a minimal positive feedback) by NSS. The rule that had been fixed for this conversation was that it should be monolingual French. We are thus in the exolingual-monolingual zone. But already in the same turn, NNS produces the next German (or English-German) word 'Jazztanz'. This time, NS doesn't reformulate, but indicates with a minimal feedback ('mhm') that she understands and NNS might keep on. The same happens again in line 21. The most revealing lexical choice occurs however in line 33, when the – French-speaking – female student

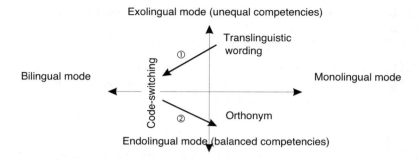

Figure 10.5

takes up the girl's German 'Jazztanz' in her own utterance. Doing this, she provides legitimacy to her partner's use of German and confirms the bilinguality of the situation again, as in Example 3, without annulling its exolinguality. The situation has thus glided from exolingual-monolingual to exolingual-bilingual as represented in Figure 10.5 (arrow ①).

In a similar way, we may interpret the evolution from lexical code-switching to borrowing as change in the interpretation of the status of the lexical form in the sense that it is considered as orthonym not only in bilingual settings (the right word comes from the other language and therefore I code-switch), but also in monolingual ones (there is a proper word in another language and therefore I propose to introduce it as a 'guest word' in the respective monolingual lexicon, (arrow ②). In other terms, a 'foreign' element can be a borrowing from its very first occurrence onwards if it is intended and interactively accepted as the orthonym in a monolingual setting. On the contrary, in a bilingual setting, with frequent code-switching, many occurrences of an embedded language word do not impede its interpretation as lexical code-switching. We assume this is the case in Example 6. The discussants are a mixed couple and their friends in Basle; B. comes originally from the French-speaking Bas-Valais; L. from the German-speaking Haut-Valais; P. and M. are from the French-speaking canton du Jura. They talk about the carnival, an important event of the year in Basle. The frequent use of the Swiss German term 'Gässli' by all the speakers does not, in our eyes, entail that it is considered as a borrowed word in the French vocabulary. It keeps the status of a lexical code-switching despite its frequency:

Example 6

P: Non mais moi j'vais aller demain. demain soir
L: demain soir demain soir
         No, but I will go [sc. to the Carnival] tomorrow, tomorrow evening
                                   tomorrow evening tomorrow evening

L: c'est bien sûr   demain soir le mardi c'est plutôt
B: ah le mardi c'est beau
         it's sure   tomorrow evening Tuesday it's rather

L: les les *Guggemusig*
M: c'est quand les /
B: oui mais dans les *Gässli*
         the the Guggemusig [= brass band playing in a rather disharmonic
         way]
                             it's when/
                                     yes but in the streets
                                     [affective diminutive]

P: dans les *Gässli*. ouais
L: oui. les *Gässli*
         in the streets, yes
                       yes, the streets

Conclusions

Our starting point was that both proficient bilinguals and foreign language learners 'mix' their languages. We have argued that formally, the resulting classes of 'translinguistic markers' (i.e. formal traces of the language contact at the surface of discourse; see Lüdi, 1987) cannot often be clearly distinguished.

In our view, the difference lies in the functions the translinguistic markers assume – e.g. the deictic or topological function in the case of the 'estacão de Pombal', the exploitation of the referential potential of the other language in the case of 'Gässli', but also of 'mast de stahl' or the function as rescue device the cases of 'was heisst Witz' and 'oder eine Schiene'. Depending on the function, that marker will get the status of code-switching or translinguistic wording respectively.

Clearly, the speaker's role in defining this status is important (e.g. hesitation markers and dubitative intonation accompanying a translinguistic wording); however, the definitive decision is taken jointly by the interacting partners in the framework of an interactive format. In other words, we would like to put forward the members' point of view in deciding about the status of a translinguistic marker (see also Lüdi, 1993).

We have also argued that the status of the translinguistic marker depends narrowly on the definition of the setting as endolingual/exolingual and monolingual/bilingual respectively. More precisely, there is a mutual influence as illustrated by the diagram: the use of specific bilingual or exolingual techniques is made possible by the expectation of a determined setting, and contributes, at the same time, to the construction of this setting. Bilinguality and exolinguality are not, in other terms, categories independent from the perception of the interacting persons; they are, on the contrary, the result of a social construction in and through the interaction. One might say that the interlocutors are, to a certain degree, free to set the parameters in the co-ordinate systems defined by the two axes mentioned at the beginning.

This is of course not a new idea as such. In cultural studies, the conception of monolithical 'Cultures' was replaced long ago by a more dynamic and constructivist one. Cultures are thus conceived as sets of norms and behaviours that are constructed and deconstructed in interaction with 'relevant others'. Our claim is that bilinguality is not an objective concept, but rather a part of a set of socially constructed norms of behaviours – and that the same holds true for monolinguality! If translinguistic markers are perceived as violations of prescriptive linguistic norms and generate social proscription in many language communities, it is because of the (culturally constructed) stereotype that monolingualism is 'natural' and plurilingualism resulted from the confusion of tongues by God and weighs on mankind like a divine curse since the construction of the tower of Babel (Genesis 11, 6–7). This idea has not only become the underlying principle of a real monolingual ideology; most linguistic theories are built upon the same premises. One of the major tasks of linguistics of plurilingualism will be to challenge this view (Lüdi, to appear).

Note
1. Some of the arguments presented here were part of our contribution to the *Symposium on code-switching in bilingual studies: Theory, significance and perspectives* organised by the European Science Foundation in Barcelona 21–23 March 1991, published in French in the Proceedings (Lüdi, 1991b).

References
Araujo Carreira, M.H. (1990) *Alternance et mélange de langues (portugais-français) chez des adolescents portugais scolarisés en France*. Paper presented at the 9th AILA conference, Thessaloniki-Halkidiki (Greece), 15–21 April 1990.
Auer, P. (ed.) (1998) *Code-switching in Conversation*. London: Routledge.
Bloomfield, L. (1933) *Language*. New York: H. Holt.

Bourdieu, P. (1982) *Ce que parler veut dire. L'économie des échanges linguistiques.* Paris: Fayard.
Broeder, P. *et al.* (eds) (1988) Processes in the developing lexicon. *Final Report of the ESF Additional Activity 'Second Language Acquisition by Adult Immigrants',* Volume III. Strasbourg/Tilburg/Göteborg: European Science Foundation.
Dewaele, J.-M. (1998) Lexical inventions: French L2 versus L3. *Applied Linguistics* 19 (4), 471–90.
Dewaele, J.-M. (2001) Activation or inhibition? The interaction of L1, L2 and L3 on the language mode continuum. In U. Jessner, B. Hufeisen and J. Cenoz (eds) *Cross-linguistic Influence in Third Language Acquisition: Psycholinguistic Perspectives* (pp. 69–89). Clevedon: Multilingual Matters.
Ducrot, O. and Todorov, T. (1972) *Dictionnaire encyclopédique des sciences du language.* Paris: Seuil.
Faerch, C. and Kasper, G. (1983a) Plans and strategies in foreign language communication. In C. Faerch and G. Kasper (eds) *Strategies in Interlanguage Communication* (pp. 20–60). London/New York: Longman.
Faerch, C. and Kasper, G. (1983b) On identifying communication strategies in interlanguage production. In C. Faerch and G. Kasper (eds) *Strategies in Interlanguage Communication* (pp. 210–38). London/New York.
Grosjean, F. (1985) The bilingual as a competent but specific speaker-hearer. *Journal of Multilingual and Multicultural Development* 6, 467–77.
Grosjean, F. (2001) The bilingual's language modes. In J.L. Nicol (ed.) *Language Processing in the Bilingual* (pp. 1–25). Oxford: Blackwell.
Gumperz, J. (1967) On the linguistic markers of bilingual communication. *Journal of Social Issues* 23, 48–57.
Gumperz, J. (1982) *Discourse Strategies.* Cambridge: Cambridge University Press.
Jake, J. (1998) Constructing interlanguage: Building a composite matrix language. *Linguistics* 36, 333–82.
Jake, J. and Myers Scotton, C. (1997) Codeswitching and compromise strategies: Implications for lexical structure. *The International Journal of Bilingualism* 1, 25–39.
Levelt, W.J.M. (1989) *Speaking. From Intention to Articulation.* Cambridge: MIT Press.
Lüdi, G. (1987) Les marques transcodiques: regards nouveaux sur le bilinguisme. In G. Lüdi (ed.) *Devenir bilingue – parler bilingue* (pp. 1–21). Tübingen: Niemeyer.
Lüdi, G. (1991a) Construire ensemble les mots pour le dire. A propos de l'origine discursive des connaissances lexicales. In E. Gülich *et al.* (eds) *Linguistische Interaktionsanalysen. Beiträge zum 20. Romanistentag 1987* (pp. 193–224). Tübingen: Niemeyer.
Lüdi, G. (1991b) Les apprenants d'une L2 code-switchent-ils et, si oui, comment?. In *Papers for the Symposium on code-switching in bilingual studies: Theory, significance and perspectives. Barcelona, 21–23 March 1991* (pp. 47–71). Strasbourg: European Science Foundation.
Lüdi, G. (1993) Statuts et fonctions des marques transcodiques en conversation exolingue. In G. Hilty (ed.) *Actes du XXe Congrès International de Linguistique et Philologie Romane* (t. III, pp. 123–36). Tübingen: Narr.
Lüdi, G. (1996) 30. Mehrsprachigkeit. In H. Goebl *et al.* (eds) *Kontaktlinguistik. Ein internationales Handbuch zeitgenössischer Forschung* (Vol. 1, pp. 320–7). Berlin: Walter de Gruyter.

Lüdi, G. (1997) Beobachtungen zur Wortbildungskompetenz fortgeschrittener Französischlerner. In G. Holtus, J. Kramer and W. Schweickard (eds) *Italica et Romanica. Festschrift für Max Pfister zum 65. Geburtstag* (pp. 159–72). Tübingen: Niemeyer.

Lüdi, G. (to appear) Consequences of the investigation of translinguistic markers for linguistic theory. In J. van Thije, Jan (ed.).

Lüdi, G. and Py, B. (2002) *Etre bilingue*. Berne, Francfort -s. Main, New York: Lang.

Myers-Scotton, C. ([1993] 1997) *Duelling Languages: Grammatical Structure in Codeswitching*. Oxford: Oxford University (1. ed. 1993; Paperback edition 1997 with new 'Afterword').

Myers-Scotton, C. (1993) *Social Motivations for Codeswitching. Evidence from Africa*. Oxford: Oxford University Press.

Myers-Scotton, C. and Jake, J. (1995) Matching lemmas in bilingual competence and performance model: Evidence from intrasentential code switching. *Linguistics* 33, 98–124.

Poplack, S. and Sankoff, D. (1984) Borrowing: The synchrony of integration. *Linguistics* 22, 99–135.

Pottier, B. (1992) *Sémantique générale*. Paris: Presses Universitaires de France.

Romaine, S. ([1989] 1995) *Bilingualism*. Oxford: Blackwell.

Sankoff, D. and Poplack, S. (1979) A formal grammar for code-switching. *Papers in Linguistics* 14: 3–46.

Schegloff, E.A. (1982) Discourse as an interactional achievement: Some uses of < uh huh > and other things that come between sentences. In D. Tannen (ed.) *Analysing Discourse: Text and Talk* (pp. 71–93). Washington, DC: Georgetown University Press.

Schütz, A. (1967 [1962]) *Collected papers I: The problem of social reality*. The Hague: Nijhoff.

Siguán, M. (1987) Code switching and code mixing in the bilingual speaker: A cognitive approach. In G. Lüdi (ed.) *Devenir bilingue – parler bilingue* (pp. 211–24). Tübingen: Niemeyer.

Slobin, D. (1973) Cognitive prerequisites for the development of grammar. In C. Ferguson and D. Slobin (eds) *Studies of Child Language Development* (pp. 175–208). New York: Holt, Rinehart and Winston.

Slobin, D. (1991) Learning to think for speaking; native language, cognition, and rhetorical style. *Pragmatics* 1 (1), 7–25.

Tarone, E. (1983) Some thoughts on the notion of 'communication strategy'. In C. Faerch and G. Kasper (eds) *Strategies in Interlanguage Communication* (pp. 61–74). London/New York: Longman.

Vasseur, M.-Th. (1990) Bilinguisme, acquisition de langues étrangères et données intuitionnelles: les autoconfrontations dans le programme ESF sur l'acquisition d'une L2 par des adultes migrants. In *ESF Network on Code-Switching and Language Contact: Papers for the Workshop on Concepts, Methodology and Data. Basel, 12–13 January 1990* (pp. 171–88). Strasbourg: European Science Foundation.

Wode, H. (1990) But Grandpa always goes like this . . . or: The ontogeny of code-switching. In *ESF Network on Code-Switching and Language Contact: Papers for the Workshop on Impact and Consequences: Broader Considerations. Brussels, 22–24 November 1990* (pp. 17–50). Strasbourg: European Science Foundation.

Chapter 11

Code-switching: Evidence of Both Flexibility and Rigidity in Language

CAROL MYERS-SCOTTON

Introduction

The goal of this paper is to use code-switching data to make an argument about the nature of language in a general sense. Specifically, I argue that code-switching (CS) provides evidence regarding both the flexibility and inflexibility of language. The argument is presented within the framework of the Matrix Language Frame (MLF) model (Myers-Scotton, 1993; [1997]) and an extended version that can apply to CS data showing convergence (Myers-Scotton, 1998; Myers-Scotton, 2002). Data supporting the argument come from both 'classic CS' and 'composite CS'. Classic CS is switching between two (or more) participating languages/varieties when speakers have strong enough proficiency in one of the languages to make it the sole source of the morphosyntactic frame that structures the unit of analysis, the bilingual CP (a clause that is the projection of Complementiser). The frame itself is called the Matrix Language and one can also refer to the source variety as the Matrix Language as well, although the Matrix Language as the frame in the bilingual CP involves only well-formedness conditions for morphosyntax. Speakers need not have a high level of proficiency in the other participating variety, called the Embedded Language. However, they must be proficient enough to provide singly occurring content morphemes as well-formed entries in a Matrix Language frame. If they attempt to realise larger constituents in the Embedded Language within the overall bilingual CP, they must have greater proficiency. Such constituents, called Embedded Language islands in the MLF model, must be well-formed in the Embedded Language and show internal structural dependency relations.

Composite CS is similar to classic CS in that they both naturally include surface-level morphemes from more than one variety. However, it contrasts with classic CS in an important way: under composite CS the source of abstract features of the morphosyntactic frame is more than one variety, resulting in a composite Matrix Language.

Compare (1) and (2). In [1], note that Swahili supplies the system morphemes (functional elements) in the mixed constituent, even though there is an Embedded Language island in English (*all the clothing*). In the mixed constituent, the English verb (*wash*) is inflected with Swahili morphemes. It is clear that Swahili is the single source of the grammatical frame. The example comes from Nairobi, Kenya. Example [2] comes from a second generation Croatian living in Australia. Here, even though Croatian is the source of all the system morphemes, there is evidence that English also contributes abstract structure to the frame.

[1] Ni-me-maliz-a   ku-tengenz-a vitanda
     1S-PERF-finish-FV   INF-fix-FV   cl.8/PL-bed
     ni-ka-<u>wash all the clothing . . .</u>
     1S-CONSEC-wash all the clothing . . .
     'I have finished fixing [making] [the] beds and I have washed all the
     clothing . . . '
     (Swahili/English CS Myers-Scotton, 1993, 1997: 80)

[2a] . . . to je možda najbolje   što   sam   ja
     that is perhaps bestNEUT/S/NOM COMP/NOM   be/1s   I
     što   ja   <u>rememba-Ø</u>   ya
     COMP/NOM   I   remember
     [2b]   Homeland Croatian:
     . . . to je možda   najbolje   što   sam   (ja)
     that is perhaps bestNEUT/S/NOM   COMP/NOM   be/1s   I
     (doživio) čega   se   sjećam
     experience/3S/M/PAST PART   COMP/GEN   REFL/ACC   remember/1S/PRES
     ' . . . that is perhaps the best thing that I have, that I remember . . . ya'
     (Croatian/English CS Hlavac, 2000: 58).

Example [2] illustrates composite CS because it both shows CS (the English verb *remember* is part of the CP) and a grammatical frame incorporating English abstract structure in various ways. First, Croatian is a pro-drop language, meaning that self-standing subject pronouns are marked and generally only used for emphasis. Yet, in [2a] *ja* 'I' occurs. Second, English *remember* is a transitive verb with the Experiencer in subject position and the Theme in object position. This is the syntactic structure of [2a]. However, in Croatian, the equivalent for *remember* (*sjećati se*) calls for a reflexive in object position while the Theme appears as a genitive object, with genitive (marked on the complementiser *čega*). Instead of *čega*, the speaker produced *što* in the nominative case and there is no reflexive.

In [2], the result is that a composite Matrix Language structures the frame. A supporting model of the MLF model, the Abstract Level model, offers an explanation for how such composite structures come about. This model is based on discussions about abstract grammatical structure of such researchers as Jackendoff (1990), Rappaport and Levin (1988) and Talmy (1985). Taken together, they imply several levels of structure. In their conceptualisation of these levels, Myers-Scotton and Jake (1995) refer to three levels: the level of lexical-conceptual structure (largely semantics and pragmatics), the level of predicate-argument structure (verbs and their relations to arguments in a CP), and the level of morphological realisation patterns (the surface realisations satisfying the well-formedness conditions of a specific variety).

They bring an innovation to earlier discussions in arguing that these levels can be split. The levels 'exist' in lemmas, abstract entries in the mental lexicon underlying morphemes. Because they can be split, levels from one lemma can be combined with levels in another lemma *from another language* in bilingual speech.

This splitting and recombining is the mechanism underlying a composite Matrix Language in composite CS. It also is involved in simple convergence (i.e. all the surface morphemes come from one variety, but part of the abstract structure comes from another variety). Positing this mechanism offers an explanation for some of the structures found in composite CS that are excellent examples of the flexibility inherent in language in general.

This paper is organised as follows. In the next section, I discuss examples from both classic CS and composite CS that give evidence of the flexibility in the structure of language. I then present examples that show areas of inflexibility; they come largely from classic CS. Concluding remarks follow.

Flexibility in Bilingual Speech

What is possible in classic CS

Even though the languages involved in classic CS may be typologically very different, there are few restrictions on the ways in which the two languages may be combined within a single mixed constituent – as long as the morphosyntactic frame consistently comes from only one participating language. The MLF model captures these generalisations in the Morpheme Order Principle and the System Morpheme Principle. That is, morphemes order and all the system morphemes that have relations external to their heads (certain inflections and certain function words) must come from the Matrix Language.

For example, consider Turkish/Norwegian classic CS (Türker, 2000). Turkish is a verb-final language that has postpositions and a rich system of case. Turkologists generally agree that it has a rather rigid SOV order, although other orders occur. In contrast, Norwegian is an SVO language that uses prepositions. In contrast with Turkish, which has no gender, both Norwegian articles and adjectives are inflected for gender. However, Norwegian has only remnants of the case system of Old Norse.

Yet, second generation Turks living in Norway – for whom Norwegian is becoming their dominant language – have no trouble realising most types of Norwegian morphemes in Turkish frames. For example, note how Norwegian nouns receive case marking in [3] and [4]. The Turkish ablative case suffix, indicating directionality ('from') has been attached to a Norwegian content word in [3] (*fylk-den*). And in [4] ablative is marked on the Norwegian noun *Stabekk* and dative case is marked on two Norwegian nouns (*centrum* and *forelesning*). Note that in both sentences, the verb-final order of Turkish.

[3] On-yedi fylk-den   gel-di-k
    Ten-seven administrative region-ABL come-PAST-1PL
        'We come [came] from seventeen administrative regions.'
        (Turkish/Norwegian CS Türker, 2000; 68)
[4] Stabekk-ten   çik-tiğ-im-da e:
    stabekk-ABL   get out-OPART-1sg-LOC hmm
    sentrum-a   gel-iyor-um   o-ra-da-ki
    centre-DAT   come-PROG-1sg,   that-DER-LOC-DER
    forelesning-ler-e gruppearbeid-e gir-mek
    lecture-pl-DAT   groupwork-DAT   enter-INF
    için.
    for/in order to
    'After leaving Stabekk – hmm – I come to the city centre to attend the lectures and group studies.'
    (Turkish/Norwegian CS Türker, 2000: 69).

CS involving another language that has postpositions, Hungarian, with English as the Embedded Language, shows that the incongruity between the prepositions of English and Hungarian is also easily resolved. With Hungarian as the Matrix Language, its patterns of morpheme configurations prevail. See example [5]

[5] ... itt a különb-öz-ö   dorm-(o)k-ba ...
    here DET various   dorm-PL-LOC
    (Talking about break-ins at dormitories on a university campus)

' . . . here in various dorms . . . '
(Hungarian/English CS Nagy, 1994: 21).

Classic CS is quite common in a number of sub-Saharan communities where a Bantu language is the first language of speakers and typically the Matrix Language of bilingual CPs. When they engage in CS with English as the Embedded Language, there is also an incongruity between the languages regarding the encoding of locational information. However, in this case, it is not a matter of prepositions vs. postpositions. Rather, Bantu languages encode locations as nouns. There are three noun classes for different types of references to locations. Still, even though the mismatch of features is relatively great between the English system of prepositional phrases (PP) and the Bantu system of locational noun phrases (NP), the conflict is simply resolved again in favour of the Matrix Language. In example [6a] Chicheŵa, the major language of Malaŵi, is the Matrix Language. Class 18 (with the noun class prefix *ku-*) encodes locations that are indicated with no specificity; thus, the city of Lilongwe is treated as a location, not an entity. Example [6b] shows classic CS involving Chicheŵa as the Matrix Language and English as the Embedded Language. The singly occurring English noun *folder* is treated as a location. Because it receives the noun class prefix of Class 17, the class for encoding 'withiness', *folder* is treated as an enclosed space.

[6a] Ku-Lilongwe, ndi-ka-kahla   ma-<u>week-s</u> a-wiri.
     CL.18-Lilongwe,   1S-FUT-stay-FV cl.6/PL-week-PL cl.6/PL-two
     'I will stay to [in] Lilongwe for two weeks.'
     (Chicheŵa/English CS Simango corpus 1995 (Myers-Scotton, 1993;
     [1997]: 190)
[6b] A-<u>mummy</u>, Justin Lewis a-na-li-be kalikonse mu-<u>folder</u> y-ake.
     HON-mummy   3S-PST-COP-without anything in folder   CL.9-POSS
     'Mummy, Justin Lewis did not have anything in his folder.'
     (Chicheŵa/English CS Simango corpus 1995).

Quite a different type of flexibility is shown in CS data sets involving NPs with Arabic as the Matrix Language. In Arabic, a set of demonstratives must be followed by a second element under DET, a definite article. However, in CS data when French is the Embedded Language, this second element can come from French, as in example [7] from Moroccan Arabic/French CS. That is, a French DET + N (*le feu rouge*) is part of the larger NP that includes the Arabic demonstrative (*dak le feu rouge* literally 'that the fire red'). From the point of view of the Matrix Language Frame model, the French NP constituent (within a larger PP constituent in the case of [7]) is termed an internal Embedded Language island. Such islands are identical

to other Embedded Language islands in that they must be well-formed in
the Embedded Language and show structural dependency relations, but
they are different in that they are part of a larger constituent headed by a
Matrix Language morpheme. This larger constituent is part of a still larger
constituent, the bilingual CP.

[7] ... hda <u>le dix-septième étage</u>   f dak   <u>le feu rouge</u> ...
       near DETseventeenth floor   at DEM ART fire red ...
       ' ... near the seventeenth story [building] at that the red light ... '
       (Moroccan Arabic, French Bentahila and Davies, 1992: 450)

In general, in mixed constituents within classic CS, it is only Embedded
Language content morphemes (e.g. nouns and verbs) that are realised in a
Matrix Language frame. As content morphemes, they satisfy the speaker's
intentions because they carry conceptual information. However, in the case
of examples such as [7], it is the requirements of the Matrix Language
morphosyntactic frame that are being satisfied by the presence of the
French form. True, under the 4-M model, a new model that seeks to explain
many morpheme distributions across diverse data, including CS data (cf.
Myers-Scotton & Jake, 2000a, 2000b), the French definite article is an early
system morpheme. Early system morphemes are different from structurally assigned system morphemes. They pattern with content morphemes
as conceptually activated and therefore they also to some degree – admit-
tedly a lesser degree than content morphemes-satisfy speaker's intentions.
Further, there is a strong link between content morphemes and the early
system morphemes that they call (i.e. in this case, the link is between DET
and N, with DET called in order to provide specificity). But here, the main
function of *le* in *le feu rouge* cannot be to add content (i.e. specificity) –
because the Arabic demonstrative already fulfils that function. Instead, the
main purpose of *le* is to meet the structural requirements of the demonstrative. That structural requirements can be met cross-linguistically is an
excellent example of linguistic flexiblity.

   Example [8] illustrates the more expected outcome: an Arabic definite
article, not an Embedded Language one, satisfies the requirements of the
Arabic demonstrative for a second element under DET. Both Arabic elements under DET modify the Dutch noun *smurf-en* 'smurfs'. This example
comes from Moroccan Arabic/Dutch CS.

[8]   ... nešri   dik   s-<u>smurf-en voor de auto</u>
       ... I buy   those   the-smurf-pl for the car
       'I buy   those the-smurfs for the car.'
       (Moroccan Arabic/ Dutch CS Nortier, 1990: 216).

Flexibility in Composite CS

As indicated above, composite CS differs from classic CS in that more than one language contributes to the specifications of the morphosyntactic frame. Example [9] shows the influence of English at the abstract level of lexical-conceptual structure, even though Hungarian is clearly the main source of the frame. Splitting and recombining of lexical-conceptual structure involves replacing the notion of a place as a 'surface' (as it would be conceived in monolingual Hungarian) with the notion of a place as a 'container'. The example comes from the speech of a young girl living in the United States. Even though Hungarian is her first language, she is increasingly shifting to English as her dominant language under the influence of the culture where she is now living.

Bolonyai analyses the example as showing 'the replacement of one of the spatial feature components integrated in a locative case by another [case]' (1999: 203). Instead of the sublative case *-ra* 'onto' (called for in Standard Hungarian), the illative case *-ba* 'into' is used. That is, instead of marking Goal and surface (with sublative case), the child marks Goal and container (with illative case). Bolonyai suggest that the classes (P.E., music, and art) are seen more as containers – as they would be in English – than as surfaces – as they would be in St. Hungarian.

[9] Hogy   megy-ünk   <u>P.E.</u>-be,   <u>music</u>-ba,   <u>art</u>-ba.
    that go-PRES/1PL P.E.-ILLAT/into   music-ILLAT/into   art-ILLAT/into
    'That we are going to P.E., music, [and] art.'
    (Hungarian/English CS Bolonyai, 1999: 203)

Another type of flexibility regarding lexical-conceptual structure is shown in conversations of 10 native German speakers for whom German is beginning to lose its dominant language status (Fuller & Lehnert, 2000). At the time of data collection, they had lived in the United States for at least five years where they are permanent residents. Some speak mostly German at home (they have German spouses), and others reported having many German friends. However, 9 out of the 10 reported having primarily English-speaking contacts outside the home. What is of interest in their use of articles in morphosyntactic frames that are mainly structured by German. Although both English and German have similar noun phrase structures, constraints on articles differ in two ways. First, personal status nouns (e.g. occupation) require articles in English, but not in German. Second, German requires articles in some NPs where they are not used in English (proper nouns, street names, and certain plural nouns).

In the naturally occurring data for these speakers, there were 37 contexts providing an appropriate slot to use an article in either English or in

German, but not in both. In 17 instances (46%) they followed an English pattern for overtly realising definiteness/indefiniteness or not with an English noun, even though the rest of the morphosyntax of the bilingual CP comes from German. For example, in [10] the prepositional phrase *für defense* has no article; however it would in monolingual German (*für die Verteidigung*). Out of the 17 NPs following an English pattern, 16 showed nonuse of an article, as in [10].

[10]... und zwar anstatt die Afrika-Hilfe die wollen
    and (EMPH0 instead of the/FEMAfrica-aid the/FEM want/3PL
    das streichen, ich weiss gar nicht wieviel,
    that strike   I   know   at all   not how much
    eine Million,   oder ... und für <u>defense</u> geb-en, gel
    one/FEM million or and for defense give-INF you know
    'And instead of aid to Africa, they want to discontinue that, I don't know how much, a million, or ... and use it for defense, you know.'
    (Fuller & Lehnert, 2000: 416).

Example [11] is the one example in which an article is used with an English noun, with the use reflecting English structure although the morpheme comes from German.

[11]Wir   hab-en   ein-en   ge-habt der   ein <u>preacher</u> war ...
    1PL Have-3PL one-M/ACC PART-have who/M   ART preacher be/PAST/S
    'We had one who was a preacher ...'
    (Fuller & Lehnert, 2000: 417).

Fuller and Lehnert argue against simply describing such a pattern of article use as 'transfer' and no more. It is much more explanatory to posit that the specifications of the English noun in these NPs regarding definiteness are combined with other levels of abstract structure from German to result in a composite structure for the DET + N combination. That is, for these speakers, German is no longer the sole source of morphosyntactic structure. In almost half of their utterances that include the possibility of DET + English N, the English noun determines whether a determiner will be indirectly elected to encode definiteness – even though the determiner is in German. That a noun in one language can control a determiner in another language shows a certain flexibility.

   Türker (2000: 174) reports similar examples of how certain collocations in Norwegian of N + V are realised in Turkish/Norwegian CS with a Norwegian noun, but then the Turkish verb that corresponds in its lexical-conceptual structure to the Norwegian collocation. (For example, the Turkish verb for 'spread' (*sür*) is used in one instance with the Norwegian noun *matpakke* 'lunch box' (as in the Norwegian collocation å smøre matpakke literally 'to spread a lunch box')). Again, this is an example of composite CS, but in this case the influence is not simply within an NP (as in the Fuller & Lehnert examples), but within a collocation involving a noun and a verb that are in different constituents from a syntactic point of view. Seemingly, the Norwegian collocation has input in selecting the Turkish verb; this input is at the level of lexical-conceptual structure.

Inflexibility in Bilingual Speech

Whether an Embedded Language verb can satisfy the Matrix Language frame and receive Matrix Language inflections for elements under INFL is an issue for some CS language pairs, pointing to an area of likely inflexibility in language. In many language pairs, Embedded Language verbs can be inflected with Matrix Language system morphemes. Example [1] comes from a Swahili/English corpus in which there are 91 tensed English verbs showing Swahili inflections. Similarly, Halmari (1997) gives many examples of English verbs inflected with Finnish system morphemes in her study of American Finnish.

However, when certain languages are the Matrix Language in classic CS, they disallow inflected Embedded Language verbs. These languages are a diverse set; many of them are verb-final languages (e.g. Japanese, Hindi, Turkish), but not all. For example, Chichewa, a Bantu language that is SVO, allows very few inflected Embedded Language verbs; instead, a 'do construction' (discussed below) is regularly employed.

One can argue that these languages show inflexibility in not allowing tensed Embedded Language verbs with Matrix Language inflections. However, at the same time they show fexibility by expressing the intended intentions in another way. They all employ a 'do construction'. This consists of the verb encoding *do* from the Matrix Language; this verb receives all the necessary inflections to express intentions. This *do* verb is typically combined with a non-finite verb (the infinitive in the case of most language pairs) that receives no Matrix Language inflections. Example [13] is an example from a Turkish/Norwegian CS corpus and example [12] comes from Turkish/Dutch CS. Both employ the Turkish 'to do' verb *yap-mak*.

[12] Diskuter-e   yap-iyo-z   tabi   ki.
     discuss-INF do-PROG-1pl   of course   CONJ
     'We (do) discuss (things), of course.'
     (Turkish/Norwegian CS Türker, 2000: 106)
[13] Ben   sen-in-ki-si-ni   <u>len-en</u>
     I you-GEN-DER-POSS-ACC borrow-INF
     yap-mak   iste-di-m   <u>toen had ik ze al</u>.
     do-INF want-PAST-1sg then had I   them   already

'I wanted to borrow yours, but then I had them already.'
(Turkish/Dutch, Backus, 1996: 238 cited in Türker, 2000:106).

Example [14] comes from Chicheŵa. The 'do' verb is -*chita*.

[14] Ngoni, ku-khomo   w-a-chit-a   <u>check</u>   eti.
    Ngoni, CL.18-door 2S-PERF-do-FV check   right?
    'Ngoni, you have checked the door, right?'
    Note: FV = final vowel (indicative mood)
    (Chicheŵa/English CS Simango corpus 1995)

Researchers can point out that in certain languages this 'do construction' is not used simply in CS; traditionally, speakers have used this construction to integrate borrowed verbs into the recipient language. However, citing the tradition of employing the 'do construction' does not explain why alien verbs cannot be inflected. Clearly, incongruence between the requirements of the Matrix Language frame that verbs must satisfy and the abstract nature of alien (Embedded Language) verbs is at the heart of the explanation. That is, in some way, the Embedded Language verb does not meet some requirements of the Matrix Language frame. Jake and Myers-Scotton, 1997 suggest that this incongruence involves inflections under INFL, but they offer no specifics.

Myers-Scotton and Jake motivate their suggestion about 'do verb' constructions with their analysis of another outcome in Palestinian Arabic/ English CS. They report findings from an Arabic/English CS corpus that shows very few English (the Embedded Language) verbs with Arabic inflections. Instead, this corpus shows a large number of Embedded Language islands that are entire INFL phrases (i.e. phrases including a tensed verb).

Overall, 86 out of the 109 English verbs in the corpus they studied occur in IP Embedded Language islands, many more than could have occurred by chance. There are only five instances of English verbs occurring with Arabic inflections and three of these involve the same verb and the same speaker.

Example [14] from this corpus shows two such IP Embedded Language island, each introduced by a complementiser or another element in Comp position of the overall CP.

[14] ʔana   ʕindi   <u>job security</u> wa   ma   feeš   <u>pressure</u> xaaliaṣ
    I   with/1S job security   and NEG there is/NEF pressure at all
    Kawnik   elṭwa_eeda [CP hina   [<u>you feel like a queen</u> IP] CP]
    GER/be/2F   the-one   here you feel like a queen
    wa ma   feeš   <u>competition</u>
    and NEF there.is/NEF   competition

huma butudfaʔooli   kul haga [$_{CP}$ *liʔanuhum* [$_{IP}$ they can afford it $_{IP}$] $_{CP}$]
they   3P/Imp/pay/1S/Obj all thing   because/3P   they can afford it
'I have job security and there is no pressure at all. Being the only one,
here you feel like a queen and there [is] no competition. They pay for
everything because they can afford it.'
(Palestinian Arabic/English Okasha, 1999 cited in Myers-Scotton &
Jake, 2001: 103)

Jake and Myers-Scotton (1997) argue that the reason for the large
number of such islands in this corpus is the incongruity between the Arabic
frame and the nature of English verbs. They point out that when other languages, such as French, are the Embedded Language in CS with Arabic as
the Matrix Language, French verbs do easily appear in Arabic frames with
Arabic inflections (D. Caubet personal communication).

What is the problem with English verbs? Jake and Myers-Scotton argue
that at the abstract level of the mental lexicon, Arabic and English verbs are
different. In Arabic, a verb, even at this abstract level, does not have an
entry for an uninflected verb stem; rather, it has two entries, each of which
is specified for tense or aspect (imperfect or perfect). In contrast, English
has a single enty for a verb stem, which is not specified for tense or aspect.
In English, tense and aspect are structurally assigned features that only
become salient at the level of the formulator when larger constituents are
assembled. Because the English verb counterpart of an Arabic verb does
not meet the specifications of an Arabic frame at the time content morphemes are being accessed in the frame; that is, an English verb cannot be
realised in a mixed constituent for which the specifications call for a verb
with tense/aspect already specified. They argue that an IP in English must
be selected if an English verb is to occur, because then tense/aspect can be
structurally assigned when such a constituent is assembled (cf. Jake &
Myers-Scotton, 1997: 33).

This scenario is an explanation of why the compromise strategy of large
Embedded Language islands is overwhelmingly the main method for introducing the intentions that English verbs encode into Arabic/English CS.
Note that there is no evidence of a composite Matrix Language in this
corpus; rather, Arabic is the sole source of the morphosyntactic frame. Similarly, the 'do construction' is a compromise strategy for classic CS (i.e. for
corpora in which one participating language is the source of the frame). At
this point in these corpora, there is no splitting and combining of abstract
structure across languages that could result in more flexible standards that
an inflected verb must meet.

A moment's reflection indicates that the flexibility reported in the
second section largely involves the abstract level of lexical-conceptual

structure. This level is conceptually activated, meaning it is realised by expressing a speaker's intentions, not so much in regard to inter-relations with other levels of abstract structure or with how larger constituents are assembled. In contrast, in some languages, elements under INFL are structurally assigned in the sense that their realisation depends on information that is not available until larger constituents are assembled at the level of the Formulator. If the language pairs participating in CS include a language in which elements under INFL are accessed late and a language in which they are accessed early, verb inflection cross-linguistically is ruled out. That is, if these elements are conceptually activated at the level of the mental lexicon in the source language of the Matrix Language frame, then INFL elements that are structurally assigned in the Embedded Language may be accessed 'too late' to be available for incorporation into the frame as tensed verbs with Matrix Language inflections.

Conclusion

This contribution describes and attempts to explain diverse examples of structures showing some flexibility in meeting the well-formedness conditions of the Matrix Language that provides the morphosyntactic frame for the bilingual CP of CS data sets. Some examples where inflexibility prevails are also discussed.

In classic CS, there are many areas of incongruence between participating languages in CS that still permit Embedded Language elements to appear in Matrix Language frames – as long as the basic requirements of the frame are preserved. But note that this simply means that incongruence between the participating languages is resolved in favour of the Matrix Language.

However, when socio-political conditions encourage speakers to shift from one language to another, then actual modifications of the structural requirements coming from the source language of the Matrix Language frame begin to occur; these modifications are in favour of structures from the former Embedded Language. What happens is that a single source language no longer entirely controls the morphosyntactic frame of the bilingual CP in CS. Instead, features of abstract grammatical structure from the former Embedded Language can combine with features from the original source language. The result is called composite CS because it is a composite Matrix Language that structures CS utterances. The details of such a composite show a good deal of cross-linguistic flexibility; some examples have been cited here.

Even so, inflexibility characterises some aspects of classic CS corpora. Tensed verbs from the Embedded Language cannot be accommodated in the Matrix Language frame in some language pairs. For these pairs, even though the frame readily allows Embedded Language nouns to receive Matrix Language nominal inflections, it does not allow Embedded Language verbs to receive Matrix Language verbal inflections. Two compromise strategies are invoked (in different language pairs); note they both preserve the Matrix Language frame. These are the 'do construction' and the large Embedded Language island (as large as an IP). Why such strategies are necessary when certain languages are the source of the Matrix Language remains unclear. However, this paper suggests that the answer lies with incongruity between the participating languages regarding the nature of elements under INFL. Cross-linguistically, these elements may be accessed at different points in language production. In some languages, they may be conceptually activated, but in others they may be structurally assigned only at a later point in production. The conflict across the language pairs involved in CS is resolved by accessing Embedded Language verbs only via compromise strategies.

In sum, in classic CS, Embedded Language elements are only realised in the Matrix Language frame when they do not violate frame requirements; it is they that must be flexible by being 'congruent enough'. In classic CS, the Matrix Language frame itself shows little or no flexibility.

Still, if sociolinguistic conditions favour a shift and some Embedded Language abstract structure becomes part of the frame, very different outcomes showing much flexibility (and variation) are possible. But language in general strives for uniformity and I suggest that the period of composite structures in bilingual CPs is short-lived. Of course, a gradual Matrix Language turnover (to the former Embedded Language) and a long-lived composite Matrix Language is possible; in fact, the composite Matrix Language may fossilise as a community's main language. However, such a gradual turnover (and subsequent fossilisation) seems to occur relatively rarely (although arrested shifts evident in some mixed languages are the remnants of gradual turnovers and composite Matrix Languages, cf. Myers-Scotton, 1998). Rather, more evidence favours a full-scale shift at some (early?) point in the composite. That is, if they are going to shift, speakers seem to shift rather abruptly to the former Embedded Language. They may retain some of the morphosyntax of the original source of the Matrix Language that is operative in the composite Matrix Language. But in their push for avoiding meaningful variation (i.e. virtual uniformity), they may also purge their language of such structures. With this monolingual uniformity comes a strong measure of inflexibility in grammatical structure. Still, as long as abstract grammatical structure can be split and recombined, some flexibility – and structural change – is possible.

References

Backus, A. (1996) *Two in One. Bilingual Speech of Turkish Immigrants in the Netherlands.* Tilburg, The Netherlands: Tilburg University Press.

Bentahila, A. and Davies, E. (1992) Code-switching and language dominance. In R. Harris (ed.) *Cognitive Processing in Bilinguals* (pp. 443–58). Amsterdam: Elsevier.

Bolonyai, A. (1999) The hidden dimensions of language contact: The case of Hungarian–English bilingual children. Unpublished PhD dissertation. Columbia SC: University of South Carolina Linguistics Program.

Fuller, J.M. and Lehnert, H. (2000) Noun phrase structure in German–English codeswitching: Variation in gender assignment and article use. *International Journal of Bilingualism* 4, 399–420.

Halmari, H. (1997) *Government and Codeswitching: Explaining American Finnish.* Amsterdam: Benjamins.

Hlavac, J. (2000) Croatian in Melbourne: lexicon, switching and morphosyntactic features in the speech of second-generational bilinguals. Unpublished PhD dissertation. Melbourne: Monash University Department of Linguistics.

Jackendoff, R. (1990) *Semantic Structures.* Cambridge, MA: MIT Press.

Jake, J.L. and Myers-Scotton, C. (1997) Codeswitching and compromise strategies: Implications for lexical structure. *International Journal of Bilingualism* 1, 25–39.

Myers-Scotton, C. (1993) *Duelling Languages: Grammatical Structure in Codeswitching.* Oxford: Clarendon Press.

Myers-Scotton, C. (1997) (2nd edn.) *Duelling Languages: Grammatical Structure in Codeswitching with a New Afterword.* Oxford: Oxford University Press.

Myers-Scotton, C. (1998) A way to dusty death: The Matrix Language turnover hypothesis. In L. Grenoble and L. Whaley (eds) *Endangered Languages* (pp. 289–316). Cambridge: Cambridge University Press.

Myers-Scotton, C. (2002) *Contact Linguistics: Bilingual Encounters and Grammatical Outcomes.* Oxford: Oxford University Press.

Myers-Scotton, C. and Jake, J.L. (1995) Matching lemmas in a bilingual language competence and production model: Evidence from intrasentential code switching. *Linguistics* 34, 981–1024.

Myers-Scotton, C. and Jake, J. (2000a) (eds) Special issue: Testing a model of morpheme classification. *International Journal of Bilingualism* 4, 1.

Myers-Scotton, C. and Jake, J. (2000b) Four types of morpheme: Evidence from aphasia, codeswitching and second language acquisition. *Linguistics* 38, 1053–1100.

Myers-Scotton, C. and Jake, J. (2001) Explaining aspects of codeswitching and their implications. In J. Nicol (ed.) *One Mind, Two Languages: Bilingual Language Processing* (pp. 84–116). Oxford: Blackwell.

Nagy, E. (1994) A study of borrowing and code-switching in the speech of Hungarians living in Columbia, South Carolina. Unpublished MA thesis. Columbia SC: University of South Carolina Linguistics Program.

Nortier, J. (1990) *Dutch-Moroccan Arabic Code Switching.* Dordrecht, Holland: Foris Publications.

Okasha, M. (1999) Unpublished Palestinian Arabic/English codeswitching data set.

Rappaport, M. and Levin, B. (1988) What to do with theta-roles. In W. Wilkins (ed.) *Syntax and Semantics, Thematic Relations* 21 (pp. 1–36). New York: Academic Press.

Simango, S.M. (1995) Unpublished Chicheŵa/English codeswitching data set.

Talmy, L. (1985) Lexicalization patterns: Semantic structure in lexical form. In T. Schopen (ed.) *Language Typology and Syntactic Description III* (pp. 51–149). New York: Cambridge University Press.

Türker, E. (2000) Turkish–Norwegian codeswitching, evidence from intermediate and second generation Turkish immigrants in Norway. Unpublished PhD dissertation. Oslo: University of Oslo Department of Linguistics.

Chapter 12

Rethinking Bilingual Acquisition

FRED GENESEE

Introduction

The study of bilingual acquisition has had a remarkably long history. The first scientific report of a bilingual child was published by Ronjat in 1913 and, of course, there was the longitudinal study by Werner Leopold of his two bilingual daughters that was published between 1939 and 1949. Relative to what is generally considered to be the beginnings of research on monolingual acquisition – that is, the work of Roger Brown in 1958, this represents an early start for the study of the simultaneous acquisition of two languages. Despite the early work of Ronjat and Leopold, further research remained sparse until the 1980s. During the intervening years, beginning in the 1950s, researchers focused on issues pertaining to bilingualism in general. The research conducted during this era made many valuable contributions to our understanding of the social patterning of bilingualism (including language spread and loss), the social psychological and cognitive consequences of bilingualism, and alternative conceptualisations of the diverse types of bilingualism. I am referring here to the classic works of Joshua Fishman, Wallace Lambert, William Mackey, and Uriel Weinreich. One of the first comprehensive textbooks of this work was published by Hugo Baetens Beardsmore in 1982. The work of these scholars, and others whom I have not been able to mention because of space limitations, were relevant to bilingual acquisition, the topic of this chapter, but in a relatively general and inferential way rather than directly.

Beginning in the late 1980s, there was an upsurge in theoretical and empirical attention devoted directly to bilingual acquisition (e.g. De Houwer, 1990; Deuchar & Quay, 2000; Hoffmann, 1991; Lanza, 1997; Meisel, 1986; Romaine, 1989). This surge in interest can be attributed to several factors. First, there is the recognition that contrary to earlier views, simultaneous acquisition of two, or more, languages is not uncommon. While we lack definitive statistics, it has been speculated that there are as many or even more children who grow up bilingual as monolingual (Tucker, 1998). Therefore, documentation of the facts of bilingual acquisition and the development of theories to explain these facts are worthy in their own right. Second, theories of language acquisition, which currently are based largely on monolingual children, must ultimately incorporate the 'facts' of bilingual acquisition if they are to be comprehensive. Much more research is needed to uncover these facts. Moreover, there is an emerging appreciation among language acquisition theorists that bilingual children provide unique test cases for important issues arising from general theories of acquisition. Slobin demonstrated the power of cross-linguistic research for our understanding of the mechanisms of acquisition and his work continues to be influential (Slobin, 1997). The study of simultaneous bilinguals pushes the power of cross-linguistic research further since bilingual children are their own controls on a number of variables (such as personality, age, cognitive ability, etc.) that can confound studies of monolingual children (see Nicoladis, 2001, and Paradis *et al.*, 2000, for examples). In short, studies of simultaneous bilingual acquisition can contribute significantly to the development of a general theory of language acquisition.

Research on infants acquiring two languages simultaneously can make a unique contribution to our understanding of the human language faculty and by extension the human mind because it permits us to examine the capacity of the mind to acquire and use more than one language. While most theories of language acquisition do not exclude the possibility of bilingual acquisition, nor do they address it explicitly or in detail – they are largely silent with respect to the acquisition of two languages simultaneously. The capacity of infants to acquire two or more linguistic systems, sometimes with radically different structural properties (e.g. English and Inuktitut, in Allen, 1996), at the same time in functionally compatible ways, has implications for our conceptualisation of the neuro-cognitive architecture of the human mind that underlies language acquisition in general. There are implications for our conceptualisation of mind and brain that are linked to bilingualism and bilingual acquisition that are only beginning to be explored.

Current work on bilingual acquisition is broad in scope and encompasses most facets of language development, including pre-verbal speech perception (Bosch & Sebastian-Gallés, in press), phonology (Deuchar & Quay, 2000; Paradis, 1996, 2000, 2001), early lexical development (Quay, 1995), syntax (see Genesee, 2001, for a review), and socio-pragmatic or communication skills (Comeau & Genesee, 2001; Genesee *et al.*, 1996; Lanza, 1997). This work extends our understanding of bilingual acquisition that began to emerge in the 1960s and 1970s by directly examining the processes and representational systems that underlie bilingual acquisition and the specific factors that influence them – for example, the role of dominance (Yip & Matthews, 2000), structural overlap in the participating grammars (e.g. Döpke, 2000), and parental input (e.g. Lanza, 1997; 2001).

This chapter charts the progress of recent research on bilingual acquisition by selectively addressing some prominent questions that have motivated work in the field, past and present. More specifically, I would like to review extant research that addresses the following questions:

(1) Is simultaneous acquisition of two languages normal?
(2) Are bilingual children initially monolingual?
(3) Is bilingual acquisition the same or different from monolingual acquisition?

Definitional Matters

Before proceeding, it is important to point out that research on bilingual acquisition encompasses a variety of different cases, including the acquisition of more than two languages; that is multilingual acquisition (see Mikes, 1990; and Quay, 2001, for example). It also includes the acquisition of signed as well as spoken languages (Petitto *et al.*, 2001; Richmond-Welty & Siple, 1999). This review will focus on the simultaneous acquisition of two spoken languages since the preponderance of empirical work has focused on such cases.

Is the simultaneous acquisition of two languages normal?

Research on bilingual children, whether focusing on acquisition directly or the consequences of bilingualism, has often been clouded by the expectation that early bilingualism is problematic and poses challenges for the developing child. The challenges facing children who grow up bilingual are often thought to be far reaching and largely detrimental. For example, in a review of early work relating bilingualism to personality formation, Diebold (1968) concluded that bilingualism leads to emotional maladjustment and, in particular, psychodynamic conflict (e.g. schizophrenia in the extreme case). Closer to the issue at hand, a number of researchers reported that bilingual children exhibited lower verbal intelligence and/or ability (Arsenian, 1945; Darcy, 1953; Macnamara, 1966).

The bilingual-acquisition-as-deficit view raises a number of important specific questions concerning the nature, pattern, and developmental rate of bilingual acquisition. In this section, I address the more general but fundamental issue of whether human infants who are exposed to two languages from the outset are indeed challenged. I seek to answer this question by asking a more controversial question, namely is bilingual acquisition normal. I have conceptualised the question in this form because I take the deficit view to mean that infants and children are biologically pre-disposed to acquire only one language and, thus, are initially unable or challenged to acquire two. The alternative view, the one that I believe the evidence supports, is that human infants possess the biological capacity to acquire two languages as normally as one. My argument in favour of the latter position draws on two bodies of research – one concerned with neo-natal and infant neuro-cognitive abilities and the other with general milestones in bilingual acquisition. In the absence of more complete empir-ical evidence on bilingual acquisition than is currently available, my arguments are inferential because they necessarily draw primarily on evi-dence from monolingual children.

The notion that bilingual acquisition is challenging presupposes that the neuro-cognitive abilities of neonates and infants are limited in ways that hamper their capacity to acquire two languages simultaneously. I would argue that the extant evidence does not support this view. Minimally, the infant must possess two critical capacities to acquire two languages simulta-neously – the ability to discriminate important language-related differences in the auditory input and the ability to remember such information. In the absence of these fundamental abilities, the infant cannot distinguish one language from another in the input and cannot remember linguistically rel-evant auditory information from the input. Memory for such information is critical for the construction of distinct language systems. Research during the last two decades indicates that infants possess these abilities and, moreover, that they are operational in the fetal stage (see Boysson-Bardies, 1999, for a review) and, thus, permit the processes that are essen-tial for bilingual acquisition to begin earlier than has previously been imagined.

Within 24 hours of birth, newborns prefer the voice of their mothers in contrast with that of another mother speaking to her baby (DeCasper & Fifer, 1980; Mehler *et al.*, 1978; see also Mehler *et al.*, 1988, for evidence con-cerning somewhat older infants). Preference for the mother's voice is not demonstrated if the voice samples are played backward suggesting that the infants' preference is tied to perception of dynamic features of lan-guage input and, more specifically, prosody. This is important since prosody is a likely cue to early discrimination of dual language input. Indeed, Mehler and his colleagues (1988) have shown that newborns can distinguish utterances in their native language from those in a foreign language; native language here refers to the language used by the parents and overheard by the infant pre- and post-natally. When the language samples were filtered so that only prosodic-cues remained, the infants continued to differentiate between the native and foreign language, again reinforcing the importance of prosody in the early discrimination of language samples. The infants' ability to distinguish a familiar, previously heard language from an unfamiliar, foreign language implies that they have formed a neural representation of the familiar language which then acts as a template against which other test languages (familiar or unfamiliar) can be compared. The ability to recognise a familiar language (or languages) also directs the child's attention to information relevant to the language to be acquired. Bosch and Sebastián-Gallés (2001) report that Spanish–Catalan bilingual infants can discriminate between their two native languages at 135 to 139 days of age and they do so at the same age that monolingual children discriminate between these same languages. In other words, the bilingual children were not delayed, or accelerated, in their discriminant capacities as a result of dual language exposure.

There is evidence that infants' impressive auditory discriminatory and memory capacities are based on *in utero* language experiences. More specifically, DeCasper & Spence (1986) have found that fetuses who were read prose passages by their mothers on a daily basis six weeks prior to birth demonstrated a preference for these passages after birth in comparison to novel passages. The infants demonstrated a preference for the previously heard passages even when they were read by another female, indicating that it was not simply familiarity with the mother's voice but rather the general acoustic properties of the speech signal that the infants were responding to. Similarly, monitoring changes in heart rates, these researchers also noted that fetuses in the 37th week of gestation distinguished between familiar and novel poems following previous exposure to the familiar poems.

Additional evidence of newborns' innate preparedness for language learning comes from extensive investigation of monolingual children's perception of segmental features of human language. It has long been known that adults perceive consonantal contrasts that are phonemic in their native language categorically – that is to say, acoustic variations within a certain range of each consonant are all perceived as the same phoneme (e.g. /la/ vs /ra/). It is believed that categorical perception of the consonantal segments that make up human languages reflects the hardwiring of the auditory system and its sensitivity to specific acoustic ranges. Precursors to categorical perception have been demonstrated in pre-verbal infants. Of particular relevance to the issue of bilingual acquisition, during the first 6 to 8 months of life, pre-verbal infants can discriminate most of the phonetic contrasts that all languages make use of (Jusczyk, 1985) whether these contrasts are in the input the infant is exposed to or not. By the tenth month, infants continue to discriminate contrasts that occur in the input, but no longer discriminate non-native contrasts.

Taken together these findings on speech/language perception in mono-linguals are important because they indicate that new-born infants are innately prepared to discriminate language-related signals, both segmental and supra-segmental, and that these discriminatory abilities focus the child's attention on acoustic information in the input that is relevant to the development of their native language. Moreover, experiences with the native language begin to shape the baby's perceptual abilities very early in development – *in utero* in the case of language discrimination and shortly after birth in the case of phoneme discrimination. Timing is important since, arguably, for the human mind to analyse and make sense of dual language input, learning must begin early. To quote Boysson-Bardies, 'We now know that not only is the brain of the baby not empty, but in a certain sense it is fuller than that of the most brilliant scientist' (1999: 13). Of relevance to the issue of bilingual acquisition, there is nothing in our current understanding of monolingual acquisition that would lead one to believe that bilingual acquisition is inherently problematic or unnatural.

To reinforce the argument that the human infant is as well prepared for dual language learning as single language learning, I would like to review our state of knowledge with respect to critical milestones in bilingual acquisition. For this purpose, I have summarised the results of studies on children acquiring two languages simultaneously that make reference to their rate or age of development with respect to three domains of language: phonology, lexicon, and syntax. In some cases, monolingual norms or comparison data are provided; in other cases, reference is made to monolingual data published by others. Both types of 'evidence' are included and each is identified. When monolingual results are provided, they often take the form of age ranges since, as is well known, there are considerable individual differences among monolingual children in all aspects of language development. There is variation among these reports with respect to the precise features that were examined, even in a given language domain. No attempt is made here to take this variation into account, although a simple description of the focus of each study is provided.

I have excluded studies from this summary that make qualitative comparisons between monolinguals and bilinguals – that is, studies that focus on the pattern or nature of changes in language with development. Issues concerning qualitative differences and similarities between bilingual versus monolingual acquisition are addressed in the next section.

In comparing bilingual development to monolingual development, I do not wish to argue that this is necessarily the most or only appropriate basis for judging whether bilingual development is 'normal'. Nor do I wish to imply that the data, monolingual or bilingual, that are provided in the reports I have summarised are adequate for making these comparisons. To

Table 12.1 Summary of monolingual–bilingual age comparisons (July 2001)

Author(s)	Monolingual milestones	Lexicon[1]	Syntax[1]	Phonology[1]	Target languages; sample sizes; age of bilingual children	Conclusions
Bosch & Sebastián-Gallés (2001)	Mono control groups			Preferential listening	Sp+Catalan; n = 28; 135–139 days old	Comparable to monolingual data
Goodz, Legaré & Bilodeau (1990)	Mono control groups	1st words & vocab dev.			Fr+Eng; n = 12; 5–44 mths old	Within monolingual range
Oller, Eilers, Urbano & Cobo-Lewis (1997)	Mono control groups			Phonological analyses	Sp+Eng; n = 17; 0.4–1.6 years old	Comparable to monolingual controls
Oller, Eilers, Urbano, & Cobo-Lewis (1997)	Monolingual data			Onset of babbling, vowel ratio	Sp+Eng; 44 mono E; 29 bil; smaller n's for longitudinal analyses	Comparable to monolingual English controls
Padilla & Liebman (1975)	Other pub. data		Brown's stages, MLU		Sp+Eng; n = 3; 1.5–2.2 yrs old	Comparable to monolingual data
Paradis (2001)	Mono control controls			Word truncation task	Fr+Eng; n = 17; 23–35 mths old	Bil's. comparable to monolingual controls
Paradis & Genesee (1996)	Other pub. data		Linguistic analyses		Fr+Eng; n = 3; 2;0–3;0 yrs old	Within monolingual range
Paradis, Crago, Genesee, Rice (in press).	Mono normal and SLI controls		Tense and non-tense morphemes		8 Bil SLI; 21 Mono E SLI; 40 norm. E mono; 10 F. mono SLI; 20 norm mono F.	Bil SLI children comparable to mono E. and F. SLI children

Table 12.1 (_contd_)

Author(s)	Monolingual milestones	Lexicon[1]	Syntax[1]	Phonology[1]	Target languages; sample sizes; age of bilingual children	Conclusions
Pearson, Fernandez & Oller (1993)	Mono control groups	MacArthur Inventory			Sp+Eng; n = 25; 8–30 mths old	Comparable to monolingual controls
Pearson & Fernandez (1994)	Other pub. data	MacArthur Inventory			Sp-Eng.; n = 18; 8–30 mths old	Within monolingual range
Pearson & Navarro (1998)	Mono control groups			Articulation test	Sp+Eng.; n = 11; 36 mths old	Within monolingual range
Schaerlaekens, Zink & Verheyden (1995)	Mono control groups	Vocab. test			Dutch + Fr; n = 114; 4–5 yrs old	Slightly delayed but measured 1 language only
Umbel & Oller (1994)	Test norms	PPVT in Eng. & Sp.			Sp+Eng; n–102; 6.7–11.6 yrs old	Within normal range for monolinguals
Vihman (1982)	Other pub. data	Linguistic analyses			Estonian+Eng; n = 1; 1.1–2;.10 yrs old	Delay in use of inflections. & word combinations

1. Entries in these columns refer to techniques/tests/indices used to assess development in each domain.
Mono = monolingual; bil = bilingual; Eng = English; Sp = Spanish; Fr = French; Other pub data = data published elsewhere

assess the adequacy of extant data would constitute a separate report in itself. The objective here is simply to survey extant research in order to form a general impression of the developmental progression of children acquiring two languages in comparison to those acquiring one. Even general trends of comparable rates of development in bilingual and monolingual development would provide reassuring evidence in support of my arguments that bilingual acquisition is normal and does not entail developmental costs.

With two exceptions, the published studies summarised in Table 12.1 report that the rate of bilingual development and/or age of emergence of certain language phenomena in bilingual children was comparable to or within the age range reported for monolingual development. The two exceptions are Vihman (1982) and Schaerlaekens *et al.* (1995); Vihman reported on the use of inflectional morphology and two-word combinations, and Schaerlaekens *et al.* reported on lexical development. Thus, although bilingual children are exposed to and must systematise two sets of language input, they appear to do so within the same general timeframe and approximately at the same ages as children learning only one language. Evidently, the challenges of bilingual acquisition can be accommodated within the same temporal parameters as monolingual acquisition and do not burden the child's mental capacities leading to delays in development. This is not to conclude that bilingual children do not experienced significantly delayed development; some do. Monolingual children do also. The focus here is on the most typical cases. Nor does it imply that bilingual children are or look the same as monolingual children. We shall see in a later section that bilingual acquisition is both the same as and different from monolingual acquisition.

Are bilingual children initially monolingual?

Notwithstanding the preceding arguments, until recently, many researchers believed that bilingualism was not the initial stage for children exposed to two languages during infancy. More specifically, it was argued by some that children exposed to two languages go through an initial stage when they do not distinguish between the languages being learned. The most explicit formulation of this hypothesis was proposed by Volterra and Taeschner (1978: 312). They proposed that differentiated linguistic systems emerge in three stages:

> (1) . . . in the first stage the child has one lexical system which includes words from both languages. A word in one language almost always dose not have a corresponding word in the same meaning in the other language. (2) In the second stage the child distinguishes two different lexicons, but applies the same syntactic rules to both languages. (3) In

the third stage the child speaks two languages differentiated both in lexicon and syntax, . . .

To their credit, Volterra and Taeschner formulated the most explicit and precise version of this otherwise general claim and in doing so they inspired much useful work in the field. Volterra and Taeschner were not alone in proposing that bilingual children go through a unitary language system stage (e.g. Murrell, 1960; Redlinger & Park, 1980; Swain, 1972).

In effect, it was argued that bilingual children are initially monolingual and that real bilingualism does not emerge until later, around three years of age. Such claims were based on the widespread finding that virtually all bilingual children code-mix during the earliest stages of productive language use. I use the term code-mixing generically in this chapter to refer to the use of elements (phonological, lexical, morphosyntactic) from two, or more, languages in the same utterance or stretch of conversation – intra- and inter-utterance mixing respectively. The term code-switching is often used with reference to adult code-mixing. I use the more neutral term code-mixing here in order to avoid any assumption that the structural and functional characteristics of child bilingual code-mixing are the same as adult bilingual code-mixing. I review recent research on the structural characteristics of child code-mixing later (see Genesee, 2001, for a discussion of the functional characteristics of child code-mixing).

There are a number of methodological shortcomings of the early studies that call their conclusions into question (see Genesee, 1989, for a review). In order to uphold the unitary language system (ULS) hypothesis, one would need to establish that, all things being equal, bilingual children use elements from both languages indiscriminately in all contexts of use. Alternatively, since one language of the bilingual child is often more developed than the other, they might be expected to use their two languages in proportion to their relative proficiency in each, regardless of language context (Nicoladis & Genesee, 1996). Evidence that bilingual children in the earliest stages of acquisition can use their developing languages differentially and appropriately with interlocutors who speak different languages would be difficult to reconcile with the proposal of fused systems. Such evidence would be more compatible with underlying differentiation of the languages. In fact, many of the early studies that argued for a ULS did not present or analyse their data by context. For example, the evidence cited by Volterra and Taeschner themselves was limited to episodes with the child's German-speaking mother; the child's language use with her Italian-speaking father are not provided. An additional shortcoming of some of the early work was the use of example-based evidence to support claims about the child's whole language system. Clearly, infrequent and isolated examples of any linguistic phenomenon cannot be taken to be indicative of the child's overall competence since they may be performance errors or some other non-systematic behaviour. It is imperative that the child's entire output during observation sessions be reported in order to provide a complete accounting of the child's language performance and, by inference, their underlying language competence. This brings me to a final methodological issue – restricting analyses to the bilingual child's code-mixing fails to reveal how frequently and under what circumstances the child does *not* code-mix.

Recent evidence refutes the ULS hypothesis, and it is now generally accepted that bilingual children do not go through an initial unitary stage, at least from the one-word stage onward (e.g. De Houwer, 1990; Genesee, 1989; Goodz, 1994; Lanza, 1997; Meisel, 1994, 2001; Petitto *et al.*, 2001). In a study of English-French bilingual children in Montreal, Genesee *et al.* (1995) systematically observed the children during naturalistic interactions with their parents in the home. The children were observed on three separate occasions: once with their mothers alone; once with their fathers alone; and once with both parents present. The parents reported using and were observed to use the one parent/one language rule for the most part when interacting with their children. Thus, the parents presented different language contexts. The children were between 22 and 26 months of age and were in the one- and early two-word stage of language development. We examined not only the frequency of the children's mixing (within and between utterances), but also the frequency with which they used single language utterances that were appropriate to the interlocutor (e.g. French utterances with the French-speaking parent and English with the English-speaking parent).

Even at this early stage of development, these children were able to use their two languages in a context-sensitive manner – they used substantially more French than English with their French-speaking parent and substantially more English than French with their English-speaking parent. When the parents were together with the children, the children likewise used more of the father's language with the father than with the mother, and vice versa for the mother's language (see Figure 12.1 for results with the children when both parents are together). That these children used their two languages appropriately with each parent, whether alone or together, argues for differentiation of the children's languages.

We conducted a follow-up study to further examine young bilingual children's ability to use their developing languages appropriately in dyadic interactions. Our initial study may have underestimated the ability of bilingual children to differentiate their languages because their parents, like the parents of many bilingual children, knew and sometimes used both

English

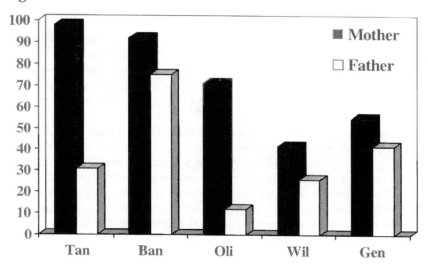

French

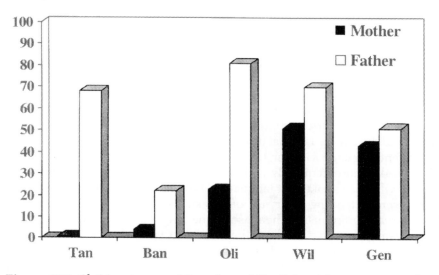

Figure 12.1 Children's use of French and English with parents together (mothers were native English-speakers and fathers were native French-speakers)

languages with their children. In short, these parents did not strictly require separation of the languages. Moreover, the differentiation that we observed might have reflected a process of associative learning whereby each child had come to associate certain words with each parent over time – French words with the French-speaking parent and English words with the English-speaking parent. True bilingual communicative competence entails the ability to adapt one's language use on-line in accordance with relevant characteristics of the situation, including the preferred or more proficient language of one's interlocutor.

In order to examine these issues, we observed a number of additional French–English bilingual children during play sessions with monolingual strangers (Genesee *et al.*, 1996). We selected strangers on the assumption that evidence of differential language use with unfamiliar interlocutors would reinforce our argument that two-year-old bilinguals' languages are differentiated and, as well, would attest to true on-line communicative competence at an early stage of bilingual acquisition. The children would not have been able to use the right language with this interlocutor through associative learning because this was the first time they had talked with her. We selected *monolingual* strangers in order to ascertain the children's ability to identify critical language characteristics of an interlocutor with minimal prior exposure. Since the language spoken by the stranger was the less proficient language of three of the four children, this was a particularly rigorous test of their abilities to accommodate the stranger.

Three of the four children gave evidence of on-line adjustments to the stranger by using more of the strangers' language with the stranger than with their parents and, in particular, the parent who spoke the same language as the stranger, usually the father (see Figure 12.2 for examples of two children's data). Also, three of the children used less of the language not known by the stranger with the stranger than with either parent. Thus, despite the fact that the children had had no prior experience with this adult and despite the fact that three of them were compelled to use their less proficient language with her, they not only used the appropriate language, they used it more frequently with the monolingual stranger than with the parent who also spoke that language. These results indicate that the children were extending their use of the strangers' language as much as possible and minimising their use of the language the stranger did not know as much as possible. That they used a great deal of the language not known by the stranger simply reflects their relative proficiency in that language, a pattern that we observed even when the children were speaking with their parents. It should not be surprising that all the children did not perform alike given the well-documented and large individual differences among children in a variety of different aspects of language acquisition.

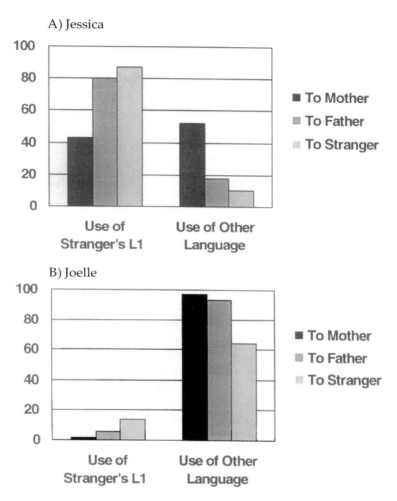

Figure 12.2 Children's use of their languages with a stranger and with parents

There is no reason to believe that the development of communicative competence (bilingual or monolingual) is not subject to the same individual variation that is demonstrated in other aspects of language acquisition.

Taken together these two studies indicate that bilingual children in the early stages of acquisition can use their languages differentially and appropriately with familiar and unfamiliar interlocutors. These findings also

Table 12.2 Mixing rates of interlocutors and children in low and high input conditions

ANTHONY	*Low condition*	*High condition*
Child	3.85% (4)[1]	14.00% (14)
Interlocutor	12.05% (44)	37.62% (196)
JONATHAN	*Low condition*	*High condition*
Child	14.84% (23)	27.36% (29)
Interlocutor	15.93% (43)	29.22% (64)
LUCAS	*Low condition*	*High condition*
Child	10.48% (11)	46.79% (51)
Interlocutor	12.26% (70)	47.61% (219)
NOAH	*Low condition*	*High condition*
Child	36.92% (24)	72.13% (88)
Interlocutor	15.58% (60)	37.46% (106)

1. Values in parentheses indicate frequencies of occurrence

challenge the unitary system explanation of child bilingual code-mixing. Further evidence that bilingual child code-mixing is not symptomatic of language fusion, or confusion, comes from a study in our laboratory that systematically examined bilingual children's ability to adjust their rates of code-mixing in response to changing rates of code-mixing on the part of their interlocutors (Genesee *et al.*, 2000). We observed four young children (all boys) who were learning English and French from their parents in their homes in Montreal. The children were between 2.4 and 2.7 years of age and were in the one-word and very early two-word stage of acquisition. After we had observed the children independently with each parent in order to collect data to assess their language development and to observe their code-mixing with their parents, we then observed them three times while interacting and playing with a trained bilingual research assistant. The assistant played with the children for approximately 40 minutes each time; the base language she used with each child was French, the less proficient language of three of the children. In session I, she code-mixed relatively infrequently – between 12% and 16% of the time. Most of her code-mixing consisted of whole utterances in English; she engaged in intra-utterance code-mixing, but much less than inter-utterance mixing. In session II, she increased her rate of mixing to between 29% and 47%, depending on the child. The objective of the study was to systematically examine whether the children would adjust their own rates of code-mixing in accordance with the rates of their adult interlocutors. Evidence of increases in the children's mixing from session I to session II would imply that the children were able to monitor the adult's rates of mixing and to adjust their own mixing accordingly. It would also indicate that they can control their rate of code-mix in accordance with pragmatic characteristics of the interaction, thereby providing evidence that code-mixing does not reflect a unitary fused system.

As indicated in Table 12.2, all four of the children increased their rates of mixing substantially and to a statistically significant degree when the interlocutor increased her rate of mixing. To confirm that this increase was not simply an artefact of the children's increased familiarity with the assistant, we recalled the children for a third play session during which the assistant reduced her rates of mixing to their previous low levels. Observing the children's code-mixing during this third session also permitted us to examine the degree of control the children could exercise over their language use. Recall that the base language of the interaction with the assistant was the less proficient language of three of the children, the exception being Lucas. Thus, downward shifts in mixing during session III would necessitate that these children refrain from using their more proficient language. Three of the children demonstrated a significant reduction in their rates of mixing from session II to session III, the exception being Anthony.

The evidence reviewed in this section indicates that bilingual children have functionally differentiated linguistic systems by at least 2 years of age or when they are in the one- and early two-word stages of development. Differentiation may occur earlier (however, see Deuchar & Quay, 2000: 34). In a re-analysis of data from Leopold's study of Hildegard, Paradis (1996) found that her 'prosodic development followed separate paths in English and German' from 1.6 to 2.0 years of age. Although somewhat surprising to early researchers working in this field, these results are not surprising in light of the evidence reviewed in the previous section which argued in favour of the infants' capacity to acquire dual systems from the outset.

Is bilingual acquisition the same as monolingual acquisition?

Volterra and Taeschner's 1978 notion of fused lexical and syntactic systems reflects another previously held viewpoint about bilingual acquisition, namely, that it must be different from monolingual acquisition. I address this issue by examining evidence concerning the syntactic development of young bilingual children. The focus is on syntax since this is where most research has been conducted and because syntax is at the heart of language development itself. A key distinction here concerns autonomous versus interdependent development (Paradis & Genesee, 1996). Autonomous bilingual development would be reflected in patterns of acquisition and linguistic representation that are the same as those of monolingual children acquiring the same languages. In effect, bilingual children 'would look' like monolinguals. Alternatively, the grammars of bilingual children might develop interdependently. Paradis and Genesee (1996: 3) define interdependent development as 'the systemic influence of the grammar of one language on the grammar of the other language during acquisition, causing differences in a bilingual's patterns or rates of development in comparison with a monolingual's'.

Interdependence could take several forms. First, the simultaneous acquisition of two languages might pose challenges to the language faculty that could result in slower development, in general or in specific domains of grammar, in bilinguals in comparison to monolinguals. For example, children acquiring English and Spanish simultaneously might be delayed in the obligatory use of subjects in English as a result of exposure to Spanish, a language that licenses the omission of subjects in certain contexts. Second, and in contrast, bilingual acquisition could accelerate language development in cases where two languages share certain structural properties and especially structures that normally emerge earlier in one of the languages when acquired monolingually. For example, for reasons that are not fully understood, monolingual French-learning children acquire finite verb forms at an earlier age than monolingual English-learning children (Pierce, 1992). Children acquiring English and French simultaneously might show an accelerated acquisition of finiteness in their English as a result of the early emergence of finiteness in their French verbs. Yet another form of interdependence is transfer, the systematic incorporation of a linguistic property from one language into the other. For transfer to be distinguished from acceleration, it would have to result in a deviant structure or pattern in comparison to the target language – for example, if English–French bilingual children were shown to place negatives after lexical verbs in English, this could constitute evidence for transfer from French. Note that these possibilities assume differentiated linguistic systems and, thus, differ from the assumptions of the unitary language system hypothesis, discussed earlier.

The language development of bilingual children need not be entirely autonomous or interdependent – certain aspects might develop interdependently while the rest develops autonomously. Furthermore, interdependence might be characteristic of certain language combinations, but not others. It has been shown that, for the most part, bilingual children acquire the appropriate syntactic structures of each language they are learning (De Houwer, 1990; Döpke, 2000; Hulk & Muller, 2000; Juan-Garau & Pérez-Vidal, 2000; Meisel, 1989; Paradis & Genesee, 1996; Yip & Matthews, 2000). Paradis and Genesee (1996), for example, found that 2–3 year old French–English bilingual children (1) used finite verb forms earlier in French than in English; (2) used subject pronouns in French exclusively with finite verbs but subject pronouns in English with both finite and non-finite verbs, in accordance with the status of subject pronouns in French as clitics (or agreement markers) but full NPs in English; and (3) placed verbal negatives after lexical verbs in French (e.g. *'n'aime pas'*) but before lexical verbs in English (*'do not like'*). These patterns characterise the performance of monolingual children acquiring these languages. Moreover, the bilingual children acquired these patterns within the same age ranges as monolingual children.

At the same time, cross-language influences, or transfer, have been noted – by Döpke (2000) in German–English bilingual children, by Hulk and van der Linden (1996) and Müller (1998) in German–French children, and by Yip and Matthews (2000) in a Chinese–English child. Döpke, for example, reports that Australian children learning English and German simultaneously overgeneralised the -VO word order of English to German which instantiates both -VO and -OV word orders depending on the clausal structure of the utterance. Working within the Competition Model (Bates & MacWhinney, 1987), Döpke argues that children learning German and English simultaneously are prone to overgeneralise S-V-O word order in their German because the -VO order is reinforced on the surface of both the German and the English input they hear. Hulk and Müller (2000: 229), have similarly argue that 'there has to be a certain overlap of the two systems at the surface level' for cross-linguistic syntactic influence to occur. Structural overlap and ambiguity in the input have also been invoked as possible explanations in phonological transfer by Paradis (2001) in a study of French–English 2–3 years olds.

It is important to note that these instances of cross-linguistic transfer are restricted – they pertain to specific aspects of the child's developing grammars and they appear to occur only under certain linguistic circumstances – where there is overlap in the structures of the two languages for the analogous property. Moreover, they are temporary since we know from research on adult bilinguals that, in the long run, bilingual children can acquire the appropriate target language forms. In short, these instances of transfer, while interesting, do not compromise the gener⁻¹ conclusion that the syntactic systems of bilingual children are different are the same in most respects as those of monolingual child stage of development. It is important to point out here that th may not obtain in all cases since there may be mitigating ci result in different patterns. For example, Paradis (19 Matthews (2000) have proposed that dominance may m that one might well expect considerably more transfer monolingual patterns in cases where exposure to or proficiency in each language is not balanced. Thus, these conclusions pertain to the capacity of the child's capacity to acquire two languages simultaneously and not to what happens in every case.

There is another domain where bilinguals clearly differ from monolinguals – they mix elements from both languages in the same utterances. This difference from monolingual acquisition is often viewed as a deviant form of language use by researchers, professionals, and parents alike. And yet research on adult bilinguals indicates that their intra-utterance code-mixing is not random but is grammatically constrained and, furthermore, complies with the grammatical principles of the participating languages (Myers-Scotton, 1997; Poplack, 1980). Although there is no consensus on the nature of the specific constraints that organise intra-sentential code-mixing in adults, there is consensus that constraints serve to avoid grammatically illicit or deviant constructions. That bilingual children ultimately acquire grammatical constraints on their code-mixing is attested by the studies on adult bilinguals. The question arises are there structural constraints on child bilingual code-mixing. Aside from its theoretical significance for our understanding of child code-mixing, this question addresses the view that bilingual acquisition is different from monolingual acquisition because it implicates the capacity to co-ordinate two grammars during on-line production, a clear difference from monolingual competence.

To date, research has examined constraints on intra-utterance code-mixing by bilingual children learning the following language pairs: French and German (Köppe, in press; Meisel, 1994), French and English (Genesee & Sauve, 2000; Paradis *et al.*, 2000); English and Norwegian (Lanza, 1997); English and Estonian (Vihman, 1998), and Inuktitut and English (Allen *et al.*, 1999). Despite the diversity of language pairs that have been examined, all researchers conclude that child bilingual code-mixing is grammatically constrained and in accordance with constraints that operate on adult code-mixing. The operation of constraints based on abstract notions of grammatical knowledge, which are at the core of Myers-Scotton's Matrix Language Frame model (1997), is most evident in bilingual children once they demonstrate such knowledge overtly (e.g. verb tense and agreement markings), usually around 2.6 years of age and older. The operation of constraints that reflect surface features of grammar, such as word order, that characterise Poplack's constraint model (1980) is evident even earlier in development, prior to overt marking of abstract grammatical relations in the child's language, from the two word/morpheme stage onward. Köppe (in press) has proposed a hybrid model, composed of linear, word order constraints _g the early stages of production and abstract, hierarchically organ-
_traints subsequently.

These findings indicate that in addition to the linguistic competence to formulate correct monolingual strings, as noted earlier, bilingual children have the added capacity to co-ordinate their two grammars on-line in accordance with the grammatical constraints of both languages during code-mixing, a capacity that permits the bilingual child (and adult) to express their bilinguality in uniquely creative ways. Returning to the central issue in this section – bilingual children demonstrate the same general patterns of syntactic development as monolingual children but differ from monolingual children in their capacity to co-ordinate their two languages on-line when code-mixing.

Conclusions

In this chapter, I have reviewed research evidence that pertains to three general questions that I believe have been the focus of attention in the field for some time. In every case, I believe that current evidence, whether it is drawn from studies of monolingual or bilingual development, challenges previous views and paints a picture of the developing infant that is eminently capable of acquiring two languages simultaneously. Indeed, findings from research on pre-natal and young post-natal infants suggest that they possess the perceptual and memory capacities that are fundamental to dual language acquisition and that they begin this process very early in development – possibly pre-natally, as has been indicated in the case of monolinguals. We have seen further that infants exposed to two languages simultaneously form differentiated linguistic systems from the earliest stages of productive language use (i.e. the one-word stage) and probably earlier (during babbling) and that their pattern and rate of language acquisition (at least in the domain of syntax) is comparable to that of monolinguals in most important respects. At the same time, there are differences between bilinguals and monolinguals in the form of cross-linguistic transfer and code-mixing. We saw that transfer is probably quite restricted in scope and time. We also now understand that code-mixing is grammatically constrained and, most importantly, reflects additional processing capacities that bilingual children possess that permit them to co-ordinate the grammars of their two languages during on-line production.

Overall, the view of bilingual acquisition that is emerging from contemporary research is in accord with current views of human development in general that attribute innate structures and capacities that facilitate development where deficiencies were previously seen. This view makes a great deal of sense because it argues that the child's developmental capacities are derived from the innate capacities of the human organism. There is no evidence to believe that these innate neuro-cognitive capacities predispose infants to monolingualism over bilingualism.

Of course, much remains to be done. Bilingual acquisition is complex, and we have only begun to understand the myriad factors that might influence this process. There are variations arising from different language combinations and different amounts and kinds of exposure that remain to be explored. Research that addresses speech perception and early speech production in pre-verbal bilingual children is virtually non-existent and waiting to be done (cf. Poulin-Dubois & Goodz, 2001; Bosch and Sebastián-Gallés, 2001). If the last decade of research is any indication, the next one promises even greater progress in our understanding of bilingual acquisition.

Acknowledgements

I would like to thank the Social Sciences and Humanities Research Council, Ottawa, Canada, for financial support of my research cited in this chapter.

References

Allen, S.E.M. (1996) *Aspects of Argument Structure Acquisition in Inuktitut*. Amsterdam: Benjamins.

Allen, S., Genesee, F., Fish, S. and Crago, M. (2000) Grammatical constraints on early bilingual code-mixing: Evidence from children learning Inuktitut and English. Paper presented at the Boston University Conference on Child Language, November 1999.

Arsenian, S. (1945) Bilingualism in the post-war world. *Psychological Bulletin* 42, 65–85.

Baetens Beardsmore, H. (1982) *Bilingualism: Basic Principles*. Clevedon: Multilingual Matters.

Bates, E. and MacWhinney, B. (1987) Competition, variation, and language learning. In B. MacWhinney (ed.) *Mechanisms of Language Acquisition* (pp. 157–94). Hillsdale, NJ: Lawrence Erlbaum.

Bosch, L. and Sebastián-Gallés, N. (2001) Early language differentiation in bilingual infants. In J. Cenoz and F. Genesee (eds) *Trends in Bilingual Acquisition* (pp. 71–94). Amsterdam: Benjamins.

Boysson-Bardies, B. (1999) *How Language Comes to Children: From Birth to Two Years*. Cambridge, MA: MIT Press.

Brown, R. (1958) *Words and Things*. New York: The Free Press.

Comeau, L. and Genesee, F. (2001) Bilingual children's repair strategies during dyadic communication. In J. Cenoz and F. Genesee (eds) *Trends in Bilingual Acquisition* (pp. 231–56). Amsterdam: Benjamins.

Darcy, N.T. (1953) A review of the literature on the effects of bilingualism upon the measurement of intelligence. *Journal of Genetic Psychology* 82, 21–57.

DeCasper, A.J. and Fifer W.P. (1980) Of human bonding: Newborns prefer their mothers' voices. *Science* 208, 1174–6.

DeCasper, A.J. and Spence, M.J. (1986) Prenatal maternal speech influences newborns' perceptions of speech sounds. *Infant Behavior and Development* 9, 133–50.

De Houwer, A. (1990) *The Acquisition of Two Languages from Birth: A Case Study.* Cambridge, MA: Cambridge University Press.

Deuchar, M., and Quay, S. (2000) *Bilingual Acquisition: Theoretical Implications of a Case Study.* Oxford: Oxford University Press.

Diebold, A.R. (1968). The consequences of early bilingualism on cognitive development and personality formation. In E. Norbeck, D. Price-Williams and W.M. McCord (eds) *The Study of Personality: An Inter-disciplinary Appraisal* (pp. 218–45). New York: Holt, Rinehart & Winston.

Döpke, S. (2000) Generation of and retraction from cross-linguistically motivated structures in bilingual first language acquisition. In F. Genesee (ed.) *Bilingualism: Language and Cognition* (pp. 209–26). Cambridge: Cambridge University Press.

Genesee, F. (1989) Early bilingual development: One language or two? *Journal of Child Language* 16, 161–79.

Genesee, F. (2001) Bilingual first language acquisition: Exploring the limits of the language faculty. In M. McGroarty (ed.) *21st Annual Review of Applied Linguistics* (pp. 153–68). Cambridge: Cambridge University Press.

Genesee, F., Boivin, I. and Nicoladis, E. (1996) Talking with strangers: A study of bilingual children's communicative competence. *Applied Psycholinguistics* 17, 427–42.

Genesee, F., Comeau, L. and Baynton, L. (2000) Parental code-mixing: Does it really make a difference? Paper presented at the Boston University Conference on Language Development. Boston, MA, 5 November, 2000.

Genesee, F., Nicoladis, E. and Paradis, J. (1995) Language differentiation in early bilingual development. *Journal of Child Language* 22, 611–31.

Genesee, F. and Sauve, D. (2000) Grammatical constraints on child bilingual code-mixing. Paper presented at the Annual Conference of the American Association for Applied Linguistics, 12 March, Vancouver, Canada.

Goodz, N. (1994) Interactions between parents and children in bilingual families. In F. Genesee (ed.) *Educating Second Language Children* (pp. 61–81). New York: Cambridge University Press.

Goodz, N.S., Legaré, M.C. and Bilodeau, L. (1990) Language acquisition in bilingual families. Poster presented at the 7th International Conference on Infant Studies, Montreal, Quebec.

Hoffmann, C. (1991) *An Introduction to Bilingualism.* London: Longman.

Hulk, A. and Müller, N. (2000) Bilingual first language acquisition at the interface between syntax and pragmatics. In F. Genesee (ed.) *Bilingualism, Language and Cognition: Syntactic Aspects of Bilingual Acquisition* (pp. 227–44). Cambridge: Cambridge University Press.

Hulk A.C.J. and van der Linden, E. (1996) Language mixing in a French-Dutch bilingual child. In E. Kellerman, B. Weltens and T. Bongaerts (eds) *EUROSLA 6. A selection of papers. Toegepaste taalwetenschap in artikelen* 55, 89–103.

Jusczyk, P.W. (1985) On characterizing the development of speech perception. In J. Mehler and R. Rox (eds) *Neonate Cognition: Beyond the Blooming, Buzzing Confusion* (pp. 199–229). Hillsdale, NJ: Lawrence Erlbaum.

Juan-Garau, M. and Pérez-Vidal, C. (2000) Subject realisation in the syntactic development of a bilingual child. In F. Genesee (ed.) *Bilingualism: Language and Cognition* (pp. 173–91). Cambridge: Cambridge University Press.

Köppe, R. (in press) Is codeswitching acquired? In J. MacSwan (ed.) *Grammatical Theory and Bilingual Codeswitching.* Cambridge, MA: MIT Press.

Lanza, E. (1997) *Language Mixing in Infant Bilingualism: A Sociolinguistic Perspective.* Oxford: Clarendon Press.

Lanza, E. (2001) Bilingual first language acquisition: A discourse perspective on language contact in parent–child interaction. In J. Cenoz and F. Genesee (eds) *Trends in Bilingual Acquisition* (pp. 201–30). Amsterdam: Benjamins.

Leopold, W.F. (1939) *Speech Development of a Bilingual Child: Volume 1.* New York: AMS Press.

Leopold, W.F. (1949) *Speech Development of a Bilingual Child: Volume 3.* New York: AMS Press.

Macnamara, J. (1966) *Bilingualism and Primary Education.* Edinburgh: University Press.

Mehler, J., Bertoncini, J., Barrière, M. and Jassik-Gershenfeld, D. (1978) Infant recognition of mother's voice. *Perception* 7, 491–97.

Mehler, J., Jusczyk, P.W., Lambertz, G., Halsted, N., Bertoncini, J. and Amiel-Tison, C. (1988) A precursor of language acquisition in young infants. *Cognition* 29, 143–78.

Meisel, J.M. (1986) Word order and case marking in early child language: Evidence from simultaneous acquisition of two first languages (French and German). *Linguistics* 24, 123–183.

Meisel, J.M. (1989). Early differentiation of languages in bilingual children. In K. Hyltenstam and L. Obler (eds) *Bilingualism Across the Lifespan: Aspects of Acquisition, Maturity and Loss* (pp. 13–40). Cambridge: Cambridge University Press.

Meisel, J.M. (1994) Code-switching in young bilingual children: The acquisition of grammatical constraints. *Studies in Second Language Acquisition* 16, 413–41.

Meisel, J.M. (2001). The simultaneous acquisition of two first languages: Early differentiation and subsequent development of grammars. In J. Cenoz and F. Genesee (eds) *Trends in Bilingual Acquisition* (pp. 11–42). Amsterdam: Benjamins.

Mikes, M. (1990) Some issues of lexical development in early bi- and trilinguals. In G. Conti-Ramsden and C. Snow (eds) *Children's Language, Vol. 7.* (pp. 103–20). Hillsdale, NJ: Lawrence Erlbaum.

Müller, N. (1998) Transfer in bilingual first language acquisition. *Bilingualism: Language and Cognition* 1, 151–171.

Murrell, M. (1960) Language acquisition in a trilingual environment: Notes from a case study. *Studia Linguistica* 20, 9–35.

Myers-Scotton, C. (1997) *Duelling Languages: Grammatical Structure in Codeswitching.* Oxford: Clarendon Press.

Nicoladis, E. (2001) Finding words in the input: Evidence from a bilingual child. In J. Cenoz and F. Genesee (eds) *Trends in Bilingual Acquisition* (pp. 131–48). Amsterdam: Benjamins.

Nicoladis, E. and Genesee, F. (1996) A longitudinal study of pragmatic differentiation in young bilingual children. *Language Learning* 46, 439–64.

Oller, D.K., Eilers, R.E., Urbano, R. and Cobo-Lewis, A.B. (1997) Development of precursors to speech in infants exposed to two languages. *Journal of Child Language* 24, 407–26.

Padilla, A.M. and Liebman, E. (1975) Language acquisition in the bilingual child. *Bilingual Review* 2, 34–55.

Paradis, J. (1996) Phonological differentiation in a bilingual child: Hildegarde revisited. In A. Stringfellow *et al.* (eds) *20th Proceedings of the Boston University Conference on Language Development* (pp. 528–539). Somerville, MA: Cascadilla Press.

Paradis, J. (2000) Beyond 'one system or two': Degrees of separation between the languages of French–English bilingual children. In S. Döpke (ed.) *Cross-linguistic Structures in Simultaneous Bilingualism* (pp. 175–200). Amsterdam/Philadelphia: Benjamins.

Paradis, J. (2001). Do bilingual two-year-olds have separate phonological systems? *International Journal of Bilingualism* 5, 19–38.

Paradis, J., Crago, M., Genesee, F. and Rice, M. (in press). French–English bilingual children with SLI: How do they compare with their monolingual peers. *Journal of the American Speech-Language-Hearing Association.*

Paradis, J. and Genesee, F. (1996) Syntactic acquisition in bilingual children: Autonomous or interdependent? *Studies in Second Language Acquisition* 18, 1–25.

Paradis, J., Nicoladis, E. and Genesee, F. (2000) Early emergence of structural constraints on code-mixing: Evidence from French–English bilingual children. In F. Genesee (ed.) *Bilingualism: Language and Cognition* (pp. 245–61). Cambridge: Cambridge University Press.

Pearson, B.Z., Fernández, S.C. (1994) Patterns of interaction in the lexical growth in two languages of bilingual infants and toddlers. *Language Learning* 44, 617–54.

Pearson, B.Z., Fernández, S.C. and Oller, K. (1993) Lexical development in bilingual infants and toddlers: Comparison to monolingual norms. *Language Learning* 43, 93–120.

Pearson, B.Z. and Navarro, A.M. (1998) Do early simultaneous bilinguals have a foreign accent in one or both of their languages? In A. Aksu-Koc *et al.* (eds) *Perspectives on Language Acquisition: Selected Papers from the VIIth ICSCL* (pp. 156–68). Istanbul, Turkey: Bogazici University Printhouse.

Petitto, L.A., Katerelos, M., Levy, B.G., Gauna, K., Tetreault, K. and Ferraro, V. (2001) Bilingual signed and spoken language acquisition from birth: Implications for the mechanism underlying early bilingual language acquisition. *Journal of Child Language* 28, 453–96.

Pierce, A. (1992) *Language Acquisition and Syntactic Theory.* Dordrecht: Kluwer.

Poplack, S. (1980) 'Sometimes I start a sentence in English y termino en Espanol': Toward a typology of code-switching. *Linguistics* 18, 581–618.

Poulin-Dubois, D. and Goodz, N. (2001) Language differentiation in bilingual infants: Evidence from babbling. In J. Cenoz and F. Genesee (eds) *Trends in Bilingual Acquisition* (pp. 95–106). Amsterdam: Benjamins.

Quay, S. (1995) The bilingual lexicon: Implications for studies of language choice. *Journal of Child Language* 22, 369–87.

Quay, S. (2001) Managing linguistic boundaries in early trilingual development. In J. Cenoz and F. Genesee (eds) *Trends in Bilingual Acquisition* (pp. 149–200). Amsterdam: Benjamins.

Redlinger, W.E. and Park, T. (1980) Language mixing in young bilinguals. *Journal of Child Language* 7, 337–52.

Richmond-Welty, E.D. and Siple, P. (1999) Differentiating the use of gaze in bilingual-bimodal language acquisition: A comparison of two set of twins of deaf parents. *Journal of Child Language* 26, 321–38.

Romaine, S. (1989) *Bilingualism.* Oxford: Basil Blackwell.

Ronjat, J. (1913) *Le développement du langage observé chez un enfant bilingue.* Paris: Librairie Ancienne H. Champion.

Schaerlaekens, A., Zink, I. and Verheyden, L. (1995) Comparative vocabulary development in kindergarten classes with a mixed population of monolinguals, simultaneous and successive bilinguals. *Journal of Multilingual and Multicultural Development* 16, 477–94.

Slobin, D.I. (1997) *The Crosslinguistic Study of Language Acquisition, Volume 5: Expanding Contexts.* Mahwah, NJ: Lawrence Erlbaum.

Swain, M. (1972) Bilingualism as a first language. Unpublished PhD, University of California, Irvine.

Tucker, G.R. (1998) A global perspective on multilingualism and multilingual education. In. J. Cenoz and F. Genesee (eds) *Beyond Bilingualism: Multilingualism and Multilingual Education* (pp. 3–15). Clevedon: Multilingual Matters.

Umbel, V.M. and Oller, D.K. (1994) Developmental changes in receptive vocabulary in Hispanic bilingual school children. *Language Learning 44*, 221–42.

Vihman, M. (1982) The acquisition of morphology by a bilingual child: A whole-word approach. *Applied Psycholinguistics 3*, 141–60.

Vihman, M. (1998) A developmental perspective on codeswitching: Conversations between a pair of bilingual siblings. *International Journal of Bilingualism 2*, 45–84.

Volterra, V. and Taeschner, T. (1978) The acquisition and development of language by bilingual children. *Journal of Child Language 5*, 311–26.

Yip, V. and Matthews, S (2000). Syntactic transfer in a Cantonese–English bilingual child. In F. Genesee (ed.) *Bilingualism: Language and Cognition* (pp. 193–208). Cambridge: Cambridge University Press.

Laudatio

Hugo Baetens Beardsmore – No Hyphen, Please!

ERIC LEE

There are certainly any number of people better placed than I to present Hugo Baetens Beardsmore the scholar and to underline the great diversity and qualities of his writings and teaching. In the various overlapping disciplines he has made his own – ELT, language learning, bilingualism, bilingual education, sociolinguistics, language planning – he needs no introduction. Yet it is my impression that the man behind the author, the very human being behind the teacher, is less well known, and that, truly, is a pity. So it is with great pleasure that I have accepted the task of writing this brief epilogue in order to set the record straight.

Hugo Baetens Beardsmore was born in the middle of the Second World War in a small village in Flemish Brabant some 20-odd kilometres northeast of Brussels. Though he feels he did not personally alter the course of the war to any significant extent, the war, in no uncertain way, was to change his family fortunes dramatically. Suffice it to say that at a very early age he found himself living in post-war England, plunged into a different language, culture and social milieu from the one already familiar to him. The shock of this initial encounter, cushioned lovingly by his mother as far as she was able and by the continuing contacts he had with his native Belgium through family visits, together with the long process of learning and adaptation that inevitably followed helped to lay the sturdy foundations of the person we know today: a man of many parts, equally at home, both socially and linguistically, in any number of countries and among people from all walks of life.

At the end of his primary and secondary schooling, he won a scholarship to the University of Wales at Aberystwyth, where he was thrown yet again – this time knowingly and willingly – into new sociolinguistic surroundings. There, under his own Milk Wood in mid-Wales, comfortably cut off from England and things English, he settled down happily to some cross-country running (like his father before him), the student life in general and the study of French in particular. It is a moot point whether this choice of subject was ultimately determined by his deep sense of belonging in Belgium or, more prosaically, by his horror of mathematics and of matters both physical and chemical. Whatever the underlying motivation may have been, the choice turned out to be a happy one, as he finished brilliantly, taking a first-class honours degree.

The next step was largely to shape his future academic career: first, because it brought him back to Belgium and so closer to his roots; second, because for his doctorate he chose to study one aspect of the bilingual situation in Brussels, namely to provide an up-to-date, rigorous linguistic portrait of the regional French of the capital, detailing the effects on that language of local Dutch. His PhD dissertation, written in French, was subsequently published in 1971 as the highly acclaimed *Le français régional de Bruxelles*, since which time he has widely, and justly, been regarded as the authority on the French of Brussels.

Hugo Baetens Beardsmore's first 'real job', his invaluable baptism of fire through which he learned the tricks of the trade, was as a teacher of English as a foreign language at the *Institut de Phonétique* of the *Université Libre de Bruxelles*, where he soon rose to assume responsibility for the department and to coordinate its work in numerous applied fields such as English for special purposes, materials creation, and language testing (especially of oral proficiency).

Following the split of the University of Brussels into two separate linguistic entities, he chose to further his career along more traditional academic lines by moving in 1970 to the *Vrije Universiteit Brussel*, where he has worked ever since, first as lecturer and, since 1981, as full professor of English. His research interests have remained essentially in the field of multilingualism in its many manifestations: languages in contact, the sociology of language, language planning, language in education, to mention only these, and have shaped much of his specialist teaching at both Brussels universities and across the world.

There are generations of students who have cause to be grateful to Hugo Baetens Beardsmore, who is and will continue to be remembered as an equitable teacher with an exceptional pedagogic gift. As his many students past and present will testify, he has a knack of stimulating real interest in complex issues by explaining them simply and clearly. Nowhere is this more apparent than in his *Bilingualism: Basic Principles*, first published in 1982 and followed by a second edition in 1986, which has enjoyed enormous success, indeed has become a standard textbook on the subject in many university centres far and wide.

The academic career of this extraordinary man has known no bounds. The author of well over a hundred publications, he has lectured in many countries, served as Dean of the Faculty of Letters and Philosophy at the VUB, and was holder of the Peter Paul Rubens Chair at Berkeley. As an acknowledged authority on language planning and language in education, he has worked as adviser to such prestigious international bodies as the European Commission and the Council of Europe, and to the governmental authorities in the USA, the Basque country, Singapore, Hong Kong and Brunei. His achievements have earned him a special entry in the *Encyclopedia of Bilingualism and Bilingual Education,* and in recognition of his work he was elected a member of the Belgian Royal Academy of Overseas Sciences in 1989, becoming its president in 2001.

Hugo Baetens Beardsmore is a meticulous worker with an unfailing attention to detail. Indeed, it is difficult to imagine what else he could have been, having fought all his life to eliminate the intrusive hyphen inserted by others, simply out of ignorance or slovenliness, into his family name.

His untiring pursuit of knowledge and love of travel, especially in the Far East, have brought him into contact with kings and paupers alike. Though more than happy to confess that he has breakfasted with ambassadors, lunched with ministers and dined with royalty, he has managed never to 'lose the common touch'. Not surprisingly, his travels and studies have also made of him a man of considerable culture, with wide-ranging tastes in music, books, the theatre and the visual arts. He is something of an aesthete with a gourmet interest in food and fine wine, a knowledgeable collector of *objets* who enjoys life in tasteful domestic surroundings decorated under his own supervision.

Under his own supervision – not steam. For there is, sad to relate, one desperate weakness hidden away among so many strengths that in all fairness needs to be ruthlessly exposed: his lack of practical skills. Not in languages, of course, for unlike many a theoretician, Hugo Baetens Beardsmore is also an accomplished polyglot, one proud of 'working in English, shopping in Dutch and being private in French'. What he uses his German, Italian and Spanish for, I am at a loss to say!

No, the only tongue that remains entirely foreign to him is DIY. The internal workings of the homely ballcock, for instance, are a source of unfathomable complexity, while replacing a simple washer in a tap will, to him, forever remain a task shrouded in impenetrable mystery. With characteristic generosity of spirit, however, our hero has only unreserved admiration for those capable of plumbing (no joke intended) the depths of such enigmas as these.

One other rather perplexing aspect of his globe-trotting persona is that he seems incapable of undertaking a trip without calling down upon his head some misadventure or other: not only will pieces of his luggage go astray but whole planes will inexplicably be diverted and fail to arrive; his coat and wallet will be removed in error from a respectable Paris restaurant; his hotel will catch fire minutes after he has checked in; he will be attacked, even arrested, on the basis of mistaken identity – enough to put the faint-of-heart off travelling for life.

Yet Hugo Baetens Beardsmore is one of life's survivors, a resilient, resourceful personality who boldly relishes life's ups and shows considerable fortitude in the face of its downs. He is a most generous, independent spirit with great warmth of character, an entertaining raconteur and purveyor of jokes in many tongues.

In both his private and professional life he is a man of great integrity, who stands by his beliefs and is unafraid to right wrongs. He regards education as a liberating force, detests obfuscation, and has always steadfastly refused to sacrifice sound academic practice to administrative expediency. He is never more critical than of himself, though he is open-minded and slow to judge others. Like the Rev. Eli Jenkins, he understands that 'we are not wholly bad or good' and is always among 'the first to see our best side, not our worst'.

And I personally know children who can vouch for the fact that not even under the severest pressure does he cheat at marbles.

If it is true, as was suggested earlier, that Hugo Baetens Beardsmore is less well known as a person than he deserves, it is largely due to his overriding sense of discretion in all things. He asks nothing for himself that he does not spontaneously grant others: a profound respect for their individuality and their right to privacy. I have tried not to fail him in this here.

For over 30 years now I have been lucky enough to know Hugo Baetens Beardsmore in his many guises: as an enlightened and far-seeing department head, as my thesis supervisor, as a colleague with whom I have worked on many a project, and, most importantly, as a valued and loyal family friend. It has been a real pleasure to write these closing words, if only to repay in some small measure the enormous debt of gratitude I owe him.

Hugo Baetens Beardsmore may be sure that these words will find an echo in the hearts of his numerous students, colleagues and friends around the world.

Index

Arabic, 14, 16, 36, 49, 50, 198

Baetens Beardsmore, Hugo, 3-4, 5, 7, 8, 10-27, 33, 56, 63, 67, 68, 88, 109, 112, 115, 123
Baker, Colin, 6, 32, 33, 59, 61, 88-111
Belgium, 1, 2-3, 12, 24
Bilingual, balanced/unbalanced, 1, 7, 38, 174-188
Bilingual acquisition, 7, 11-13, 29, 45, 62, 63, 93, 100-102, 204-228
Bilingual education, 4, 6, 11-13, 15, 17-20, 29, 56-66, 67-87, 103-105, 112-113, 123-124
Bilingualism,
    advantages/disadvantages of, 2, 28-42, 117-118
Brunei, 4, 6, 67-87, 112-127

Canada, 2, 24, 36, 49, 58
Chinese, 6, 15, 49, 50, 74, 119-120, 132-140, 163, 221
Clyne, Michael, 6, 43-56
Code-switching, 7, 29, 72-83, 114, 174-188
Culture, 13-17, 40, 65, 88, 99
Cummins, Jim, 6, 12, 13, 18, 48, 56-66

Dutch, 2, 4, 22, 35, 46, 48, 141, 194

Education, 6, 11-13, 15, 17-20, 29, 56-66, 67-87, 103-105, 112-113, 123-124
Edwards, John, 5-6, 8, 28-42, 67, 113, 115
English, 4, 6, 34, 36, 37, 45, 48, 49, 58, 59, 60, 69, 109, 112, 120, 123, 124, 141, 143, 183, 190, 198, 214, 221, 222
Europe/European Union, 56, 58, 93

European schools, 4, 18

Fishman, Joshua, 17, 44, 47, 68, 93, 94, 95, 115, 128
French, 2-3, 4, 12, 14, 16, 21, 22, 35, 37, 46, 48, 51, 58, 174, 214, 221, 222

Genesee, Fred, 7, 19, 116, 204-228
German, 12, 22, 28, 35, 37, 43, 45, 46, 49, 50, 51, 179, 182, 183, 184, 196, 221, 222
Greek, 35, 40, 58

Identity, 5-6, 16, 29, 41, 64, 88
Ideology, 5, 20-25
Italian, 35, 46, 48

Language maintenance, 44, 51, 94, 128-140
Language shift/loss, 44, 94, 128-140
Li, Wei, 1, 116, 128-140
Linguistic diversity, 88-111
Luxembourg, 1, 4

Mackey, William, 17, 90
Majority, 40, 62, 94
Malay, 6, 7, 67-87, 112-127, 141-173
Minority, 40, 62, 94
Myers-Scotton, Carol, 7, 175, 189-203

Singapore, 2, 4, 6, 120, 121, 132-140
Skutnabb-Kangas, Tove, 15, 18, 61, 89
Spanish, 48, 49, 50, 60, 179

USA, 22, 23, 36, 57, 59, 60, 61

Welsh, 34, 98-109